Two books in one spe

C.S. Lewis had a Wife

Marshall had a husband

WILLIAM J. PETERSEN

Tyndale House Publishers, Inc.
Wheaton, Illinois

First printing, February 1985
Library of Congress Catalog Card Number 84-51763
ISBN 0-8423-0202-6, paper
Copyright © 1985 by William J. Petersen

CATHERINE MARSHALL HAD A HUSBAND
First printing, October, 1986
Library of Congress Catalog Card Number 86-50455
ISBN 0-8423-0204-2
Copyright © 1986 by William J. Petersen

First Combined edition for Christian Herald Family Bookshelf: 1986

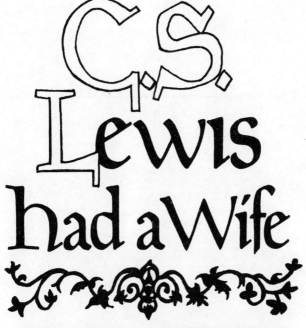

C.S. Lewis had a Wife

WILLIAM J. PETERSEN

LIVING BOOKS
Tyndale House Publishers, Inc.
Wheaton, Illinois

First printing, February 1985

Library of Congress Catalog Card Number 84-51763
ISBN 0-8423-0202-6, paper
Copyright © 1985 by William J. Petersen
All rights reserved
Printed in the United States of America

CONTENTS

They *"feasted on love;*
every mode of it—
solemn and merry,
romantic and realistic,
sometimes as dramatic
as a thunderstorm,
sometimes comfortable
and unemphatic
as putting on your
soft slippers."

C. S. LEWIS
A GRIEF OBSERVED

INTRODUCTION

This is a book about some outstanding Christians and about a side of them that is seldom seen, their personal lives—the marriages of people whom God has used. In each chapter there are a few surprises.

Interestingly, the marriages of great Christians may not differ much from those of people you know, perhaps even from your own marriage. But as you read how these people coped with the strains and stresses of their marriages, you will get some insights into how you can grapple with the challenges of your own marriage.

John Knox had a most unusual mother-in-law. She was sometimes a problem for him, but in a most unlikely way. Hudson Taylor had no mother-in-law problem; his problem was with prospective fathers-in-law. Evangelist Billy Sunday had a problem with a prospective father-in-law, too, but he seemed to need a business manager more than a wife.

Then there was Grace Livingston Hill, a strong-willed woman with a tender heart. What kind of a man would she marry? Well, she married twice, and the men were as different from each other as you can imagine.

Last, you will see how the noted bachelor, C. S. Lewis, finally got married when he was nearly sixty years old, and to a woman who had trouble getting along with people. It was a surprising marriage in other ways, too.

Through these five marriages, you will see how God develops His servants through marriage. Each of the five were developed in different ways, but undoubtedly their service for the Lord would have been greatly limited if they had not married.

Marriage is seldom easy. It needs to be worked at. Even these men and women whom God has used so spectacularly—perhaps *especially* these men and women—had to work at marriage.

At one point I was thinking of calling this book *Great Christian Marriages*. But you will soon discover that while the Christians I am writing about were certainly great Christians, there is no guarantee that their marriages were great. And that's what makes these sketches both entertaining and helpful. While they loved and served God greatly, they were also human. And so are we.

William J. Petersen

CHAPTER
ONE

Meet
John
and
Marjory
Knox

**W**HAT John Knox, the tell-it-like-it-is Scottish Reformer, really needed was a good press agent.

How could an old curmudgeon like John battle a young romantic like Mary Queen of Scots and hope to win?

Why did he take his mother-in-law on his honeymoon?

How could he virulently blast the rule of women when the reign of Queen Elizabeth was about to start?

Yes, John Knox could use a good press agent, even today.

But what about his wife Marjory Bowes? Was she only a toy that John played with while he waited to talk with her mother? Was she a real person? For that matter, was the marriage of John

Knox and Marjory Bowes a real marriage?

And was John Knox really the woman-hater he is alleged to have been?

Granted, John Knox was more of a Howard Cosell than a Walter Cronkite. Things always seemed to happen around John Knox. He was a lightning rod, no doubt about that. But he was also the spark plug, the energizer, not only of the Scottish Reformation, but also of the Scottish Revolution. Yet the question remains: what about his marriage?

In Scotland, the memories of Robert Burns, Walter Scott, and John Knox can still be felt across the bonnie braes and heathered hills. While Burns and Scott are more beloved, it was Knox who shaped the country. His influence on Scotland was more pronounced than Luther's was on Germany or Calvin's on Switzerland.

It was John Knox who challenged his nation to struggle for freedom and to fight against unjust rulers. In doing so, he laid the groundwork for modern democracy. Modern Presbyterianism owes as much to John Knox as it does to John Calvin.

But few men in history have been so castigated and vilified—unless you count Nero and Attila the Hun—as John Knox.

And what about his mother-in-law? Historian Will Durant writes, "Rarely in history has a mother-in-law been so loving and so loved." He claims that John Knox married Marjory Bowes "because he loved her mother."

Let's take a closer look at John and Marjory Knox, a most unusual couple in a most unusual time in history.

First, let's admit that John Knox didn't seem to have a very good sense of timing. For years he had looked for a close friend. Finally, at the age of thirty-one, he found one, a man named George Wishart. Two months later, Wishart was strangled and burned as a heretic.

For years Knox had been a priest without a parish, a minister without a congregation. Finally, at the age of thirty-three, he received his call and preached his first sermon. Three months later the town was invaded by the French; he was captured and forced to become a slave on a galley ship.

At the age of thirty-eight, he asked a young woman to marry him. She was willing, her mother was willing, and her father finally gave his reluctant approval. Seven months later, "Bloody Mary" came to power in England, and John had to flee the country, leaving his fiancée behind.

Poor timing? Maybe. But timing wasn't the only thing that seemed awry in the relationship between John Knox and Marjory Bowes.

Consider the picture when they first met. John was thirty-five, and an old thirty-five at that. He had spent nineteen months as a galley slave, had served as a chaplain to a gang of assassins, and had lost his best friend who was burned at the stake. Marjory, only fourteen, was the daughter of a country gentleman and had been reared in a rather genteel style in Norham Castle.

He was a Scotsman from a town repeatedly ravaged by the British, and as one contemporary wrote, he was "descended but of lineage small." She was from one of the most influential families of northern England, a section of the country whose citizens made a point of belittling the Scots.

Though Marjory was flattered by John Knox's interest in her, her father was understandably irate. The age difference wasn't a problem to him; that was commonplace in those days. But he didn't approve of any daughter of his (and he and his wife, Elizabeth, had ten daughters) marrying a low-class Englishman. A low-class Scotsman was a hundred times worse, and a low-class Scottish refugee priest was unimaginable. Priests had no business getting married to anyone.

That was the way Richard Bowes viewed the relationship. His wife, Elizabeth, had another view. For that matter, she always seemed to look at things differently, and that was getting to be politically embarrassing to Richard Bowes.

When Henry VIII repudiated the authority of the Pope in 1534, the Bowes family, as a leading family in northern England, was expected to follow their political leader. It wasn't easy for Richard, but he did it; yet at heart he remained a nominal Catholic. However, his wife, Elizabeth, took the change seriously. She started reading her Bible and began asking questions about what she read.

"Why do you always have to ask so many questions?" Richard Bowes must have queried his wife many times. He knew that people kept their heads on their shoulders a lot longer when they didn't ask questions. Besides, it wasn't normal for a woman to ask questions.

So when John Knox arrived on the scene in 1549, Elizabeth had fifteen years of unanswered questions bottled up within her. And for the first time in her life she found someone who took her questions seriously.

Now that you've met the principal characters, let's take a closer look at the enigma known as John Knox.

John Knox was born in Haddington, Scotland, near Edinburgh in about 1514, twenty-two years after Columbus discovered America and four years before Luther nailed his famous theses to the door in Wittenberg, Germany.

Scotland was at the rim of the civilized world in those days; one of Knox's contemporaries said it was "almost beyond the limits of the human race." Another said it was separated from the society of man. To Europeans it was the land where the devil lived; to the British it was infested with barbarians.

Whenever the British invaded Scotland, they

seemed to march through Haddington, massacring a few men, women, and children along the way. If the British weren't invading, the clans were marauding and feuding. When John Knox was six, the Hamiltons battled the Douglases, leaving eighty-seven men dead in the streets of Edinburgh.

For a hundred years, every Scottish monarch had met a violent death. None had lived beyond the age of forty-two.

While violence wracked the nation, corruption riddled the church, which possessed half of the country's wealth. The feudal lords who ruled the countryside were a law unto themselves and intimidated even the king. The common people were caught in the middle.

The Knox family was among those caught in the middle. John's mother probably died when he was only an infant, perhaps even in giving birth to John; but his father was able to get him an education in the local schools. Because John was quite bright, it was decided that he should study for the priesthood; that was the only way a poor boy could better his station in life.

In those days priests were more plentiful than churches, so John, after his studies at the University of St. Andrews and after his ordination as a priest, became a lawyer and a grammar tutor back in his hometown of Haddington.

John had read the Bible occasionally while at university, but it wasn't until he was back in Haddington that the seventeenth chapter of John's Gospel grabbed him. He called it his "anchor" and it formed the basis of his future theology. Verses such as, "This is life eternal that they may know You, the only true God and Jesus Christ whom You have sent" not only gave him an assurance of salvation which he had never had before, but also transformed his life.

However, it wasn't until he met George Wishart that his newfound Protestantism was really activated.

Wishart, tall, young, and possessing a strange habit of washing himself in a bathtub every night, was taking Scotland by storm. But Knox's section of the country was leery of strangers and made it a habit to duck unannounced visitors in the village pond, or worse. So Wishart needed a bodyguard, and the feudal lord whom Knox was serving as a tutor volunteered John's services. As a result, John, though still a priest in good standing, carried a two-handed sword as he accompanied Wishart for the next five weeks.

John was certainly not an activist or a revolutionary at this point. Life as a tutor to wealthy students was fairly comfortable; and he wasn't thinking of a career change. He might have carried a sword to protect Wishart, but he wasn't eager to use it.

As biographer W. Stanford Reid puts it, "He enjoyed the relative obscurity of a member of a laird's household, where he could study and expound the Bible, teach grammar, and encourage intellectually two or three teenagers without having to face the hurly-burly of the violent world around him."

When his five weeks of service with Wishart were ended, Knox had mixed emotions. He idolized Wishart; the man had become the closest friend he had ever had. Yet at the same time he was ready to return to his teenage charges. "Return to your bairns [pupils]," Wishart told him and then added prophetically, "One is enough for the sacrifice." A few hours later Wishart was arrested for Protestant heresy; within a few weeks he was executed.

Knox was shaken. As a priest who had betrayed his position by serving as a bodyguard for a Protestant heretic, he was a marked man. Sooner or later, they would track him down; sooner or later he would face the same destiny as Wishart.

He thought of fleeing to Luther's Germany, where he could study in tranquility, but first he consulted with the lairds whose sons he was tutoring. What did they think he should do?

Not wanting to lose an able tutor, they suggested that John take their sons to St. Andrews, the Protestant stronghold university city in which Knox had been educated.

St. Andrews could hardly be confused with a haven of rest. Scotland's Roman Catholic archbishop had just been assassinated and the perpetrators of the crime were holed up in St. Andrews Castle. So it was not exactly an ideal spot for a young teacher trying to stay out of trouble.

At first he was simply a tutor at St. Andrews.

But when some of the men overheard him teaching, they asked him to become chaplain of the castle. When he refused, saying, "I will not run where God has not called me," they held a public meeting and voted him in unanimously.

John burst into tears. There was no turning back now. He was in the middle of the fray and there was no way out.

The following week he preached his first sermon. His congregation was a strange mix of assassins and saints, peasants and professors.

In the sermon he stressed the importance of reliance on Scripture and the necessity of the doctrine of justification by faith alone. While criticizing the Roman Catholic church, he also called upon his Protestant congregation to repent. He censured them for their conduct and told them that unless they humbled themselves, God would send the French to capture them.

"Our walls will protect us," they shouted back.

"Your walls are like eggshells," John retorted.

Less than three months later, the French took the castle. Along with the others, John was condemned to the galleys as a common criminal to spend the rest of his life rowing for the king of France.

It might have been worse. If he had been released to the Scottish authorities, he would have suffered the same fate as Wishart.

Chained in irons, at times dangerously close to death, he spent nineteen months on the high seas.

Then early in 1549, when he was thirty-five, John was released, thanks to the negotiating efforts of the British government.

Returning to Scotland was out of the question; instead he took up residence in Protestant England and before long he was given a church in Berwick in northern England, near the Scottish border. It was as W. Stanford Reid says, "a typical rough, tough border town." The mix of this congregation was not much better than his previous one. It was composed mostly of British soldiers who hated Scotsmen and Scottish refugees who hated the British. Having developed stomach ulcers and kidney problems while on the galleys, John didn't find Berwick the place to recuperate—except at Norham Castle.

Norham Castle was a retreat from the storms of the parish. But more than that, at Norham Castle, perhaps for the first time in his life, he was able to interact with women who were not afraid to use their minds. It fascinated him.

Elizabeth Bowes became a mother-figure for John Knox. She had two sides to her. As Reid says, "She was a person with strong convictions who at times strengthened even him when he was faint. . . . On the other hand she had continual doubts and fears about her own spiritual condition: whether she had true faith, whether she was of the elect, whether she had committed the unpardonable sin."

At times John found her endless questions "a cross to bear," yet he delighted to teach her. Her questions challenged him to go back to the Scriptures and examine them for answers. By eliciting his warmth and devotional practicality, Elizabeth helped John as much as he helped her.

When she told him that the devil was tempting her so much that she doubted if she could really be a Christian, he responded, "The devil is a roaring lion, seeking whom he may devour; whom he has devoured already, he seeks no more." The fact that Satan was troubling her was a good sign, not a bad one.

When she felt she had committed the unpardonable sin, he wrote her, "Despair not, mother, your sins (albeit ye had committed thousands more) are remissible. . . . I am just as certain of your election in Christ as I am that I preach Christ to be the only Savior."

It was because of her urging that he wrote a very practical tract on prayer. In it he defined prayer as "an earnest and familiar talking with God," to whom we declare our miseries, from whom we ask help, and to whom we give prayer and thanks.

Because most of his letters to Elizabeth discussed biblical and doctrinal issues, they were deemed valuable and were kept for posterity. Letters written to her daughter Marjory were more personal and probably didn't deal with such weighty matters. Regardless of the possible reasons, we have many letters addressed to Elizabeth but only one letter addressed to Marjory.

One letter to Elizabeth is admittedly controversial. "Call to your mind," John wrote to her, "what I did standing at the cupboard in Alnwick; in very deed I thought that no creature had been tempted as I was. And when that I heard proceed from your mouth the very same words that he troubles me with, I did wonder, and from my heart lament your sore trouble, knowing in myself the dolour thereof, and no other thing, dear sister, meant I; and therefore think not that I either flatter you, or yet that I conceal anything from you; no, for if I had been so minded, I had not been so plain in other cases."

As biographer Jasper Ridley says, "It would be interesting to know what Knox had done at the cupboard in Alnwick." Our minds immediately read sexual innuendoes into such a letter. But Ridley concludes, "The more we read Knox's letters to Mrs. Bowes, the more obvious it becomes not only that there was nothing physical and sexual in their relationship, but that there was nothing strange or abnormal about it."

It was to Elizabeth that John revealed most candidly his innermost self. Sometimes he did so in the process of assuring her that he was tempted just as much as she was. "Externally, I commit no idolatry, but my wicked heart loveth the self, and cannot be refrained from vain imaginations. . . . I am no mankiller with my hands; but I help not my needy brother so liberally as I may and ought." And again, "There is a spiritual pride which is not hastily suppressed. . . . I write to you by my own experience."

Years later, Knox explained that Mrs. Bowes had a "troubled conscience . . . which never suffered her to rest." He went on to add that "her temptation was not in the flesh . . . but in spirit; for Satan did continually buffet her. . . . I have seen her . . . pour forth tears and send to God dolorous complaints, ofter than ever I heard man or woman in my life. Her company to me was comfortable (yea, honorable and profitable, for she was to me and mine a mother); and yet it was not without some cross; for . . . my mind was seldom quiet, for doing somewhat for the comfort of her troubled conscience." In other words, as much as he appreciated her, even admired her, she sometimes got on his nerves.

Even before his engagement John depended on Marjory to keep her mother on an even emotional keel. Once he wrote to her, "The Spirit of God shall instruct your heart what is most comfortable to the troubled conscience of your mother."

The biggest spiritual problem that Marjory seemed to have was how to live a Christian life as the daughter of the captain of Norham Castle. She had been reading in the Epistle of James that Christians should not give the seat of honor to the wealthy guest while ordering the poor to stand in a corner; she wondered how that applied to her when, in Norham Castle, guests were seated according to rank.

John answered her that in Jesus Christ, all who profess Him are equal before Him, and that riches and worldly honors are regarded as nothing in His sight. "True Christians," John wrote to Marjory, "should have more respect to the spiritual gifts" that God gives His servants.

Meanwhile, Marjory's mother asked questions, the answers to which could fill an encyclopedia. Some of her questions were philosophical ("Why do some philosophers teach that the world has always existed?"); some were biblical ("Did Jacob's sons act properly when they killed the Shechemites shortly after the Shechemites agreed to be circumcized?"); but more often they dealt with her personal doubts and her feelings of sinfulness ("I think I have committed the sins of Sodom and Gomorrah").

In the two years after John Knox had begun his ministry in Berwick, his clerical stock rose rapidly, and as it rose Richard Bowes started thinking that maybe the outspoken Scotsman might not be such a bad catch for his daughter after all. By the fall of 1551 he was touted as the most famous preacher in northern England and he was being talked about in the halls of Westminster and Canterbury. In 1552 John was preaching before the king of England himself and had been named as one of the royal chaplains.

John was not a tall man; in fact, he was slightly shorter than average, but he was broad-shouldered, and his black hair and beard added dignity as well as authority to his bearing. With deep-set gray-blue eyes, he seemed as if he could see straight through you.

Richard Bowes was still not overjoyed about having John Knox as his son-in-law, but finally, in December 1552, he consented to a prenuptial contract between his daughter and the Scotsman. Marjory was about seventeen; John about thirty-eight.

John had just come from London where he had preached to the king, and rumors were flying that he might be the next bishop of Rochester. How could a prospective father-in-law refuse him?

But in the next couple of months Richard Bowes got word from his brother in London that the king's health was failing, and if he died there was a better than fifty-fifty chance that Catholic Mary Tudor would become England's next ruler.

On hearing this, Richard Bowes thought that maybe he had been a bit hasty in agreeing to the engagement. Maybe he had let his wife talk him into it. There had to be something he could do to nullify it; the most important thing he could do now would be to delay it as long as possible.

By the following July the king had died, Mary Tudor was on the throne, and John Knox was a hunted man. His friends, one by one, were being imprisoned in the Tower of London. Burning at the stake awaited most of them.

It was amazing how rapidly his fortunes had turned. By now, not only was Richard Bowes dead-set against the wedding, but John wasn't so sure he wanted to push for it either. With Mary Tudor on the throne, what future could a Protestant preacher offer a seventeen-year-old bride?

But Elizabeth Bowes wasn't giving up. Her husband could switch religions at the drop of a monarch, but she knew what she believed in and nothing could change her. She also believed that John Knox was the man for her daughter and nothing would change that, either.

She urged John to contact her brother-in-law, Robert Bowes, in London. If Robert could be convinced, then he might be willing to try to convince Richard.

It wasn't a good idea, but John tried it anyway. Robert was even more opposed to the wedding than Richard was. In fact, he blamed all the problems of the Bowes family on Elizabeth and John. They were trying to arrange the wedding apart from Richard's better judgment, he said, and he was probably right.

"I am not a good orator in my own cause," John wrote back apologetically to Elizabeth.

Emotionally, John was hurt. Insults had always been hard for him to swallow. Depressed, he wrote, "My life is bitter unto me." He despaired that the marriage would ever happen; and having talked to Robert Bowes in London, he despaired of his own life. Robert Bowes would sooner see him handed over to the authorities than married to his niece Marjory.

There was no way he could think of marriage

now. Already his own life was in jeopardy; but if he married Marjory he would jeopardize the lives of two others: Marjory and Elizabeth. John was certain now; the marriage would have to be postponed.

But there was another problem. Richard Bowes was already thinking of other suitors for Marjory. The prenuptial contract could easily be nullified, for John was a Catholic priest, wasn't he? And under Mary Tudor it would be once again illegal for priests to marry.

Before long, the handsomest prospective bachelors in all of northern England would be parading to Norham Castle, and there would be little that John could do to stop it. How long could he expect a seventeen-year-old to remain faithful under such circumstances?

John struggled with the decision. Should he stay in England and suffer a martyr's death? Or was it wiser to flee to Europe? It seemed wiser to flee; but, of course, that would mean deserting Marjory.

Then he got another letter from Elizabeth. Could he come to Norham Castle and talk to her husband? To her, it seemed to be the only hope.

John didn't think it would work any better than the visit to Richard's brother. On the other hand, he wanted to see Marjory again, so he decided to give it a try. He wrote ahead to Elizabeth to tell her that he planned to come. "If I escape sickness and imprisonment, you will see me soon. Yet, mother, depend not upon me too much, for what am I but a wretched sinner? Whatever becomes of me, remember, mother, the gifts of God are not bound to any one man."

Frankly, John was scared. Going to Berwick would be dangerous because he was so well known there. John couldn't even trust what Richard Bowes might do. In a neighboring town he stayed with some fellow Protestants who begged him not to go on to Berwick and Norham Castle. "Partly by admonition, partly by tears, they compelled me to obey, somewhat contrary to my own mind."

So without seeing either Marjory or her mother, John turned around. He had to flee the country, but he didn't like the prospect of doing that either. "Some will ask then, 'Why did I flee?' Assuredly I cannot tell, but of one thing I am sure, the fear of death was not the chief cause of my fleeing." Soon afterward, he crossed the English Channel to France.

In Dieppe, France, he sat in a small room, considering himself to be a failure. He had deserted his fellow Protestants in England; he had forsaken his fiancée, and he had left behind a future mother-in-law whom he had urged to be strong and courageous. He asked himself how strong he had been. His heart, as he puts it, was "sore trubillit." He admits that "in the beginning of this battle I appeared the fainthearted and feeble soldier, yet my prayer is that I may be restored to the battle again." He was also praying that he would be restored to Marjory.

For the next eighteen months, Knox traveled between Dieppe, France (the message center that kept him in contact with both England and Scotland), Frankfurt, Germany (the publishing center of Europe and a haven for many English Protestant refugees), and Geneva, Switzerland (where John Calvin was transforming the city into what Knox later called "the most perfect school of Christ").

During those months, the news from England did not get any better. Mary Tudor was earning her nickname "Bloody Mary"; and the news from Norham Castle indicated problems there as well. John wrote to Elizabeth Bowes, "Be not moved with any wind, but stick to Jesus Christ." He confessed that he doubted that they would ever meet again on earth.

Elizabeth's closest friends were returning to Roman Catholicism. Richard, of course, was one of the first to do so, and now he was demanding that Elizabeth and Marjory follow his lead.

The pressure on Elizabeth and Marjory was intensifying week by week; by her letters Elizabeth made sure that John was kept up to date on all the developments. And along with the news, she kept inserting subtle (and some not-so-subtle) reminders that his presence was needed in both England and Scotland. England needed him, Scotland needed him, and above all, Marjory needed him.

John wasn't easily convinced. All the other reports that he was getting indicated that it definitely was not safe to return to England. The traffic was all going the other way. English Protestants were flocking into Frankfurt with their horror stories of what life was like under Mary Tudor.

And from what he could tell, Scotland didn't look any better. John hadn't seen his native Scotland for eight years, and the idea of returning now and facing immediate arrest was, as he put it, "most contrarious" to him.

But Elizabeth kept prodding. Biographer Geddes MacGregor says, "Evidently heart triumphed over head." More likely, it was Elizabeth who triumphed and finally Knox decided to venture back into his native Scotland for a brief visit. He had two items on his agenda: first, to marry Marjory at long last; and second, to assess the spiritual climate of his homeland. Later he acknowledged that he wouldn't have returned at this time at all if it hadn't been for Elizabeth's prodding.

So it was that in September 1655 John Knox slipped as quietly as possible into Scotland. First, he met Marjory and married her, although historians do not agree on exactly when and where it took place.

Some say that John went across the border to Norham Castle in England and married Marjory there. But that's unlikely. Richard Bowes had become increasingly embarrassed (perhaps angered would be a better term) by the two staunch Protestants in his home. By refusing to go to Mass, they faced arrest. To have his wife and daughter arrested would be politically embarrassing for a man of Richard Bowes' standing in northern England. For the past two years he had been trying to cajole them into some religious compromises, but he knew how stubborn his wife was; now he was convinced that his daughter Marjory was equally stubborn. They refused to cut their loyalties to their Protestant faith and, even more reprehensible to Richard, they refused to cut their ties with that blustery Scots preacher.

Finally, Richard Bowes gave his ultimatum. They had to choose: attend the Mass or else. The "or else" meant "get out." They would have to leave Norham Castle and all its rights and privileges.

They chose to leave Norham Castle.

It must have taken considerable courage for those two women, one twenty years old, the other about fifty, to leave the comfort of upper-class life in a British castle, sneak across the border into Scotland, and wait for John Knox to come, hoping that he would risk his life as they had risked theirs to enter Scotland.

But he came. And it was probably in Edinburgh, Scotland, shortly after his arrival, that John at last married Marjory after a thirty-month engagement.

Now that he was in Scotland, he had to check out the religious climate for himself. There were both similarities to and differences from England. Like England, Scotland was ruled by a queen named Mary. Like Mary Tudor of England, Scotland's Mary of Guise had forced the Protestant Christians underground. But in the crags and crannies of sparsely settled and still clannish Scotland, she was finding it more difficult to round up the heretics than Mary Tudor was in England. So house churches were sprouting up all over. During his visit John took the opportunity to visit as many house churches as he could.

Everywhere he went, he was greeted enthusiastically. He writes of the "fervent thirst of our brethren, night and day, sobbing and groaning for the bread of life." To his mother-in-law, waiting for him to return to Edinburgh, he writes, "If I had not seen it with my eyes in my own country, I could not have believed it." His speaking tour was extended longer than he had originally planned; he apologized to Elizabeth and Marjory for the delay and he asked them to "patiently bear . . . for depart I cannot, until such time as God quench their thirst a little."

By the following spring, the authorities, alarmed by the way that John Knox was criss-crossing the land, decided to put a halt to his unauthorized preaching. When he was summoned to a trial, he decided it was time to think of leaving. He put Elizabeth and his bride, Marjory, on a boat to Dieppe, France, while he wrapped up his business. He stayed a few more months, teaching the Scots how to conduct their worship services and urging them to read the Bible every day, even if it might seem monotonous. "Every day you eat bread, don't you?" he asked them.

Hardly had he fled the country when another

summons was issued for his arrest; he was hanged in effigy. Once again, he had gotten out just in the nick of time.

He took his wife and mother-in-law to Geneva, Switzerland, where he had been called to the pastorate of a thriving English congregation. It was as much of a honeymoon as John and Marjory would ever enjoy. John joked about Geneva being his "den of ease," and certainly in comparison to what was going on elsewhere, it was.

It was an adjustment for John at the age of forty-two to settle down to married life. In one letter he requested prayer because he was "now burdenit with dowbill cairis." Not only did the congregation impose demands on him, but so did his family, which included, no doubt, more questions from his mother-in-law. In addition, he felt he was also pastor-at-large to Protestants in both England and Scotland.

The following May a delegation arrived in Geneva from Scotland urging him to return. They said that they thought the situation might be improving. John wasn't convinced. He had other reasons why he didn't want to leave Geneva too quickly. First, Marjory was pregnant, and he didn't think he should leave her now. Second, he felt his presence in Scotland would do more to incite a political revolution than a religious reformation; and third, his congregation in Geneva was just starting to show some spiritual progress. But he replied to the messengers that he would come with "reasonable expedition," which apparently meant that he would come as soon as he felt he could.

Five months later, he said good-bye to his congregation and family and ventured 400 miles north to Dieppe, France, en route to Scotland. Shortly after arriving in Dieppe, however, a letter arrived from Scotland indicating that it might be better if he didn't come now.

John was irked, and he didn't hide his feelings. "To some it may appear a small and light matter that I have cast off and as it were abandoned . . . my house and poor family destitute of all head, save God only, and committing my small flock to the charge of another."

For two months he waited in Dieppe, corresponding with his Scottish brethren and writing religious tracts, but it wasn't a happy two months. What was God's purpose in uprooting him from Geneva to come on this wild goose chase? He finally returned, still disgruntled, to Geneva.

Back in Geneva, he spent a busy year, writing letters and tracts prolifically. Marjory assisted him with the correspondence, as well as in the transcription of his manuscripts, because she "wrote with a good hand." Jasper Ridley remarks that "not many married women would have been sufficiently literate and well-educated to render such assistance." One letter written to John Foxe (author of *Foxe's Book of Martyrs*) shows a flare for style and a graciousness of expression which could have been learned only through her upbringing at Norham

Castle. In the letter Marjory thanked Foxe for the gifts sent to her and her mother. Because of her able assistance, John referred to her as his "left hand."

John didn't speak openly of his affection for her; it was not easy for a Scotsman in that era to do so. But he did refer to her as "of earthly creatures most dear to me." Calvin spoke of Marjory as "the most delightful of wives," and called her "suavissima." Geddes MacGregor adds, "Only such gentle sweetness as was hers could have been powerful enough to hold as it did the enduring affection of so stormy and dominating a personality as John Knox." Undoubtedly, the next few years revealed John Knox at his stormiest.

It had been during those two disgruntled months in Dieppe that he began penning his most famous work, "The First Blast of the Trumpet against the Monstrous Regiment of Women." John Knox was, to put it mildly, against women rulers.

Everywhere John turned he saw nations ruled by women. His native Scotland was ruled by the Queen Regent Mary of Guise. John hadn't minded the fact that she had permitted him to be hanged in effigy, but what he didn't appreciate was the fact that she had considered one of his writings a joke. France's influence was rising in Scotland, and if Mary had her way, Scotland would follow France in religion as well. John feared that.

In France, John witnessed the ruthless power of Catherine de Medici, who later ordered the St.

Bartholomew's Day Massacre of the Protestant Huguenots. And in England Mary Tudor ("Bloody Mary") had burned many of John's friends at the stake and sent many others to rot in the Tower of London.

Admittedly, it was surprising in that day to have women monarchs. After all, women generally had few rights; they could hold no political office (except the office of queen); they had no legal authority even over their own children. To John, it didn't make sense.

Unlike many of his contemporaries, both Protestant and Catholic, John was not a woman-hater. Far from it. More than half his letters (of which we have record) were addressed to women. When he refers to women, it is usually with dignity and consideration. As far as friendships go, his closest, most intimate confidences were with women—not only his wife and mother-in-law, but also Anne Locke, Mrs. Hickman, and Janet Adamson. He may have consulted with a man such as John Calvin, but it was to Elizabeth Bowes that he unburdened his soul.

However, when he saw women as leaders of the most powerful nations of the world, he judged it to be completely unnatural and against God's plan. Jezebel was his prime example. Of course, he had to acknowledge that some women—such as Deborah in the book of Judges—might be exceptions, but you can't use an exception to change a rule.

The main thrust of John's argument was directed

against Queen Mary Tudor of England and "the cruelties and tyrannies" that characterized her reign.

In fact (and here is where John made everyone sit up and take notice), John urged that nobles and clergy had the responsibility "to remove from honor and to punish with death such as God has condemned by His own mouth."

That was treason. John Calvin himself was scandalized by the book (he banned it in Geneva) and was chagrined that such a report could be printed in his fair city. Other Reformers were also shocked. No Protestant leader had ever gone as far as John Knox had gone. Previously, Protestants had held, "We must obey our kings whether they are good or evil." John Knox was arguing that if you went along with unjust rulers, you yourself were incurring the wrath of God. In fact, people who failed to seek to overthrow wicked regimes by revolution should be punished.

Once again, John's timing got him into trouble.

Less than six months after he had published his literary blast, Mary Tudor died, and Queen Elizabeth, a Protestant, took the throne. Since John's condemnation applied to all women rulers (though admittedly to Mary in particular), Elizabeth never forgave him, and John could never again think of returning to live in England.

But, fortunately, it wasn't the English church that called him to return; it was the Scottish church. A letter was sent to him and another letter to John Calvin, who was urged to apply pressure to John Knox to make him want to return to Scotland.

Once again, John dallied. Marjory was expecting their second child, and John didn't want to leave until he was sure that Marjory had delivered the child safely.

Then a few more months passed before he finally left Marjory, their two children, Nathaniel and Eleazar, and his mother-in-law, Elizabeth Bowes. He asked a colleague to take care of them until he felt it safe for them to join him in Scotland; he didn't know how long that would be.

It was in May 1559 that forty-five-year-old John Knox set foot once again in Scotland. And he was made to feel "at home" immediately. Five days after he arrived he was officially proclaimed an outlaw. A reward was offered to anyone who would either seize or kill him; bounty hunters lurked everywhere. One of his first letters from Scotland asked for money so he could buy a faster horse.

But John was not going to be stopped now. Everywhere he went, he roused the citizenry. He had little time to write letters. He complained, "In twenty-four hours I have not four free to natural rest and ease of this wicked carcass."

Outwardly, the growing Protestant force seemed ineffective. As Knox says, "We do nothing but go around Jericho, blowing with trumpets as God giveth strength, hoping victory by his power alone."

After only a month in Scotland, despite the

turbulent atmosphere, John asked Marjory to come. He was eager (he said "thirsty") to have her join him. So Marjory, her mother, and their two sons, along with Christopher Goodman, Knox's ministerial colleague, left Geneva, went to Paris, and there applied for permission to pass through England. Unlike John, who was refused permission by Queen Elizabeth herself, Marjory and Mrs. Bowes had no trouble at all getting a visa. In fact, they stopped at Norham Castle.

But things weren't the same there. Elizabeth's husband, Richard, had passed away nine months earlier, only a few weeks before Mary Tudor had died and Queen Elizabeth had come to the throne. It was also about the time that Knox's seditious "First Blast" had begun circulating in England.

Neither Elizabeth nor Marjory were mentioned in Richard's will. He bequeathed his estate to his other children, including four unmarried daughters; but the daughters could receive the inheritance only if their uncles approved their marriages.

Obviously, Marjory had married John against Richard's will, and thus had forfeited her right to an inheritance. As far as Elizabeth was concerned, how could he leave anything to her when she chose to be associated with the man who had written the "First Blast," advocating revolution against his queen?

Temporarily Mrs. Bowes stayed in England with relatives until the fighting in Scotland cooled down. Intrepidly, Marjory and the two boys,

Nathaniel, two, and Eleazar, ten months, entered Scotland at its most perilous time. They joined John in Dundee in northern Scotland.

Marjory must have been concerned that John was working himself to death. A month before she arrived he had been ill. Immediately she pitched in. Besides managing the children, she did a considerable share of John's correspondence. Knox wrote, "The rest of my wife hath been so unrestful since her arriving here that scarcely could she tell upon the morrow what she wrote at night."

Those were some of the most eventful days in Scottish history. About a month after Marjory and the boys arrived in Scotland, the Queen Regent of Scotland, Mary of Guise, was deposed. Fighting continued, however, between Mary's allies, the French, and the motley band of Scottish Protestants for another eight months.

John was only the cheerleader for that band, but what an effective cheerleader he was! The English ambassador reported that Knox's voice could "put life into them more than 500 trumpets."

While the fighting continued, John and Marjory lived in St. Andrews where he had served as chaplain twelve years before. Then in mid-April 1560 the Knoxes moved to Edinburgh where John became minister of St. Giles Church. Two months later Mary of Guise died, and a treaty ending the civil war was signed in July.

In Edinburgh, John and Marjory lived in a house on the west side of Trunk Close, north of High

Street. It had a garden and some extra land attached. The Edinburgh council paid the rent as well as the cost of furnishing the house. They also paid for a lock on the door. Apparently, not everyone in Edinburgh loved John.

At last he and Marjory could settle down. Geneva was pleasant, but he was a pilgrim there. Edinburgh was home; finally he could begin life as a parish preacher and enjoy his family again.

However, it was only a half year after they had moved into their new home on Trunk Close in Edinburgh that Marjory suddenly died. She was only twenty-five.

No one knows the cause of her death. Some have suggested that she wore herself out during the previous year and was not able to resist one of the epidemics that ravaged Edinburgh periodically. Or perhaps she died in childbirth.

We do not know. What we do know is that John was devastated by her death. Although he had known her for the previous ten or eleven years, they had been married for only five years, and during those years John had been absent from her for months at a time.

Years later, in the writing of his will, he still referred to Marjory as "darrest spouse" of "blessit memorie." His friend Goodman commented on the severe blow it had been to Knox to lose his wife so suddenly.

In his *History of the Reformation in Scotland*, John made it a point to omit most personal matters, and certainly emotional reactions to personal matters; but he could not refrain from commenting on Marjory's death by saying that he "was in no small heaviness by reason of the later death of his dear bedfellow."

From Geneva, John Calvin wrote to console him, "As you have rightly learned where to seek consolation in sorrow, I am sure that you are bearing this calamity with patience."

John, now forty-six, was left with two small boys under four years old, the leadership of a brand new national church, and a national government in tumultuous transition.

Elizabeth Bowes returned to help John raise the two lively boys. But by this time, she was nearly sixty years of age and was no match for the youngsters.

Two years later, John Knox took a second wife, Margaret Stewart. A few eyebrows were raised that John, who was now fifty, was marrying a girl of only seventeen. But the shocking thing in Edinburgh was that John, a man of humble birth, should marry into the Stewart family, a family with royal connections.

Margaret was descended from James II. She was the daughter of one of John's strongest Protestant backers, Lord Ochiltre. Jasper Ridley comments, "It is evidence either of Lord Ochiltre's Protestant zeal or of Margaret's affection for Knox." It may also be evidence of John's need of a vigorous young woman to be mother to his two young children.

It, too, was a good marriage, and in the coming years John and Margaret had three children of their own.

John had no problem with his wives, his first mother-in-law, or his second father-in-law, Lord Ochiltre. But he did have continuing problems with queens—Mary Tudor and Elizabeth of England, Mary of Guise, and ultimately Mary Queen of Scots. Mary Queen of Scots was the latest female monarch to plague John, or vice versa. She was beautiful, young, charming, clever, and full of intrigue. She was also Roman Catholic and deathly afraid of John Knox. John had fought too long and hard to get Protestantism recognized in Scotland to let a charming young queen take it away. Her tactics reminded him too much of Mary Tudor's to allow him to rest easily.

The English ambassador wrote back to London about the reception that Mary Queen of Scots had received in Edinburgh. Everyone had been favorably impressed by Mary, he said—everyone "saving John Knox, that thundereth out of the pulpit. . . . One day he will mar all. He ruleth the roost, and of him all men stand in fear."

For six years the battle raged between the pretty, young queen and the man "that thundereth from the pulpit." Though politically he was much less active, yet as a pulpiteer he remained as vigorous as ever. His home life also became more precious to him. MacGregor writes, "For years he had known scarcely any privacy. He had seen too little of his

children, and he had enjoyed too few of the pleasures of friendship. . . . Now in the company of
his young wife he felt he could enjoy what he had
missed. After striving with royal courts he could
appreciate her ingenuousness. Her artless laughter
soothed him. Her simple, girlish earnestness in the
regular family devotions filled with peace the heart
of the man who had thirsted after righteousness."

After John married Margaret, Elizabeth Bowes
returned to England. Interestingly, a few years later
the two boys were sent to England for their education, where they spent considerable time with their
grandmother Bowes. At least once, John came to
visit them there.

When Mary Queen of Scots was forced to abdi-
cate in 1567, her infant son, James, was crowned
king, and John Knox preached the coronation sermon. To John that was a great victory. But his
ultimate triumph came in December of that year
when the Protestant Church of Scotland was recognized as the official church of the nation.

Five years later, at the age of fifty-eight, John
Knox lay dying. He asked his young wife, Margaret,
to come and read the fifteenth chapter of 1 Corin-
thians (the resurrection chapter) to him. Then late
in the afternoon he asked Margaret to read another
passage of Scripture. "Go read where I cast my first
anchor," he asked.

She knew the passage well. Automatically she
turned to the Gospel of John and read the seventeenth chapter, which had been so instrumental in

his conversion. He passed away shortly thereafter.

During the past 400 years biographers as well as psychologists have puzzled over John Knox and his attitudes about women. They often conclude their studies with more questions than answers.

However, this much is certain. What could have been a disastrous triangle of John, Marjory, and her mother, Elizabeth, worked out surprisingly well. Each had strengths and each had weaknesses. John and Marjory developed a strong love for each other that Elizabeth not only respected but also sought to strengthen.

John appreciated Elizabeth's strength of character, her sensitive spirit, and her inquiring mind. She was teachable and John liked that in a woman. But even more admirable in John's estimation was her strength in standing for what she believed in, in spite of the loss of all her physical possessions and earthly friendships. Early in his life, John was ashamed of how often it seemed that he had run away from conflict; Elizabeth faced conflict head on.

Of course, having Elizabeth in the home was, as John put it, "not without some cross. For my mind was seldom quiet, for doing something for the comfort of her troubled conscience."

Marjory, despite her youth, was the steadying influence in the family. She kept her mother from groveling in introspection and gave John a "left hand" of constancy, stability, and love that he needed.

Though John never seemed eager to get involved in anything (including marriage), once he got involved, he was in it to the hilt. And his mind insisted that he follow everything to its logical conclusion.

On his deathbed he gave this revealing statement: "I know that many have complained much and loudly, and do still complain of my too great severity, but God knows that my mind was always free from hatred to the person of those against whom I denounced the heavy judgments of God. In the meantime, I cannot deny but that I felt the greatest abhorrence of the sin in which they indulged; still, however, keeping this one thing in view, that if it were possible, I might gain them to the Lord. . . ."

To Elizabeth, he was a teacher as well as a son-in-law; to Marjory, he was a husband with convictions (unlike her father who waffled with every political wind).

As vitriolic as John often seemed to outsiders, both Elizabeth and Marjory saw his tender side. John may have blasted his trumpet against the mighty queens of his day, but for the women who were closest to him, he played softer notes.

CHAPTER
TWO

Meet
hudson
and
Maria
Taylor

UDSON Taylor was a Yorkshire lad, the son of a small town druggist.

Half a world away, in Malaya, lived a girl named Maria Dyer. She was an orphan.

From the day Hudson was born, his father had rattled on and on about the exotic land of China. Of course, he never expected to go there, nor did he expect that his son, sickly as he was, would ever go.

When Maria was just a small girl, her father had talked about China, too; she could vaguely remember it. He went and never came back.

By the time Hudson was twenty-three, he had been engaged twice and jilted twice. About this time he wrote a letter home, saying, "There is something in my nature that seems as if it must

49

have love and sympathy." And it was about the same time that he wrote, "Whatever I set my heart on, I lose."

Maria was under the watchful eye of an eccentric schoolmarm who was sometimes mistaken for a witch. When Hudson expressed some interest in Maria, the schoolmarm forced Maria to write a letter to him rejecting him as a suitor.

It looked as if he had lost again.

Hudson Taylor, missionary innovator, founder of the China Inland Mission, father of the faith mission movement, and a nineteenth-century stalwart who exemplified his motto of "living by faith," may seem an unlikely man to be the romantic lead in this true-life drama with Maria Dyer.

And she, the orphan who grew up in a cocoon-like atmosphere and who was expected to emerge as a caterpillar, burst forth as a butterfly.

Yes, Hudson and Maria were both full of surprises.

Fun-loving, brash, affectionate, imaginative, with a hobby of collecting insects, he hardly seems the type to launch a pioneering mission to reach 400 million souls in China's interior.

Man of faith, yes; but he was a romantic at heart. Martin Luther's favorite book of the Bible may have been Romans; John Knox's favorite book may have been Jeremiah; but Hudson Taylor's seems to have been the Song of Solomon.

Together, Hudson and Maria made a great missionary team, although for a while, it didn't look as if they would become teammates at all.

It was Christmas 1856 when they first took a serious look at each other. He was twenty-four; she was nineteen. All the English missionaries housed in the Ningpo, China, compound were guests at a beef and plum pudding dinner given by one of the senior missionaries.

In a way, neither Hudson nor Maria fit in.

Technically, Maria was not a missionary. It was her sister who had accepted a position with the Ningpo mission school under Miss Aldersley, and Maria had tagged along. The two orphaned sisters didn't want to be separated.

As for Hudson, he did not fit in either.

The Ningpo mission compound was a pocket of Victorian propriety on the coast of China. And Hudson Taylor was anything but a symbol of Victorian propriety.

He had come to China under a maverick mission board that required him to live on empty promises. Without any other missionary philosophy, he developed his own. He thought he would be more effective as a missionary if he didn't seem to be a foreigner. So, much to the embarrassment of the rest of the missionary community, Hudson wore Chinese clothing and sported a piebald pigtail. He had a reputation, says biographer J. C. Pollock, "for meandering around China without denomination or settled purpose."

A fellow missionary referred to him as "a mystic absorbed in religious dreams. Not idle, but aimless."

You can imagine what Miss Aldersley thought of him.

Hudson had had a difficult time that year, especially in the previous few months. He had been working out of Shanghai until a fire had destroyed all his medical equipment. Shortly afterward, a servant had robbed him of almost everything he owned.

So he was a sorry, pigtailed sight as he hobbled into the Ningpo compound seeking refuge. Hobbled is the correct word, for he had been wearing the Chinese calico stockings and flat-soled black satin shoes with turned-up toes which were most uncomfortable. Earlier he had written to his sister that "average toes decidedly object to be squeezed out of shape, nor do one's heels appreciate their low position in perfectly flat-soled shoes."

That was when he could joke about it.

But between Shanghai and Ningpo, he had lost his sense of humor.

In Ningpo his discouragement increased. He was in love with a girl ten thousand miles away. He had asked her to marry him and it was taking a long time for her to respond. Whether she loved him or not is hard to tell. She certainly didn't relish the notion of spending the rest of her life in the shadow of the Great Wall of China, married to a man who wore a pigtail and a silk Chinese gown. Her father felt even more strongly than that about it.

Hudson wrote home: "At times I have felt so discouraged . . . that I have . . . even thought of giving up the missionary work, for her father said if I were living in England he would have no objections."

While Hudson was mooning over his unrequited love, a girl he had not previously noticed, Maria, thought that things might be looking up for her.

Eligible young women were not plentiful in Ningpo. In fact, since her sister Burella had just gotten engaged, that left Maria in the field by herself.

Maria, described by Hudson as "a good looking girl, despite the slightest cast of the eye," spoke Chinese fluently, and that may have been what impressed one of the members of the British Consular service so much. But when he proposed marriage to her, she turned him down. And then there was the missionary stationed in Shanghai who had also expressed keen interest in her, but she wasn't interested in him.

Hudson Taylor was another matter. There was something about that pigtailed Yorkshireman that intrigued her. She wrote: "I met a gentleman and, I cannot say I loved him at once, but I felt interested in him and could not forget him. I saw him from time to time and still this interest continued. I had no good reason to think it was reciprocated; he was very unobtrusive and never made any advances."

She decided to pray about it.

Then came Christmas. Maria and her sister were asked to play some duets on the pianoforte. Hudson seemed more impressed with the pianoforte than he was with the musicians.

But from then on, something was different.

Hudson wrote, "Ere I was aware of it, my acquaintance with Miss M. Dyer ripened into an attachment, which, as soon as I perceived, far from encouraging though unable to repress it, I strove to confine the knowledge of it to my own bosom."

He confined it quite well.

A couple of weeks later Maria confided to a friend her feelings about Hudson. The friend remarked that "she had not seen anything which would lead her to think that he was interested in me and remarked that it was a dreadful thing to love without that love being returned."

Biographer J. C. Pollock says cryptically, "Hudson was riding two mares." Gradually he was losing interest in his fiancée in England, but since he had proposed marriage to her, he felt honor-bound to "confine" his interest in Maria as long as possible.

Then he began comparing the two girls. Maria he felt was "a dear sweet creature, [who] has all the good points of Miss S and many more, too. She is a precious treasure, one of sterling worth and possessed with an untiring zeal for the good of this poor people. She is a lady, too."

In March, Hudson was temporarily in Swatow, China. He still hadn't received a reply to his proposal that he had sent several months before to England, but he couldn't wait any longer about communicating his feelings to Maria. He decided to write her a letter.

For Hudson, there was no beating around the bush.

Maria tells of the letter this way: "I had a sort of hope that it might be from Mr. Taylor, but I could not think that it was—that was not likely. . . . I then opened my letter and read of his attachment to me and how he believed that God had given him that love for me which he felt. He asked me to consent to an engagement to him. He begged me not to send him a hasty refusal which he intimated would cause him the intensest anguish."

Walking on air, Maria shared the exciting letter with her guardian and employer, Miss Aldersley, who responded curtly, "I presume you would not think of accepting him?"

Then Miss Aldersley gave several good reasons why she should immediately turn him down. First of all, she said, "He is an unconnected nobody." Besides that, he was not a gentleman, he was not educated, he had no position, he wore Chinese clothes, he was short (while she was tall), and he was associated with the Plymouth Brethren (while she belonged to the Anglican Church).

Miss Aldersley gave Maria no choice. She had to refuse him immediately. So as her guardian watched over her shoulder, Maria penned a letter to Hudson, "My dear sir: I had made the subject of your letter a matter of earnest prayer to God, and have desired I think sincerely only to know His will and to act in accordance with it. And though it does indeed give me no pleasure to cause you pain, I must answer your letter as appears to me to be according to God's direction. And it certainly appears to me to be my duty to decline your proposals. . . . I request you not to refer to the subject again as I should be obliged to return you the same answer."

And so it looked as if the unconnected nobody from Yorkshire and the orphan from Malaya would never get together.

James Hudson Taylor, born in 1832 in the Yorkshire mining town of Barnsley, was converted at the age of seventeen, after reading a gospel tract; six months later he committed himself to go to China as a missionary.

Soon there developed another interest in Hudson's life; he fell in love with a music teacher who unfortunately had no desire at all to go to China.

"I know I love her. To go without her would

make the world a blank. But I cannot bring her to want," he wrote.

He felt that sooner or later the music teacher would change her tune, so in the meantime he went about preparing himself for the rigors of the Orient. "I soon found that I could live upon very much less than I had previously thought possible."

He gave away much of his modest salary and lived mainly on oatmeal and rice. "One's spiritual muscles require strengthening," he said.

But beyond that, he learned lessons in prayer. "When I get out to China," he said, "I shall have no claim on anyone for anything; my only claim will be on God. How important, therefore, to learn before leaving England, to move man, through God, by prayer alone."

The next problem was finding a mission board to take him. His family was Methodist, but the Methodists had no work in China. He wrote to the London Missionary Society, but they didn't bother to answer his letter.

Then, in 1852, when he was just turning twenty, he heard of a newly formed mission, the Chinese Evangelization Society, composed mostly of Plymouth Brethren. Its founders, J. C. Pollock says, "were intensely sincere and impractical. They had scanty funds, one missionary, who later was dismissed for dabbling in the coolie traffic, and a journal."

Hudson loved the journal and didn't bother questioning anything else.

Within months he was training in a London hospital to be a missionary doctor under the new mission.

Convinced that he needed a wife when he went to China, he renewed his courtship of the music teacher, and within weeks they were engaged.

But the engagement was short-lived. She had second thoughts and so did Hudson. "I know I loved her, and she says she loved me, but I know she does not love me as she did. I fear it will have to be broken off."

Her father agreed. Hudson would be a suitable husband for his daughter if he were willing to reside in England and be a doctor. If he went to China, however, the marriage was out of the question.

A year later, without finishing his medical course, and without a wife, Hudson, now twenty-one, sailed for China, the only passenger on the sailing vessel. After an adventurous five-month voyage, he walked into the city of Shanghai.

He learned much in his first two weeks, including the fact that his mission board didn't know what it was doing. But Hudson wasn't going to let that stop him from being a missionary.

While learning the language, he became acutely homesick. He wrote long letters back to England: "Oh, I wish I could tell you how much I love you all. . . . I never knew how much I loved you all before."

In his room in Shanghai he grew three flowers—

a violet and two forget-me-nots. "I look on them with the greatest affection and have even given them names; one I call Amelia, and another Louisa [his two sisters]—what I have called a third is no matter of yours. . . . But you know we must have something to love."

Chances are, the third was named either after the music teacher or else after Elizabeth Sissons, who had written him a consoling letter after his engagement to the music teacher was broken.

It didn't take him long to propose to Elizabeth, and it didn't take her long to respond. She wrote that she would accept his proposal of marriage although her father wanted her to wait awhile. Hudson was willing to wait, but not indefinitely.

For the first year as he was learning the language and engaging in some rather unspectacular missionary treks ("We see no fruit at present, and it needs strong faith to keep one's spirit from sinking"), Hudson took the bold step of adopting native dress. The other missionaries were appalled. The British consulate reacted with scorn. But Hudson thought it was a necessity if he was to minister effectively to the Chinese. "You wouldn't know me," he wrote home, "were you to meet me in the street."

To test his new "when in Rome, look like the Romans" approach, he established a mission base inland, at a distance from Shanghai. For a few weeks he seemed on top of the world. Then two calamities befell him: (1) the British authorities told him he couldn't establish a base there and (2) Elizabeth wrote him that she had decided she didn't love him after all.

Hudson didn't like to give up on things too readily, and that applied to such things as venturing inland and pursuing a wife.

So he continued to preach in places where few other missionaries would venture, although he did leave his forward base as the authorities had ordered him. "I do love the Chinese now," he wrote home. But he explained to his younger sister that letter writing was quite a chore. "Sometimes I stop in the middle of a sentence, kill three or four fleas and one or two cockroaches and then go on again."

But it was Elizabeth who was giving him more problems than the fleas and cockroaches. "I don't know what I shall do if I get an unfavorable letter in this mail."

It was only a few months later that he trudged desolately into Ningpo.

Five years younger than Hudson, Maria Dyer had already seen a great deal of the world. Her father, who had died when she was only six, had been one of the early British missionaries to the Chinese in Malaysia. He had dreamed of evangelizing mainland China itself, but he never got there. He died off the coast of China in 1843. Four years later, his wife died.

The three orphans—Maria, Burella, and a brother Samuel, were shipped back to England to be looked after by an uncle and to be educated at a boarding school.

According to J. C. Pollock, "Maria was tall, dark-haired, dark-eyed, vivacious, and warm. She had a squint, which did not make her less attractive. She was demure, the dutiful younger sister, and no one suspected the strong currents within."

So, in 1855, when her sister responded to a missionary call to become a teacher at Ningpo, China, nobody thought it strange that Maria should want to go along with her. She knew that her parents would have been pleased to see her become a missionary to China, and so she went.

On board ship, she struggled inwardly. She couldn't understand exactly what was wrong. She was lonely, so it was understandable that she should want to stay with her sister. She was dutiful, so it was understandable that she would want to do what would have pleased her parents.

But all her life she had been reacting to shattering events. And no matter how dutiful she was, she never felt truly accepted. She even suffered pangs of guilt that maybe somehow, inexplicably, she had caused the problems of her life. No matter how dutifully she lived her life, she never had confidence that God Himself really accepted her.

However, on her voyage to China, she gained that peace. Geraldine Taylor tells it this way: "Previously she had striven to be a Christian in her own strength. . . . Gradually it dawned upon her that she was redeemed . . . because He had suffered in her stead. God had accepted Christ as her substitute and savior, and she could do no less. . . . 'There is therefore now no condemnation to them which are in Christ Jesus.' "

No longer was she responding out of fear and duty; now she was going to China out of freedom and love. On her way to become a missionary, she had become a new creation.

Under Miss Aldersley's exacting supervision, Maria also developed into an excellent teacher of the Chinese children at the Ningpo school.

One of Miss Aldersley's other contributions to her life was to help her brush aside undesirable suitors. Probably, to Miss Aldersley, they all would have been undesirable—especially Hudson Taylor.

It was difficult for Maria to think poorly about Miss Aldersley. She wrote later to her brother, "O dear Samuel, those days were days of trial indeed. . . . It seemed to be His will that Mr. Taylor and I should love each other and yet Miss Aldersley so strongly opposed it. It seemed as if God's will and Miss Aldersley's were opposite."

She couldn't understand how such a godly woman as Miss Aldersley could possibly be wrong. "Yet it seems to me that Mr. Taylor is just the sort of person as my dear father, were he living, would approve of for me." Still she wondered: "Who was I that I should set myself up against Miss Aldersley and old established Christians?"

At first, Hudson was crushed by Maria's formal

"Dear John" letter. While he didn't write home to his sister all that he was going through, he did say that he was "in much sorrow" and that he had been "tried at times almost beyond endurance."

In Shanghai for several months, he plunged into missionary efforts, aiding victims of a disastrous famine and preaching whenever he had a chance. But still he couldn't forget Maria. He had a hunch that Maria's letter could have been prompted either by a sense of duty to Miss Aldersley and the school, or that maybe Miss Aldersley had had an even more direct hand in it.

When he returned to Ningpo, his suspicions were confirmed. "Miss Aldersley got into a great stew when I came down," he wrote home. No doubt about it, he recognized that she was a formidable opponent.

But as soon as he discovered that Maria was as interested in him as he was in her, he decided to go around Miss Aldersley and write a letter to Maria's legal guardian (her uncle) in England, seeking his permission to marry Maria.

Hudson, however, wasn't the only person writing the uncle. Two weeks earlier, Miss Aldersley had already written him, informing him of the brash upstart nobody who was brazenly tampering with Maria's affections.

Maria, too, had written the uncle: "The greatest earthly pleasure that I desire is to be allowed to love the individual whom I have mentioned so prominently in this letter."

Third, but not least, Hudson wrote him his request.

No reply could be expected for at least four months.

Miss Aldersley and several others of the missionary community decreed that Hudson must not attempt to see Maria until word came back from the uncle. Most of them took Miss Aldersley's side in the matter.

One usually mild-mannered missionary said that Hudson "ought to be horse-whipped" for talking to Maria against the wishes of Miss Aldersley. Others called the relationship disgraceful. Hudson was termed "fanatical, undependable, diseased in body and mind." Besides that, he was "totally worthless." In fact, one mission leader told Hudson that he "could in no way recognize him as a Christian. He was no gentleman either."

Hudson couldn't understand what all the uproar was about. He wrote his mother: "Why? Because I don't think a maiden lady qualified to judge in love affairs?"

One other suggestion—and one that Hudson considered seriously—was that he should return immediately to England to get his medical degree. Of course, there were ulterior motives behind the suggestion. Maria responded: "If he were to leave the Lord's work for the world's honor, I would have nothing further to do with him."

Not all the attacks were flung against Hudson. Hudson wrote his mother that "dear Maria is charged with being a maniac, being fanatical, being indecent, weak-minded, too easily swayed, too obstinate, and everything else bad."

When Maria tried to heal the breach between Miss Aldersley and herself, she only made matters worse. "I have suffered persecutions for righteousness' sake," she wrote her brother, but she still couldn't understand how a saintly woman such as Miss Aldersley could be in error. "How could she be in the wrong and I in the right?"

Separated from Maria, Hudson once again threw himself into his missionary work. He drove himself at such a pace that his health broke. Recuperating from his illness, he adopted two Hebrew words as his life mottoes: Ebenezer and Jehovah-Jireh. Ebenezer means "Hitherto the Lord has helped us." Jehovah-Jireh means "The Lord will provide." Those two words were the foundation of the mission that he would later begin.

In November, about the time that he had expected a reply from the guardian, Hudson arranged a secret meeting with Maria. According to the official biographer, "they sat side by side on the sofa." According to Pollock, "It was very naughty by contemporary standards." According to Hudson himself, he was only "trying to make up for the number of kisses I ought to have had these last few months."

When they parted, they agreed that they were engaged to be married, no matter what the response from the guardian might be. Her twenty-first birthday, after all, was only two months away.

The announcement of the engagement almost split the Ningpo mission community. Some charged Hudson with "exhibiting a total ignorance of the common amenities and proprieties of life."

Two weeks later, a letter from the guardian in England finally came. In it, he said that he saw no reason to oppose Maria's wish to marry Hudson, but he thought it would be best if they waited until her birthday. The couple was ecstatic.

They lived in an age of Victorian propriety, but Hudson and Maria were certainly not typical Victorians. One missionary wrote: "When [Hudson] fell in love it was a headlong plunge, and by no means a slight or evanescent passion. And his fiancée, with her strong, emotional nature, was in this respect not unlike him."

The wedding was quickly arranged, and they were married four days after Maria's twenty-first birthday.

However, two weeks before the wedding, Hudson was broke. He and a fellow missionary had been providing breakfast for sixty to eighty Chinese famine victims every morning, and they were paying for it out of their own pockets. "How the Lord would care for us on Monday we knew not, but over our mantelpiece hung two scrolls in Chinese characters—Ebenezer and Jehovah-Jireh—and He kept us from doubting for a moment."

But then he thought about Maria. How would

she adapt to his unusual life style? Maybe it was too much to ask.

He asked her if she wished to reconsider her commitment to him: "I cannot hold you to your promise if you would rather draw back. You see how difficult our life may be at times."

She hardly paused before replying: "Don't forget that I was an orphan in a faraway land. God has been my Father all these years. Do you think I shall be afraid to trust Him now?"

Two weeks later they were married. Maria wore a silk gown and wedding veil; Hudson had only a plain cotton robe. He had sold everything else he owned in order to feed the famine victims.

Marriage pleased him. Six weeks later he wrote, "Oh, to be married to the one you do love, and love most tenderly and devotedly, that is bliss beyond the power of words to express or imagination conceive."

In the following years Maria helped Hudson mature and display more common sense. As Pollock says, "She made him take holidays. . . . He shed his moods of melancholy, he forgot to be introspective. . . . He became more assured, he was no longer on the defensive, no more a prig. Imperceptibly, she polished him."

Two years later, in 1860, they returned to England. Hudson's health had broken, and he had no choice but to take his wife and one-year-old daughter back home. In England, Hudson reverted to

Western clothes and finished his course at medical school.

But more significant was his revision of the Ningpo New Testament, the recruiting of new missionaries for China, and the founding of a different kind of mission society, the China Inland Mission.

Burdened with the spiritual need of inland China, he began traveling up and down England, announcing that "a million a month were dying without God" in China. Half the heathen population of the world lived in China, and the number of missionaries there was decreasing instead of increasing.

He prayed and pleaded for twenty-four missionaries—lack of education was no barrier—to return to China with him. His new mission society would be financed—here was the revolutionary part—entirely by faith. If he made appeals for funds, it might interfere with the finances of existing denominational missions.

Within a few months, more than a score of recruits—including a blacksmith, a carpenter, a mason, a governess, a Bible woman, and a leisured daughter of a wealthy businessman—gathered at the spartan Taylor home for their missionary indoctrination. The group came not only from all walks of life but from all denominations—Baptists, Methodists, Presbyterians, and Anglicans were all represented.

Hudson Taylor had a strange kind of attraction. His illness had worn him down, but within him there was a certain magnetism. One of the recruits commented: "I half despised him at first. A sickly looking, hesitating young man, no kicking power in his makeup much."

"God chose me," Hudson Taylor said later in life, "because I was weak enough. God does not do His great works by large committees. He trains somebody to be quiet enough and little enough and then He uses him."

Hudson was certainly God's man for the hour. Six years earlier David Livingstone had ignited Great Britain with his presentation of the needs of Africa. Now Hudson Taylor was doing it regarding China. "China, China, China is now ringing in our ears," reported the great London pulpiteer Charles Haddon Spurgeon, "in that special, peculiar, musical, forcible, unique way in which Mr. Taylor utters it." Hudson normally spoke for two hours, sometimes demonstrating the use of chopsticks or Chinese ink in the course of the lecture. And though he never asked for money, the money began to roll in.

Thus, in 1866, Hudson and Maria Taylor, their four children, and fifteen missionary recruits sailed together for China. Hudson was thirty-four, Maria twenty-nine, but they were the veterans, the old China hands. One of the recruits wrote later that Hudson was "quite one with the young men of the party. Mrs. Taylor, quieter, in some ways perhaps more mature, such rare judgment; calm sweetness about her face always; most restful. She was very thoughtful and gave much time to study of the Bible and prayer. She gave a good deal of time to the children, too—used to gather them to the cabin for a little reading."

In China, Hudson had all his men immediately shave their heads, don pigtails, and dress like Chinese teachers. This jolted the established missionary community. Six years earlier when Hudson had been the only one wearing a pigtail, they had looked upon him with amusement; but now all his disciples wore pigtails, too.

Maria wasn't so sure that all the women should wear Chinese dress. She had reservations because "the Chinese despise their own females while they respect foreign ladies; will they treat us with as much respect and shall we have as much weight with them, if we change our dress?" Hudson asked her to try it for a while. She did, and soon she was convinced that his system was right.

Hudson's philosophy on missionaries wearing Chinese clothing wasn't a gimmick. "Why should a foreign aspect be given to Christianity?" he wrote. "The Word of God does not require it. It is not the denationalization but the Christianization of these people we seek. We wish to see . . . men and women truly Christian, but truly Christian in every right sense. We wish to see churches of such believers presided over by pastors and officers of their own countrymen, worshipping God in their own tongue, in edifices of a thoroughly native style."

For that day, it was a shocking missionary philosophy.

In its early years, the China Inland Mission had more than its share of problems. Hudson and Maria were severely criticized by missionaries of established societies, were attacked by the Chinese, and even faced dissension from within their own group.

Most of their young band, however, stuck with them. One of them said about Hudson, "If he were not in the habit of casting his burdens upon the Lord, I quite believe that what he has passed through he would have sunk under."

Maria was the second in command. Some members felt "she was the backbone of the mission at the time. Hudson Taylor had so learned to value her judgment and prayerfulness that he never took a step without consulting her."

She was still young, but already she had been beset by serious illness. Tuberculosis was slowly emaciating her and she didn't have the strength to withstand the diseases that struck the missionary community.

She was called "a woman of indomitable perseverance and courage, through troubles of every kind." Another commented, "She always sympathized with everyone and everybody. It showed often in little things." Another called her "humble, retiring, almost to shyness."

Hudson and Maria remained obviously in love. Once when he went inland on a preaching tour, he wrote her, "My darling one, I can now only in

imagination hold your loved form in my arms. . . .
For my sake and for the Lord's sake take great care
of your health. . . . O if I could but give you one
kiss."

A fifth child was born to Hudson and Maria not
long after their return to China.

But in 1867 their oldest child, Gracie, became
seriously ill. Hudson wrote home, "I am trying to
pen a few lines by the couch on which my darling
little Gracie lies dying. Her complaint is hydro-
cephalus. . . . God is the strength of our heart and
our portion forever. . . . And He has not left us
now."

A few weeks later he wrote his mother in England, "I know not how to write. Our dear little
Gracie! How we miss her! As I take the walks I
used to take with her tripping by my side, the
thought comes anew like a throb of agony, Is it
possible that I shall never more feel the pressure of
that little hand. . . . And yet . . . she is far holier,
far happier than she could ever have been here."

Gracie's death may have been a turning point
in the history of the China Inland Mission. The
missionaries rallied in sympathy around the Taylors,
and a new unity emerged.

Hudson and Maria brought a new dignity to the
role of women missionaries. For the first time single
female missionaries were sent out—dressed in
Chinese garb, of course—to do evangelizing without a male missionary to accompany them. For this

innovation, Hudson and Maria faced criticism; but the results were outstanding. One woman wrote, "I think when I go out I often speak to more than 200 persons. Yet I am never treated in any way rudely, but with all kindness."

When Maria heard that the criticism had spread to England, she wrote in response, "I believe ten Miss Fauldings and ten Miss Bowyers could easily find work in Hangchow tomorrow."

Meanwhile Hudson pleaded for missionaries of both sexes: "Are there no servants of our common Lord rusting away at home or at least doing work that others could do if they left it, who might be out here among these numberless towns and villages?"

In June 1868 Hudson and Maria moved their headquarters to Yangchow, having lived in Shanghai and Hangchow since their arrival in China. Yangchow was their boldest incursion yet into China's hinterlands. Since the time of Marco Polo, few Westerners had spent much time there.

Yangchow was anything but cordial. First, rumors started spreading. Foreign doctors were accused of making pills out of patients' eyes; missionaries of salting down children. Then came an anti-missionary handbill campaign. Westerners were going to impoverish their country by selling opium.

The worst was yet to come. Stones began crashing through their windows, and that was just a warning.

According to an anonymous letter that Hudson received, much more would happen if the missionaries didn't leave Yangchow immediately.

Hudson went to Maria and suggested that perhaps the men should stay and the women and children go. She disagreed. "For us to go away," she said, "would only increase the danger to the men." The women and children stayed.

Then one day a mob—150 to 200 angry Chinese—filled the street in front of the mission headquarters. They threatened to batter down the door if the missionaries didn't open up. Some of the rioters were obviously drunk. Many were half-naked.

The missionaries prayed. Hudson reminded his fellow workers of the verse, "Lo, I am with you always," and bid them pray some more.

The sky darkened; thunder boomed through the heavens. One missionary was writing a letter. "As I write He is sending thunder and the threatening of rain, which will do more for us, Mr. Taylor says, than an army of soldiers. The Chinese shun the rain." The mob dispersed.

But a few nights later they returned with flaming torches. They heaved bricks at the shuttered windows.

Maria calmly put her children to bed. The other missionaries were amazed at her serenity. "She was as calm as when in the parlor in London." Hudson knew that he had to get help from the Chinese military. And it was needed as soon as possible.

He kissed Maria, slipped out a door, and ran into the darkness. "When we turned into the main street," he recalled later, "we were assaulted with stones, and a mob gathered behind us. . . . We were nearly exhausted and our legs so hurt with the stones and bricks thrown at us that we were almost fainting."

Back at the missionary house, two male missionaries along with Chinese servants tried to keep the mob out. Upstairs the women were praying. Maria was six months pregnant. Her youngest child had dysentery. Another missionary wife was eight months pregnant.

The rioters seemed to grow louder every minute. Time passed—a half hour, then an hour, then an hour and a half. Still no Hudson, and still no soldiers to come to the rescue.

Then came a voice from downstairs. "Mrs. Taylor, they are setting the house on fire." The missionaries began climbing out a back window to be lowered on knotted sheets and blankets to concealment in a wellhouse.

Before Maria could escape, a naked rioter stormed into the room. He grabbed her by the wrist and demanded money.

"I will cut off your head," he threatened. He saw her wedding ring and pulled it violently from her finger.

"Jump," hollered a missionary from the ground

below. It was twelve to fifteen feet, but she had no alternative. She wrenched herself loose from her attacker and leaped downward.

A missionary half caught her, breaking her fall, but she landed on her side.

By the time soldiers arrived, the riot had subsided. Of course, the missionaries had to vacate Yangchow temporarily, but they prayed to be able to return. Maria was asked if she wanted the rioters to be punished. "The revenge I desire," she replied, "is the wider opening up of the country to our work."

When the British authorities got wind of the riot, they sent gunboats up the Yangtze River to Yangchow. "Foreigners traveling in the interior have a perfect and legal right to claim legitimate local protection," the British consul had told Hudson.

It was not the response that Hudson and Maria wanted. An international incident ensued.

Maria's only desire was to be able to return to Yangchow in time to have her baby born there. And ten days before Charles Edward Taylor was born, Hudson and Maria were able to return to Yangchow. Maria wrote, "God has given me the desire of my heart." She had wanted the baby to be born "in this city, in this house, in this very room." It seemed as if her prayer had been answered.

But it didn't take long before news of the Yangchow affair reached London. Soon the name of Hudson Taylor became a household word, but not in a favorable sense. The *Times* of London denounced him: "The Apostles and early missionaries certainly did not propagate their faith under the protection of fleets and armies." The American ambassador to China called the Yangchow affair a "high-handed action."

Even the British government itself, embarrassed by how world opinion had turned against it, wondered if there was some "efficient and stringent mode of dealing with these missionaries."

Other missionaries to China were angry with the Taylors for having placed all mission work in jeopardy.

Outwardly, Hudson seemed to bear up quite well with all the misinterpretations. Inwardly, he was "desperately hurt." Long-time friends and supporters had now believed the accusations.

But it was a time when other problems were looming large as well. Hudson was concerned about the quality of his missionary recruits. "Some persons seem really clever in doing the right thing in the worst possible way or at the most unfortunate moment," he wrote home. "Really dull or rude persons will seldom be out of hot water in China."

Besides these outward pressures were inner conflicts. One missionary called Hudson "toiling and burdened" at this time.

He wrote his mother, "I have often asked you to remember me in prayer. That need has never been greater."

Later he described the time, "I began the day

with prayer, determined not to take my eye from Him for a moment, but pressure of duties, sometimes very trying, constant interruptions apt to be so wearing, often caused me to forget Him. One's nerves get so fretted in this climate that temptations to irritability, hard thoughts, and sometimes unkind words are all more difficult to control. Each day brought its register of sin and failure, or lack of power. . . . Instead of growing stronger, I seemed to be getting weaker and of having less power against sin; and no wonder, for faith and even hope were getting very low. I hated myself."

Emotionally, he was deeply depressed and he faced even "the awful temptation . . . to end his own life."

One constant that he had was Maria's love. And his love for her remained as strong as ever. "It hasn't worn off or worn out."

Biographer J. C. Pollock says that it was Maria who stood between Hudson and suicide.

When separated by travel, Hudson wrote her warmly. "I dreamed last night that I was once more by your side. . . . When I awoke . . . I was so disappointed. When shall I really see you and once more fold you in my arms?"

And Maria responded, when sending him some supplies: "My priceless treasure . . . I should like to put myself among the things that are coming."

Hudson felt that there might be a danger that they actually loved each other too much. "Oh, may He ever give us both to love Him best, most constantly and with unfailing constancy. Then we shall not love one another too much."

As Hudson traveled, he talked to his missionary crew about his own "spiritual needs." Many of them shared the same inner discomfort of which he spoke. But one of them wrote, "As for Mrs. Taylor, she wondered what we were all groping after."

A few weeks later he received a letter from one of his missionaries named McCarthy, an Irishman with a quick temper. McCarthy said that he had found the secret in "abiding, not striving or struggling." This was a breakthrough for Hudson as well. "Ah, there is rest," he wrote. "I have striven in vain to rest in Him. I'll strive no more. For has He not promised to abide with me, never to leave me, never to fail me, and . . . He never will."

It was at this time that Hudson learned the secret of the serenity that "full identification with Christ brings. . . . Can Christ be rich and I be poor?"

Maria summed it up simply, "It was just resting in Jesus and letting Him do the work."

The trials of running the mission didn't subside with his spiritual discovery, however. By 1870, when Hudson and Maria were celebrating their twelfth anniversary, the China Inland Mission had thirty-three missionaries in twelve stations in three provinces. But it was, as Hudson later wrote, "a time of great trial, a time of the greatest difficulty I have ever known in China. From Peking to Canton the people were agitated. We did not know from day to day what would take place in our inland stations. But I had unspeakable rest in my soul."

In February, their third child, five-year-old Samuel, always "exceptionally delicate," died, and Hudson and Maria felt that they needed to send their other children—Bertie, nine, Freddie, seven, and Maria, three—back to England with one of the missionaries. They would keep the baby with them in Yangchow.

It was difficult to see their children go. Hudson wrote his mother to "pray specially for Maria. When all the bustle of preparation and the excitement of departure are over, then will come the trying time of reaction. But the Lord, whose work calls for the separation, can and will support her."

Maria was pregnant again. It was her eighth pregnancy in twelve years of marriage. She continued teaching her classes as usual, despite the fact that tuberculosis had ravaged her body. She seemed happy that she had been able to complete a Chinese-English vocabulary which had now gone to the printer. Hudson was more concerned than ever about her. "My heart ached," he said, "when I saw her thin wasted frame."

The baby came in mid-July. Maria was thankful that it had been an easy delivery, perhaps her easiest. But a day or two later, she was hemorrhaging internally and was weakening perceptibly.

Within two weeks the baby died, and Maria had very little strength remaining.

Hudson went to her and asked her, "Darling, do you know that you are dying?"

"Dying? Do you think so? What makes you think that?"

"I can see it, darling. Your strength is giving way."

"Can it be? I feel no pain, only weariness."

"You are going home. Soon you will be with Jesus."

There was silence for a moment. Then Maria whispered, "I am so sorry."

Hudson looked at her gently and said, "You are not sorry to go to be with Jesus."

"Oh no, it is not that. . . . But it does grieve me to leave you alone at such a time. Yet He will be with you and meet all your needs."

She kissed him over and over again, one kiss for each of the children.

A missionary who stood nearby said later, "I never witnessed such a scene. As dear Mrs. Taylor was breathing her last, Mr. Taylor knelt down . . . and committed her to the Lord, thanking Him for having given her to him and for the twelve and a half years of happiness they had had together."

He had to buy a coffin immediately because of the extreme heat. He looked at her in the coffin for a long while. Then he rushed upstairs to be alone.

A few days later he wrote: "I cannot describe to you my feelings. I do not understand them myself. I feel like a person stunned with a blow, or recovering from a faint, and as yet but partially conscious. . . . My Father has ordered it, so . . . therefore I know it is, it must be best, and I thank Him for so ordering it. I feel utterly crushed. . . . Oftentimes my heart is nigh to breaking, but withal I had almost said I never knew what peace and happiness were before—so much have I enjoyed in the very sorrow."

Those months were devastating to Hudson. He had lost his wife, had lost a baby, and had shipped three other children to England.

In a few days he wrote to his three in England: "How happy darling Momma must be! I am so glad for her to be with Him. I shall be so glad to go to her when Jesus thinks it best. But I hope He will help me to be equally willing to live with Him here so long as He has any work for me to do for Him and for poor China."

The Lord had more work for Hudson in poor China, much more.

A year later, he returned for a much needed furlough to England. He needed to recuperate both physically and emotionally from the twelve-month period in which he had lost his wife and two of his children. He also longed to see his other children again in England.

By coincidence, missionary Jennie Faulding was returning on the same ship. She had booked passage on another vessel, but after being unavoidably delayed, had to take the same ship that carried the head of her mission, Hudson Taylor.

The long voyage together was good for both of them. Hudson had always admired Jennie, and Jennie had always been a faithful fan of his.

The daughter of a London merchant and a convinced Baptist, Jennie was well educated, gracious, and cheerful. In fact, even when no one else found anything to rejoice about, Jennie could.

She had been among Hudson's first recruits for missionary service in 1866. On her first day aboard ship heading for China, she had written home, "Oh, I have enjoyed today! The sea is so lovely and the air is so beautiful, I never thought a voyage could be such a treat. It makes my blood tingle with pleasure."

When she arrived in China, she wrote, "It seemed like a dream to be really surrounded by pigtails and little feet."

When some of the missionaries began grumbling about adopting Chinese clothing, Jennie commented that, with the exception of Hudson Taylor, she thought everyone seemed "improved by the change."

When she traveled inland, she reported, "The canals are like beautiful rivers and if the strawberries have no taste, the wild raspberries are very nice (we have had a pie made of them) and the birds sing to one's heart's content."

Hudson characterized her with the phrase, "She never thought anything could be better."

She was only twenty-three when she ventured to China, and at the time Hudson took almost a father's concern for her. In response, she admired him as a "plaster saint."

"I have known him under all circumstances," she wrote her father, "and if you could see him daily you would indeed admire his self-abnegation, his humility and quiet never-flagging earnestness."

But there was more to Jennie than just cheerfulness. She was always loyal even when other missionaries questioned his leadership, and Hudson appreciated it. He could share concerns with her, even some of his personal struggles, as he could with his wife.

So it wasn't especially surprising that, aboard ship, the depressed Hudson Taylor and the ever-cheerful Jennie Faulding developed a romance. The following year they were married. She was twenty-nine; he was forty.

It wasn't the same kind of a marriage that he had had with Maria. With Maria, there was constant romance. With Jennie, it was different, but no less happy.

They were often separated in the following years. Jennie often stayed in London taking care of the stepchildren while Hudson traveled to China making the rounds of the mission stations.

In 1878, however, just after Hudson had returned from a sixteen-month tour of the field, he received word of an unprecedented famine in North China. Six million people were starving; tens of thousands were dying; thousands of children were orphaned and homeless.

Hudson saw the need for a woman to head a team of relief workers, invading that remote section of China with the gospel, with love, and with provisions. But who could do it?

It had to be Jennie. She was the only woman who spoke Chinese, who had the respect of the other workers, and who also had his complete confidence.

At first, she wasn't convinced. She thought she was needed just as much in London—for Hudson's sake, for the children's sake, for the mission's sake. But Hudson urged her to go, for Jesus' sake.

It wasn't that she was afraid. It was simply that she wasn't convinced it was the Lord's will. "I felt like Gideon," she wrote. "I wanted some fleeces to confirm my faith." She asked for fifty English pounds to outfit her for the strenuous trip. It came within a few days.

Then on the day she was scheduled to depart, an anonymous check for a thousand pounds arrived. It was specified for an orphanage in North China she was to found.

No foreign woman had ever ventured into that part of China, but Jennie led the team composed of one man and two women.

When Hudson heard that her mission had been successful, he wrote her: "I do thank my God for giving me such a wife. . . . Every day I look at the little Bible marker you gave me, with the words, 'For Jesus' sake,' and I am thankful for the reminder."

After establishing an orphanage and a new mission outpost, she rejoined her husband a year later when he returned for another visit to China.

Hudson continued to use the motto: "For Jesus' sake." The true joy of life, he said, was to do all for Jesus' sake, even as Jennie had done.

As Hudson and Jennie grew older and no longer could take the frequent trips to China, they handed over the control of the mission to others. For Hudson, this was most difficult. "It's hardest of all to do nothing for Jesus' sake," he said.

Jennie died in 1904 at the age of sixty-one; Hudson died a year later when he was seventy-three. At the time of his death, the China Inland Mission, which he had founded a generation earlier, had 825 missionaries on the field.

The afternoon before he died, a group of missionaries were talking with him about bringing everything to God in prayer. One of them said that sometimes he found it difficult to bring the small things to God.

Hudson Taylor replied, "There is nothing small, and there is nothing great; only God is great, and we should trust Him fully."

CHAPTER
THREE

Meet
Billy
and
Nell
Sunday

AS Billy Sunday a boy who never grew up?

Why did he always refer to his wife, Nell, as "Ma"?

To what extent did Nell, who was Billy's business manager, control his life?

Billy liked the macho image. After all, it was the Teddy Roosevelt era. But he needed Nell's sure direction. Once he said that his wife "wouldn't take first prize at a beauty show, but she's got more good horse sense than any woman I ever saw in my life." And one thing that Billy respected was horse sense.

Though Billy was always up front and Nell was behind the scenes, they were a team. At first, you might think that it was Billy Sunday, the sensational evangelist, who was sure of himself; but underneath the blustery boldness was a core of insecurity. Billy was mercurial in more ways than one. Nell was hardworking and hardheaded.

Those who worked with both of them loved Billy even though he might fly off the handle once in a while. But when Nell talked, they obeyed.

Evangelism a la Billy Sunday was approached like a business with Billy as the chairman of the board and Nell as the chief executive officer.

But marriage is more than a business relationship.

You could never be neutral about baseball-player-turned-evangelist Billy Sunday.

Some called him the greatest evangelist since the Apostle Paul. Others called him a charlatan, the prototype of Elmer Gantry.

Some likened him to the Renaissance reformer Savonarola. Others said that if he had concentrated on winning souls, instead of battling booze, his ministry would have been much more effective.

Some said that his meetings topped everything since Pentecost. Others said that his acrobatic style, his flare for promotion, and his insistence on making sure that finances were amply covered brought discredit upon the cause of Christ.

Sunday once said, "I'd stand on my head in a mud puddle if I thought it would help me win souls to Christ." No doubt, if he had, Nell would have been right there rounding up an audience.

When they first met, Billy was Methodist by background, but nothing by practice. Nell was a strict Scottish Presbyterian. Billy never really had a father; but Nell's father, a prominent ice cream producer in Chicago, was very concerned, not only about his daughter, but also about the company she kept.

The year that William Ashley Sunday was born, 1862, his father enlisted as a private in the Union Army. He never returned. His widow was left with three boys under five years of age.

She remarried and had two more children. Troubles multiplied for her in the next decade. When he was six, Billy, who did not get along with his stepfather, moved into his grandfather's home a few miles away. One of his brothers was kicked in the head by a horse and had to spend the rest of his life in a home for the feeble-minded. A sister was burned to death when her clothes caught fire as she tended a bonfire. Then in the midst of the depression of 1874, Mrs. Sunday's second husband walked out on her. He apparently couldn't take any more.

When Billy was twelve, he and an older brother were shipped off to a Soldier's Orphanage where they spent two years. At the orphanage he completed the equivalent of grammar school, and learned that, while he wasn't very good in math, he was quite competent in running and fighting.

At fourteen, he returned to live with his grandfather. But both Billy and his grandfather had strong tempers, and the mix was highly inflammable. Billy soon ran away from home. In Nevada, Iowa, he collected three jobs: as a stable boy, an errand boy, and a school janitor; and he was able to earn a high school education in the process.

In 1883, when he was twenty and working as an undertaker's assistant in Marshalltown, Iowa, he played baseball for the local team. When his team won the state championship, Billy attracted the attention of "Pop" Anson, manager of the Chicago Whitestockings, owned by A. G. Spalding.

Billy went directly from the sandlots of Marshalltown to the major leagues. The small-town boy was awe-stricken. In fact, he struck out his first thirteen times at bat. In time, however, he established himself as an exciting all-around player.

His lifetime average was a so-so .259 (though he did bat .359 one year), but his fielding and his speed were almost legendary. He circled the bases in fourteen seconds and stole ninety-five bases in one season, a record which until 1962 was topped by only one other player, Ty Cobb.

One sportswriter commented: "Sunday probably caused more wide throws than any other player the game had ever known, because of his specialty of going down to first like a streak of lightning." He loved to stretch singles into doubles, though he was criticized for taking too many chances. But the fans loved him.

Every day, on his way from the hotel to the Whitestockings baseball field, Billy had to pass a Presbyterian church. It was the church that the team's batboy attended, and the batboy promised Billy that he would introduce him to his sister if he ever showed up in church.

So one Sunday evening, Billy Sunday walked into a youth service of the Jefferson Park Presbyterian Church. The first thing he noticed was Nell Thompson leading the meeting. (She also happened to be the batboy's sister.) Because she had been in charge of the youth meeting, she thought it was her responsibility to invite the newcomer to a forthcoming youth social.

That was the way it all began. The year was 1885. Nell was seventeen, Billy, twenty-two, and the road ahead was anything but smooth.

Helen "Nell" Thompson, who had made her profession of faith in Christ at the age of twelve, was now teaching a Sunday school class as well as being a leader of the youth group, and her father did not like the idea of his daughter running around with an unsaved professional ballplayer who spent his off-season as a locomotive fireman.

Of course, the biggest strike against Billy was that he wasn't a Christian; but besides that he wasn't educated and there were no indications that he was cut out for anything else in life except playing baseball.

Billy knew that prospects of developing a serious relationship with the dairyman's daughter were slim, but he didn't give up.

The first big development came a year later in 1886. One Sunday afternoon, after "tanking up" in a saloon in Chicago's Loop, Billy and several of his teammates sat down on the curb. Across the street, a group of musicians—trumpeters, flutists, trombonists—were playing gospel songs. Billy recognized the tunes; they were the songs his mother used to sing to him when he was a boy. Some of them were also sung in Nell's church.

A young man walked across the street and invited the ballplayers to come to the Pacific Garden Mission where they could hear the stories of former burglars, drunks, and prostitutes who had become Christians at the mission.

None of the other players responded. But Billy accepted the invitation, walked to the mission, and went forward to receive Jesus Christ as his Savior.

Undoubtedly, Nell was a factor in his decision. As Billy put it later: "I was hot on the trail of Nell. . . . She was a Presbyterian, so I am a Presbyterian. Had she been a Catholic, I would have been a Catholic." But there is no doubt that Billy's conversion was genuine.

The change in his life was obvious to his teammates. He gave up drinking, swearing, and gambling. Soon he requested and got a contract that allowed him not to play ball on Sundays. As he traveled with the team to various cities, he frequently gave talks in YMCAs about his conversion. He even joined Nell's church.

However, Nell's father still wasn't satisfied that Billy Sunday was the man for his daughter. Nell had another suitor, a young man from a good family, who seemed to know where he was going and was destined to get there.

As Billy became more serious about Nell, he told her about his past. For the three previous winters he had been dating the daughter of the engineer on the Chicago and Northwestern Railway, where he had been working.

The news shocked Nell. Immediately she responded: "Put on your hat and coat, go out the door, take the next train for Iowa, and fix it up with Clara, before we go any further." Billy put on his hat and coat and went out the door.

A week later, Billy was at Nell's doorstep again. "What did she say when you told her?" asked Nell before she let him in.

"Well," Billy sputtered, "I didn't exactly tell her. I decided to write her a letter instead."

Billy had written the letter, but the handling of the matter didn't please Nell's father. "No daughter of mine," said Mr. Thompson, "is going to go with a fellow who kept a girl on the string for three years." It seemed to be an uphill battle for Billy.

In 1887, while Nell was attending business college, Billy felt that some higher education wouldn't hurt him a bit, especially if he wanted to impress

Nell's father. He tried to get into Northwestern University, but his high school credentials weren't strong enough. So in exchange for agreeing to become baseball coach at the university, he was allowed to matriculate at Northwestern's prep school. With a little brushing up at the prep school, he would be able to pass the necessary entrance exams for the university.

But he never got to the university. He didn't need to. The following year, William Thompson, Sr., gave in. Convinced that Billy was a sincere Christian and a passable Presbyterian, Mr. Thompson reluctantly agreed that Billy might even amount to something in this world. In addition, he knew that his daughter was determined to marry no one else, and Nell's determination was something to contend with.

On Labor Day weekend in 1888, Billy and Nell were married in her Presbyterian church. She was twenty; he was twenty-five.

Their honeymoon was spent with the Chicago Whitestockings on the team's final road trip of the year. By now Billy was earning a substantial salary as a ballplayer. The following season, Nell frequently accompanied him on the road trips; but of course, when their first child arrived, her traveling days were over.

To complicate their married life, Billy was traded away from Chicago. Traded first to Pittsburgh and then to Philadelphia, Billy was away during much of the summer, but during the winter he was back in Chicago working for the YMCA. The more he became involved in a Christian ministry, the more he felt that this was what the Lord wanted him to do with his life.

Admittedly, he was no great speaker. He says, "When I first started out to be a Christian, I couldn't stand up in a prayer meeting and use three sentences consecutively." But in talking to men individually about their need for Jesus Christ, he was quite effective.

He and Nell talked about whether he should leave baseball and work for the YMCA. But the problem was he had just signed a lucrative three-year contract with Philadelphia. In the past he had sent some of his money to his mother and some to care for his institutionalized brother. Now he also had a wife and baby daughter to support.

Did the Lord really want him to give up baseball and work at one-sixth the salary for the YMCA, which was often six months behind in paying? He didn't know what to do.

He asked the Lord to make it very clear to him. Though it seemed unlikely, he requested the Philadelphia team to release him from his contract. His prayer was: "Lord, if I don't get my release by March 25 [when spring training was scheduled to start], I'll assume you want me to keep playing ball."

On March 17, his release came in the mail. In the same mail, however, he received an offer from the Cincinnati Reds to pick up his contract, providing an attractive salary on a one-year basis.

For Billy that clouded the issue again. Why didn't the Lord make it crystal clear?

He went to Nell and asked her what she thought. She was always good at analyzing difficult problems. And she had no doubts whatever about this one. She responded, "There is nothing for you to consider; you promised God to quit."

For the next two years, Billy and Nell lived on starvation wages at best, but more often on empty promises, while Billy passed out tracts, led prayer meetings, and aided down-and-outers to find "salvation and jobs." It was quite a comedown for a young man who had enjoyed the limelight for the previous eight years.

Then in the financial crash of 1893, the YMCA couldn't even make promises to Billy, and once again he was in a quandary about his future. Just at this time he was asked by evangelist J. Wilbur Chapman, perhaps the outstanding evangelist of the day, to become his "advance man." Eagerly he accepted the opportunity.

Prior to each of Chapman's evangelistic campaigns, Billy went into the city, organized committees, raised money to rent a hall and pay for ads, and trained the volunteer workers. It was great experience.

But in 1895, another traumatic experience engulfed the Sundays. It was during the Christmas holidays. A telegram came from Chapman. It stated simply that he was returning to the pastorate and quitting evangelism. It meant, of course, that they were once again without financial support. Billy and Nell, now with two young children, had no money saved. "We worried and prayed what to do and discussed if I should go back to play baseball," Billy recalled.

A few days later, before any other decisions were made, Billy received an invitation to conduct an evangelistic campaign himself. It was from a small town in Iowa, population one thousand. The size of the town didn't matter at all.

"We knew it was a direct answer to our prayers," said Billy.

But the meetings were scheduled to begin within ten days and Billy had no sermons. When Billy got there, he found they had no song leader, so he led the singing himself, "though I did not know a note from a horsefly."

As a direct result of the one-week crusade, one-hundred decisions for Christ were recorded, and Billy's new career had been launched.

In the next five years Billy held more than sixty revival campaigns in small midwestern towns. Free-will offerings on the last day of the crusade provided his somewhat uncertain income.

Each year Nell seemed to become more involved. She helped him with organization and soon became regarded as his business manager. After all, she had graduated from business college. "He hated managing finances, and I love figures," she explained simply.

Two more children were born in 1901 and 1907, but Nell spent as much time as she could helping Billy. Besides being his business manager, she also led prayer meetings, conducted Bible classes, spoke at women's meetings, and occasionally even led the singing.

"The children," says William G. McLaughlin, Jr., in *Billy Sunday Was His Real Name,* "were left with their grandparents and later sent to boarding schools."

An article in the Columbus, Ohio, *Citizen,* told of one example: "Sunday evening when Billy Sunday had closed an inspiring sermon in Memorial Hall and the people were halting on decision, Nell stepped into the breach, lead the choir, and swung several hundred penitents to a public acknowledgment of God." And the beauty of it all was that she was not striving to establish something. No, she was just trying to show herself a real, live helpmate. Just trying to help Billy, that was all.

Sunday's official biographer, William T. Ellis, says, "Mrs. Sunday's influence upon her husband was extraordinary. He was a devoted husband . . . and had complete confidence in her judgment. She was his 'man of affairs.'

"He made no important decisions without consulting her. She traveled with him nearly all of the time, attending his meetings, and watching over his work and his personal needs like a mother."

After a few years, Sunday's preaching style began to change. At first, he emulated J. Wilbur Chapman's dignified style. After all, some of his sermons had been borrowed from Chapman. But gradually he adopted a more popular, dramatic style and his audiences were entertained as well as inspired when they attended his revival meetings.

Perhaps it was simply that he began to be himself on the platform. He was no dignified scholar; he was best qualified as an athlete. His biographer calls him "a gymnast for Christ." The Boston *Herald* later referred to him as "a virile, agile man, sometimes a clown, sometimes a stump speaker, sometimes a minstrel monologuist, sometimes an actor, sometimes a preacher."

One of his most famous sermons was one he customarily addressed to men. It ended with Sunday's version of the poem, "Slide, Kelly, Slide." At the climax of it, he made a running dive across the full length of the platform. Then he would leap to his feet, imitating the "Great Umpire of the Universe" and yell, "You're out, Kelly."

McLaughlin says, "It was estimated that he walked a mile back and forth across the thirty-foot platform in every sermon—one-hundred and fifty miles in every campaign. But it was not merely walking; it was running, sliding, jumping, falling, staggering, whirling, and throwing himself around the platform. He did not remain in one spot or one position for thirty seconds."

His lack of formal education and his humble background frequently caused Billy to feel inferior. He had no theological training at all, so it may have been due to Nell's prompting that he sought ordination in the Presbyterian church. While his acquaintance with Scripture had been growing through the years, he still had huge gaps in his knowledge of theology and church history. Consequently, during his ordination examination, his most frequent answers were, "That's too deep for me," and "I'll have to pass that one up."

Finally, a friend moved that the remainder of the examination be waived. After all, he said, "God has used him to win more souls to Christ than all of us combined."

Although he was ordained to the Presbyterian ministry, hardly ever was he referred to as "the Reverend Mr. Sunday."

His earliest meetings were conducted in churches; by 1898 he seemed to prefer evangelistic tents, usually erected in a vacant lot near the middle of town. Then, in the early 1900s, he had a wooden tabernacle constructed, replacing the tent. And from then on he required that a wooden tabernacle be constructed in every city he was scheduled to visit.

For several years, Nell was reluctant to have her husband hold meetings in large cities. She kept the statistics and could demonstrate that when a city was larger than thirty thousand, Billy had difficulty being as effective as he would like to be. "When they're larger than that," she said, "it is impossible to reach everybody." Their goal was to see the conversion of 20 percent of the town's population during their crusade.

Actually, in Billy's first ten years of evangelism, 90 percent of his meetings were conducted in cities under ten thousand. Gradually, however, despite the statistics, he and Nell accepted invitations to larger cities. By 1914 he was speaking in such cities as Denver, Pittsburgh, Philadelphia, Kansas City, Detroit, Boston, New York, Chicago, Washington, D. C., Atlanta, and Los Angeles.

Along with the size of the crusades, the size of the Sunday evangelistic team also expanded. His staff in 1917 consisted of nearly a score of workers, including Homer Rodeheaver, the well-known gospel musician. His team also included six women in addition to his wife.

Though Billy tended to be conservative on most political issues, he was progressive on women's suffrage, and he backed his views up by giving women prominent positions on his team. Women served as his directors of businesswomen's work, extension work, Bible study, children's work, and students' work; as his assistant Bible teacher, and as his reservations secretary. Of course, Nell was his business manager and she was in charge of hiring and firing of the staff, so she might have had something to do with the number of women on the team.

Billy also had a personal masseur, a former prizefighter, on his staff, who gave him a rubdown at the close of each of his strenuous sermons.

Although their oldest son, George, was listed as business manager in 1917, Nell still made the decisions. No important moves were made without her approval. She selected the cities in which to hold campaigns and controlled his schedule. Speaking of her husband, she later said, "While supreme in his own province of preaching, he was otherwise dependent upon me. He fretted if I was not near. He seemed helpless without me."

As a crusade's opening night approached, Billy grew increasingly unpredictable. Sometimes he would lose his temper; at other times when he was slighted or when he imagined an insult, he would sulk to his room like a little boy.

It was Nell's job to be the peacemaker or, as she put it, "My job is to be the safety valve." During his rest hours, no one was allowed to interrupt him. One biographer called Nell the buffer between Billy and the outside world. Biographer Lee Thomas says that Nell watched over Billy as "a mother hen watches over her chicks."

Nell also had to watch out for Billy's excessive generosity. He often extended himself too far in both time and money. Even in the midst of a crusade he might agree to take extra meetings that Nell would be obliged to cancel out.

By 1908 Billy and Nell asked the local committees to provide a private house (or houses) for the entire crusade team. The team would eat together like a family, and each meal took on the atmosphere of a meeting of the board of directors. Billy and

Nell would sit at the head of the table and hear reports from each team member. Billy was referred to as "the Boss." Nell was usually called Mrs. Sunday, although some would call her "Ma" as Billy did.

The group may have operated like a business, but everything was handled prayerfully. Both Billy and Nell made sure of that.

Both of them prayed informally. Nell would pray, "Father, this is Ma. You know Mr. Smith has invited us to come to Pittsburgh. What should we do about it?" Her prayers, like her husband's, were devoid of "thees" and "thous."

Billy's personality was attractive to the team members. He tended to be fun-loving, with a boyish enjoyment of practical jokes. Even though he might lose his temper in the pressure of a difficult situation, he would quickly forgive and forget all about it.

On the other hand, Nell was regarded with respect, but not especially with affection. She expected obedience and she got it. Extremely hardworking, she called on others to work as hard as she did.

Later, a grandson said, "Ma reminds me of the early American woman, the type that would get in a covered wagon with her family and head for the western plains to help pioneer that great land. I can picture her in the driver's seat, with a shotgun across her lap and a nursing baby in her arms, while she held the reins."

Ma herself wrote, "At home, and between meetings, I had to care for Billy in every way. . . . During our campaigns, he spent most of his time between meetings in bed, and I waited on him. I would get him the food he liked, and in every way would relieve the terrible strain of his preaching work."

While Nell tended to exaggerate a bit on such matters, the assessment is reasonably accurate.

Billy was greeted as a celebrity wherever he went. At fifty-five, he invaded New York City. He was still healthy, slim, and bouncy; his platform antics hadn't changed. Five-feet, eight-inches tall, he dressed immaculately in a business suit. He hardly looked like a country boy from Iowa.

When he got off the train and saw the local committee coming to meet him, he was in his element. He recognized one of the men, John D. Rockefeller, Jr., threw an arm around his shoulder, and said, "Hello, old chap."

When opening night came, it was understandable if Billy was a bit tense and excitable. Crowds often lined up outside the tabernacle eight to ten hours before the doors opened. Sometimes police were called upon to escort Billy and Nell into the tabernacle. In his Philadelphia crusade, seventy-thousand came to hear him on the first day; thirty-five thousand were turned away in the evening.

In the larger cities Billy often stayed eight to ten weeks; usually the final days of the crusade brought the greatest response. In New York City, for instance, more than seven thousand came forward on the final day.

Each evening before the service began, Billy would rehearse his sermon even though he probably had given it scores of times before in other cities.

And early in the service Billy always introduced his team to his audience. After he presented his assistants, his choir leader, his soloist, and his instrumentalist, he completed his introductions by beckoning Nell. "And this is Ma," he said. It was spoken warmly, with obvious endearment.

A controversial aspect of Billy's ministry was the freewill offering with which Billy paid the salaries of his staff as well as of Nell and himself. Never before had such financial figures been made public. But because they became public and because they were often large, the critics had a field day.

In Sunday's earliest crusades the love-offerings hardly paid to keep his children in diapers. But as he went to larger cities, the offerings increased to what in that day seemed to be astronomical sums.

But Billy had a rationale. He explained it this way: Many major denominations spend several hundred dollars to win a convert for Christ. "What I'm paid for my work makes it only about two dollars per soul, and I get less proportionately for the number I convert than any other living evangelist."

Then the critics started looking at his supposed converts, and found that many of them were simply rededicating themselves to the Lord and others were making pledges to refrain from alcoholic beverages.

One of Billy's most popular messages was his "Booze Sermon." It became a part of every crusade.

Early in his ministry, during the summer months when evangelistic meetings were not held, Billy would go on the Chautauqua circuit, speaking in small towns across the Midwest. McLaughlin says, "Preachers like Sunday were sandwiched in between performances by ventriloquists, scientific lecturers, hypnotists, opera singers, acrobats, concert violinists, returned missionaries, traveloguists, minstrels, actors, and magicians. These performers were signed up for a season by a managing agency which provided steady work throughout the summer to one town after another."

It was during one such summer circuit that he developed his famous "Booze Sermon." In that day when the Prohibition movement was building up steam, it came to be Billy's most famous sermon. As a result, Billy was in the forefront of the Prohibition movement for a number of years.

How influential he was in the passage of the Prohibition Amendment is questionable; it is also difficult to say whether his "Booze Sermon" helped or hindered his total evangelistic ministry. It is certain, however, that many who came forward to give up drink had no genuine interest in Jesus Christ as Lord and Savior.

In 1910, Billy and Nell bought a home in Winona Lake, Indiana, and moved their family there. They were in good company. Evangelist J. Wilbur Chapman had already retired there and the Interdenominational Association of Evangelists met there every summer.

The Winona Lake home was a nine- or ten-room bungalow, overlooking the lake. It was rambling, but not pretentious. Billy said that it cost him $3,800 to build. Inside, on the walls, were portraits of various members of the Sunday family, as well as some oil paintings which Nell had painted in earlier years.

Around the house, Billy dressed casually and spent as much time as possible outdoors, doing yard work, tending plants and flowers, and working on his lawn.

In addition, the Sundays also owned a fruit farm in the Hood River district of Oregon, and they often spent part of their summers there.

A reporter for the South Bend *Tribune* interviewed the Sundays in their Winona Lake home, and some of the informal conversation is revealing.

In the middle of the interview Nell turned to Billy:

"Papa," she interrupted, "I wish we could get some grass seed in before the rain."

"So do I."

"Hadn't you better put it in?"

No answer.

"There's a bucket back there. Why don't you use that?"

"All right."

A minute later a pacified Billy Sunday crossed the lawn lugging a big tin wash boiler of grass seed. Then his wife pointed out where he should sow it while she called to young Billy (their second son, about ten years old at the time) to go take his music lesson.

One of her children addressed a letter to her: "Dearest Mother, General Manager, General Fix-it, General All-around healer of the troubles of the world." That's the way she was regarded by those closest to her.

Increasingly, "Ma" Sunday became a celebrity in her own right and was sought out for interviews. Interviews with her husband were always more colorful, but Nell's comments were short, direct, and opinionated. They were also quite conservative politically.

In Detroit, in the middle of World War I, she was asked her thoughts about the war. She commented that it was a political necessity; there always had been wars and there always would be. In Philadelphia, she was asked about unemployment. She responded, "I haven't got any patience for a man who can't find a job. He has usually wasted his strength and his brain through drink or cigarettes or women. . . . A good Christian is always successful."

Billy loved Nell. There's no question about that. His personal letters are filled with warm phrases: "Lover, I can hardly wait to be with you again."

The peak years for Billy and Nell were 1914 to

1918. When World War I ended, Billy's major ministry slowed down as well. He had conducted campaigns in virtually all of America's major cities; now his campaigns were once again in the secondary cities.

But other things were disturbing, too. Billy's best friend J. Wilbur Chapman ("Next to the members of my family, I loved him more than anyone else") died in 1918.

Then there were family problems, problems that "Ma," though she may have been regarded as "General Fix-it" by her family, was unable to fix. Their son George, who had assisted as business manager of the New York campaign, attempted suicide in 1923. In 1929, he was arrested for auto theft and bail jumping. In 1930 he was divorced, and in 1933 he jumped from a window to his death.

Their second son was divorced in 1927, remarried in 1928, and divorced again in 1929. The grounds were extreme cruelty. A test pilot, he was killed in a plane crash a couple of years later.

Their youngest son, Billy, Jr., was killed in an automobile wreck near Palm Springs, California, and their only daughter died in 1933. Her death was perhaps the most crushing of all to Billy Sunday. Nell described her husband as "terribly broken."

That was the year Billy had his first heart attack. He was preaching in a church in Des Moines, Iowa. He staggered and his song leader rushed to catch him. But Billy refused to halt the service. He begged his song leader to give the invitation for him, while he continued to lean against the pulpit for support. "I'd rather die on my feet than quit now," he said. The invitation was given and many responded.

Billy recovered from that attack, but two years later, at the age of seventy-three, he was stricken again and died. He had given "Ma" instructions regarding his funeral: "No sad stuff when I go."

Shortly before his death, Billy wrote, "I care not what is said about me. . . . I am and always have been plain Billy Sunday, trying to do God's will in preaching Jesus and Him crucified and arisen from the dead for our sins."

During his career he had spoken to more than 100 million people and he had seen approximately one million walk the sawdust trail.

Nell survived Billy by more than twenty years, living in Winona Lake, Indiana, until the time of her death.

Bruce Lockerbie, in his book on Billy Sunday, wrote, "Perhaps no other woman in the history of American Christianity has held such a place in the life of her husband. . . . He depended on her."

As the star on stage, Billy had his name in lights, but it was Ma who was the producer and director.

CHAPTER
FOUR

Meet
Frank
and
Grace
Livingston
hill

MILLIONS of people around the world have read Grace Livingston Hill's novels, but few know anything about her personal life. Fewer still know her husband, Frank—or for that matter have ever heard of him.

All her novels (and she wrote more than eighty of them) end with happiness. Most of them are love stories with the girl marrying the fellow in the final chapter.

But her readers never found out what characterized Grace Livingston Hill's own marriage. Did it have a happy ending, too?

Grace didn't like to write of unpleasantness. "I feel that there is enough sadness and sorrow in the world, so I try to end all my books as beautifully as possible," she once said. And that was one reason why she seldom talked about her second marriage, to a music teacher named Flavius Josephus Lutz.

Few American writers, either secular or religious, have sold more books than Grace Livingston Hill. More of her books have been reprinted than books by Dickens, Scott, or even Zane Grey. Yet the facts of her own life, her marriages, and her family are largely unknown.

What was she really like? Who was the woman behind the novels that continue to sell hundreds of thousands of copies a generation after her death? And who was Frank Hill?

Perhaps if Frank Hill had lived, Grace might never have written a novel. Perhaps she would have settled down to be the kind of minister's wife that she envisioned in some of her novels.

But Frank and Grace did not live happily ever after. He died suddenly at the age of thirty-four, leaving Grace with two small children.

And that's where Grace's life had a second beginning, as she picked up the shattered pieces. A bereavement that brought her close to a nervous breakdown turned into a new life.

As 1899 began, life seemed idyllic for the Rev. and Mrs. Frank Hill. The Wakefield Presbyterian Church in the Germantown section of Philadelphia had been under their care for the previous six years. A brilliant student, Frank had developed into a powerful preacher. Grace was coming up with creative ideas for use in the Christian education outreaches of the church.

Less than twenty-five years old, the church already had more than six hundred members in its Sunday school. Its Christian Endeavor groups enrolled nearly one hundred young people, and Frank's messages kept the congregation coming to both morning and evening services.

Their two children, though still young, were both showing signs of the same mental quickness that characterized the parents.

It was the life that Grace Livingston Hill had dreamed of.

Though she wrote occasionally for Sunday school and Christian Endeavor publications, she seemed to be finding her contentment and fulfillment as a pastor's wife, not as a writer.

It was not really surprising. After all, in her immediate family were seven ministers. Even her name Grace was bestowed upon her because of its theological content. In her mind there could be no higher calling for a woman than to become the wife of a minister.

Then a few days before Thanksgiving, after only seven years of marriage, Frank Hill was stricken with acute appendicitis. He never recovered.

For a while, friends wondered if Grace would ever recover from it either.

Grace was born in 1865, two days after Abraham Lincoln was assassinated. She died in 1947, two years after Hiroshima. In those fourscore years she was no stranger to unpleasantness.

Her father, Charles Livingston, a Presbyterian minister from a good New York family, was strict, determined, and frequently stubborn. He was also a good father, a wise counselor, and a dedicated family man. Family is something that meant a lot to the Livingstons.

In Grace's novels, Charles is sometimes seen as an older minister or father-figure. In *Beauty for Ashes*, Grace writes of the main character, "It seemed to Gloria that her father was the wisest man living." That's how Grace thought of her father.

He never sacrificed his principles; some of his parishioners called him bull-headed. His strong stands frequently precipitated church conflicts; as a matter of fact, the Livingstons seldom stayed very long in any one parsonage.

Little Grace, the only child in the Livingston home, dreamed of a permanent home, a large stone house with a big backyard. Jean Karr, in her biography, writes, "Grumbling and complaining about their lot in life was not a part of the Livingston family tradition, so the child's dream world grew and gave her whatever was lacking in her material existence."

In the sixteen years between 1876 and 1892, Grace and her parents lived in at least nine different parsonages. They moved from Watertown in northern New York to Greensburg, Indiana, to Cincinnati to Cleveland to Orange, New Jersey, to Campbell, New York, to Sorrento, Florida, to Winter Park, Florida, to Hyattsville, Maryland. The biggest church for Charles was his first; it had 225 members. Some were only mission churches, such as the one in Sorrento, Florida, with 26 members. His last church, Hyattsville, had 100 members.

Instead of breeding insecurity or perhaps disillusionment, this bouncing from one parsonage to another every two years knit the Livingston family close together. They trusted a sovereign Lord and they deeply loved one another.

It was because of her family that Grace put her trust in Jesus Christ. And her extended family included not only mother and father, but also aunts, uncles, and cousins. "After we had hustled through the dishes, we all gathered in the big sitting room around the open fire for family worship. In the evening we would all recite verses in turn before the prayer. I listened as my family talked with God, and I became inevitably acquainted with the Lord Jesus. . . . The secret of this is that my family lived the faith they preached. I saw Jesus Christ in their daily lives."

Between his many pastorates, Charles Livingston served as a home missionary in Missouri, Ohio, and Florida. This gave his daughter a deep awareness of the needs of the underprivileged.

Grace often accompanied her father when he spoke at small rural churches. She liked being his assistant, playing the organ, teaching a Sunday school class for the children, and sometimes singing a solo.

Growing up, she was probably closer to her father than to her mother. She learned to play tennis on a homemade court that he had built behind one of their parsonages. She rode horseback with him. And it was a great achievement when she could beat him in chess.

As they drove by horse and buggy through the Ohio and New York countrysides, she was flattered when he discussed politics and theology with her. "My father taught me to think," she said later.

It was from her mother's side, however, that her literary interests developed. Her mother wrote romantic love stories of the Civil War period and occasional Christmas pieces for weekly magazines during the 1860s and 1870s.

Her mother was not only Grace's severest critic—always correcting her diction, grammar, and spelling—but also her mind-expander to the beauties of nature and to the possibilities of the imagination.

No one, however, exerted a stronger literary influence on her than her Aunt Isabella, whom she called Auntie Belle. Auntie Belle was known to hundreds of thousands of young readers across the country as Pansy, the popular author of a series of best-selling novels for youth.

At the peak of her popularity she and her husband stayed with Grace and her parents. Youthful, imaginative, and lively, Auntie Belle was a "combination of fairy godmother, heroine, and saint" to Grace. "I thought her the most beautiful, wise, and wonderful person in my world, outside of my home. I treasured her smiles, copied her ways, and listened breathlessly to all she had to say. . . .

"I measured other people by her principles and opinions, and always felt that her word was final. . . . I even corrected my beloved parents sometimes when they failed to state some principle or opinion as she had done."

Besides being a minister's wife and writing one "Pansy" book after another, Auntie Belle also edited a magazine for children called *The Pansy* and answered fanmail from boys and girls who belonged to the Pansy Society. Grace was enthralled by it all.

In her early teens, Grace pitied the other children in the Pansy Society. "They could only write letters to her, while I could often be with her every day, sometimes for weeks, and could talk with her all I pleased."

The Livingston family read books together every night. In their various parsonages, they went through the novels of George MacDonald, William Dean Howells, Charles Dickens, and Walter Scott. But a special treat came when Auntie Belle had completed writing another of her Pansy novels. Then they would interrupt their reading of Dickens or Scott and enjoy the latest "Pansy," fresh from the typewriter.

Occasionally, Auntie Belle allowed Grace to peck away on her typewriter (it was one of the first all-capital Remingtons) and try to write her own stories. And one Christmas Auntie Belle gave her niece a thousand sheets of typing paper and suggested that she turn the thousand sheets "into as many dollars."

In a few weeks Grace turned out a nine-chapter, 4,000-word book called *The Esselstynes; or Alphonso and Marguerite*. The story describes what happens when two street urchins (Alphonso and Marguerite) are taken into the home of a wealthy and childless couple (the Esselstynes).

Auntie Belle was so impressed by Grace's efforts that she took the manuscript and inveigled her publisher to print a limited edition of it. It was a surprise for her twelve-year-old niece, and it became the first big step in Grace's writing career.

Grace was always a better storyteller than a student. She disliked writing themes, but if she could write a story instead, she excelled. Her education had begun in the home with her mother tutoring her in the early grades. Once she had been sent away to a boarding school, but Grace became so homesick for her parents that she begged to return home.

She also had a flair for art. As a teenager she sometimes accompanied Auntie Belle on speaking tours. While her favorite aunt told one of her "Pansy" stories, Grace would illustrate the talk with a blackboard sketch.

Aware of her talent, her family convinced her to go to art school. So she studied at Cincinnati Art School and later at Elmira College in New York, where a famous artist was teaching.

Despite her abilities in writing and art, she ended up working as a physical education instructor at Rollins College in Florida. Her father was serving a church in Winter Park at the time.

A Congregational college, the school tended to be quite puritanical. While Grace, like her father, may have been quite uncompromising on doctrinal and biblical principles, she was not rigid about general customs and styles.

As a physical education instructor, she asked permission from the board of directors to let girls wear bloomers. The board of directors vetoed the "liberal" idea.

She approached the board members one by one; finally they consented to let her give them a demonstration.

A few days later, while they solemnly met in their board of directors' room, she went into an adjoining room and changed into her bloomers—full, wide-pleated, blousing below the knee.

As she returned to the room, their eyes lowered in embarrassment. Then, one by one, they cautiously peered up to check her garb. Finally, one of them took a deep breath and uttered, "Well, I suppose that is not too bad." And with that begrudging approval, Grace won her point.

The following year, when Grace was twenty-six,

she accompanied her parents to their next church. It was in Hyattsville, Maryland. The church membership was barely at the one-hundred mark.

Though Grace had written a couple of stories for the *Christian Endeavor World* and had done a longer piece for the Chautauqua Assembly where her family vacationed almost every summer, she didn't think of writing as a career. In Florida, when she wasn't teaching at Rollins College, she had spent a great deal of time assisting her father in his home missionary activities. But she realized that this was his work and not her own. So at the age of twenty-six, she was still living under her parents' umbrella and had not found her niche in life.

That summer at a Bible conference, however, as she was going out to play tennis, she met the man of her dreams. It was almost as though he had walked out of the pages of a novel.

In her own novels Grace often borrowed from real life, and it is quite possible that her first meeting with Frank Hill is described in *Beauty for Ashes:*

She heard whistling. . . . It wasn't like any whistling she had ever heard before. . . . It was like a bird in the early morning, and sweet quaint tunes that she had never heard before, though occasionally there was a melody she recognized. . . . The whistler was familiar with fine music, that was evident. Sometimes there was a bit of Scotch melody, and then hymn tunes, whistled with such perfect rhythm that one could almost hear words with the melody.

Then she looked up and "saw a very good looking young man with a tennis racket under his arm, coming toward her."

In the book he is Murray MacRae, "tall and straight and fine."

In real life he was the Rev. Thomas Guthrie Franklin Hill, tall and straight and fine.

By the time Grace met him, Frank had already graduated from Washington and Jefferson College, south of Pittsburgh, had received his divinity degree from Western Theological Seminary, and had taken postgraduate work in Edinburgh, Scotland.

Like Grace, he had grown up in a manse, and also like Grace, his father was a Scotch-Presbyterian. His first two names had been bestowed on him in honor of a Scottish cleric who had launched "Ragged Schools" to reclaim juvenile delinquents.

He seemed a perfect match for Grace. Though she was never a serious scholar herself, she admired others such as her father (and Frank) who delighted in poring over books. His enjoyment of athletics, his concern for underprivileged young people, his sense of humor—these were things in which Grace shared as well. But underlying all of that was his spiritual commitment. Her parents agreed that Frank was right for their daughter.

A few weeks before Christmas 1892, when both Grace and Frank were twenty-seven, they were married in her father's small church in Hyattsville. Charles Livingston conducted the ceremony.

At the time, Frank was the minister of a small church in western Pennsylvania; but four months after the marriage, he received a call to the Wakefield Presbyterian Church in the Germantown section of Philadelphia. It had a new church building, but was not large in numbers (about two-hundred members). The Sunday school, however, had over four-hundred on its rolls. Both Frank and Grace were excited by the chance to work with so many boys and girls. In March 1893 he accepted the call; his annual salary would be $2,500.

They wasted no time in making changes. Frank began a men's club which he called The Vicar of Wakefield Club. The first action was to prepare a baseball field and tennis court for church young people (as well as young adults the age of Grace and Frank). The name, "The Vicar of Wakefield," was a reference to the title of Goldsmith's eighteenth-century novel. Apparently, however, some of the Presbyterians thought that the word "vicar" sounded too Episcopalian. After a year Frank consented to have the name changed. The group renamed itself the Wakefield Men's Club.

Besides providing athletics, the men's group held discussions on current political topics as well as theological issues; Frank even offered to teach a course in Latin to any man who wanted to learn. The official church records do not indicate, however, whether anyone signed up.

Frank also started a Boys' Club; and then to promote attendance at the Sunday evening Christian Endeavor meetings, he changed the time of the church's evening service.

But it was in the pulpit where Frank showed his greatest strength. Word was spreading that the young minister at Wakefield was developing into a powerful preacher.

In their first year of ministry, the church grew from 200 to 266 members, and the Sunday school expanded to a membership of nearly 600. The Christian Endeavor groups were also mushrooming. In the following years, growth continued.

While Grace played a creative role in the Sunday school and kept a hand in Christian Endeavor, her major concern during those years was her children. Her first daughter, Margaret, was born late in 1893, and the second, Ruth, was born in 1898. In any spare moments, she sat down at her typewriter and wrote short stories for the Christian Endeavor weekly publication. She also did some oil painting.

Then came November 1899. Frank and Grace were attending a church social one Friday evening. Complaining of stomach pains, he went home early. That night the pain became worse, and he was taken to the hospital. The next day he underwent an appendectomy. The operation appeared to be successful, but afterward an infection set in. Without antibiotics, Frank fought a losing battle; three days later he died.

Grace knew very well the comfort of the Scriptures in those days, but the loss of her husband devastated her, nonetheless. Church friends and relatives rallied to her support. The church session drafted a message of comfort to Grace: "That He might give beauty for ashes, the oil of joy for mourning, and the garment of praise for the spirit of heaviness."

But nothing could bring Frank back to her.

It was a time of insecurity for the entire family. "I remember many tears," her daughter Ruth recalls. Ruth also remembers crying in her crib because she was in terror of the dark. Grace came in, took her in her arms, and told her of the Shepherd Jesus who held her in His arms like a little lamb.

"I never forgot that," said Ruth. In those difficult days of bereavement, Grace was trying hard not to forget it either.

With her two little girls, Grace tried to pick up the pieces. Frank had left $5,000 in life insurance, but Grace knew that they could not live on that for very long. As soon as the church called another minister, she and her daughters would have to vacate the parsonage.

Her first thought was to return temporarily to live with her parents. That would give her time to think of other options. Then came the second shock. Her father died.

Within a few months the two men in her life whom she had idolized and upon whom she had depended had been snatched from her. Nothing had meant more to her than her family, but now

God had chosen to disrupt both the family in which she had been raised and the new family she and Frank had been building.

How could she possibly manage? She would have to care for her widowed mother as well as her children. Though depressed by the twin losses, she couldn't allow herself to become paralyzed. She had to go on.

With an uncle and a church elder providing advice, she moved to the suburban town of Swarthmore. It was a college town, and that seemed to be the main reason it was chosen. Though her daughters were young, Grace was concerned that they be given the best education possible. When they grew up, they could live at home while attending college.

Temporarily, the family rented a small house, but Grace had other plans for the future. Throughout her early years she had persistently dreamed of owning her own home. She had grown up in a succession of small parsonages; since her marriage she had lived in another one. Her daydreams envisioned a spacious stone house with a large lawn, big trees, a huge porch, and a winding staircase. The house had to be made of stone because stone spoke to her of permanence.

But if she used Frank's life insurance to build a house, she wouldn't have enough money to live on month by month. She needed additional income.

Of course, she had continued to write her short stories for Christian Endeavor. She had even begun to write weekly Sunday school lessons which were syndicated to several small suburban newspapers in the area. But none of that brought in a great deal of income for the family. Either the Lord would have to bring a second husband into her life who could help support the family, or else He would have to provide income some other way.

With her small children she knew she couldn't go out and get a job; she also knew that she couldn't make money as an artist. But she remembered how Auntie Belle had succeeded quite well by writing novels at home. Perhaps if she wrote a full-length novel and had it published, it might ease some of the money pressures.

So she sat down at her typewriter and wrote a novel, calling it *The Story of a Whim*. The setting was a college in Florida. From her experience at Rollins College, Grace could picture it well. In the plot, a new church is started amid the orange groves. That was the kind of home missionary work she and her father had been doing fifteen years earlier. Grace began the story, however, with another image in mind. The scene opens in a stone house on a hill. A stone house for her family is what Grace hoped would be the outcome of selling her book.

The Story of a Whim was not extremely successful. Though it did not bring in much income, Grace was sufficiently encouraged to move ahead with plans for her stone house. More than anything else, however, the publication of the book opened Grace's eyes to a new ministry.

From the start, Grace's real motive in writing was more spiritual than financial. "Ever since I was a little girl," she said later, "I wanted to make other people feel the same way about God that I did. I think He knew that and made it possible for me to have my wish."

The two men Grace had most admired had their pulpits, and now the Lord had provided a pulpit for Grace through writing.

Grace's daughter Ruth tells how her mother's dream house became a reality. "She got a friend, an architect, to design a house with many stone arches. She wanted stone arches and refused to let him cut down a beautiful beech tree next to the front window."

She told the architect how she thought a stone porch could be built around the tree, making a stone turret wall.

The architect didn't like the idea, nor did he like the notion of a woman telling him how to do his job. "Impossible," he replied. "Such a thing would look very out of place."

Grace wasn't convinced. That night she sat up for several hours building a cardboard model to depict what it might look like.

She proved her point. Her stone house was built according to her wishes.

Her daughter added: "This was typical of her. If she was determined that some plan should be carried out, nothing would stop her—unless she could be persuaded that it was unscriptural."

The following year, the same determination that built a house got her into serious trouble.

It was in 1903, shortly after *The Story of a Whim* had been published, and while the builders were constructing her new stone house in Swarthmore, that she met Flavius Josephus Lutz.

Grace was thirty-eight; Flavius was several years younger. Like Grace, he was a newcomer in the suburb of Swarthmore. Like Grace, he had recently moved from Philadelphia and now attended the Swarthmore Presbyterian Church.

Flavius enjoyed the arts—music especially, but also art and literature—as did Grace. In fact, he was a music teacher and played the organ at the church.

The previous two men in her life—her father and her first husband—had been scholars, not artists. Flavius was different.

In addition, he was a charmer. Although he didn't charm Grace's mother and other relatives, he did sweep Grace off her feet. And she was flattered that a younger man would show such interest in her.

Grace was vulnerable. She liked to have a man to talk with and Flavius was a great conversationalist. Perhaps financial pressures also prompted her to move quickly into marriage.

Family members warned her not to get serious about Flavius; they said it would be a tragic mistake. But, of course, she thought they didn't know Flavius as well as she did. And in 1904, Grace married Flavius Josephus Lutz.

The problem was that Flavius was accustomed to getting his own way. He had grown up in a household that had catered to him, probably because of his musical talent. In Grace's family, however, emotional outbursts were thought of as childish; people gained respect for their logical arguments, not for their emotional tantrums.

When Flavius didn't get his way, "he could be impossible," reported one family member.

He tried to dominate his house by tirades, but Grace would not be bullied. He only lost her respect when he displayed his irrationality.

As the children grew up, they were embarrassed to have their friends come inside the house, for their stepfather's behavior was totally unpredictable and frequently unspeakably rude. He wanted to rule his house, but he didn't know how.

In her book *Job's Niece*, Grace describes a spoiled young man who bears an interesting resemblance to Flavius Lutz. Doris Dunbar, who is trying to care for a family, is talking with her suitor Milton, but the words might have come originally from Grace and Flavius.

Doris: "Nobody has the right of authority over another human being who is grown and of sane mind. Especially where a matter of right and wrong is concerned. . . . I must do what I think is right. It is my own conscience I must follow, and if you really love me you will not hurt me by talking this way."

Milton: "This is all a pose in order to make me allow you to slave for your family and take them into my lap for life."

Afterward, Doris muses, as Grace may have done: "Could one love a person and not love at all those they loved? Or did he just love her because he had chosen her for his own? How terrible that Milton should think of her dear ones as burdens."

For Grace, her family was vital, primary, essential. For Flavius, it seemed a bothersome appendage. He found, of course, that he had not married only Grace, but her family as well. It was an adjustment he could not make.

Before long, Grace saw that the marriage was not working out, but she didn't know what to do. She had always opposed divorce, so that was not an option for her. Meanwhile, the tension in the home continued to mount.

For a while Grace and her mother had tutored her daughters in the home; but then, after Grace's marriage to Flavius, as Margaret was ready for sixth grade and Ruth for second, she sent them to public school.

This gave Grace more time to write, and her family was urging her to write another novel. No doubt they felt that with her second marriage in a shambles she needed something to occupy her mind.

Her publisher suggested that she try her hand

at a historical novel. Grace wasn't so sure. She wouldn't enjoy the research that would be necessary to produce it.

But then she received unexpected help. A great aunt over 100 years old told her about a Livingston who had become a substitute bride in the 1830s. As Grace heard the fantastic true story, she recognized that it had the makings of a strong plot. A cousin, who was an artist specializing in drawings of the 1830s, took time to tell her about the costumes and traditions of the period. It was enough to get Grace going again.

Out of those ingredients came Grace's first truly successful novel, *Marcia Schuyler,* published in 1908.

Literary magazines, however, did not treat it kindly. One commented: "Little new, brilliant, or finished in the way of narrative writing can be discovered. The book needs a very hot day and a hammock."

A year later, she wrote a sequel called *Phoebe Dean.* Commented *The New York Times:* "A pretty wholesome story of the most artificial kind."

Perhaps the most blistering review came from the *Saturday Review of Literature:* "Mrs. Hill's latest story is a singularly sentimental and pious tract, clumsily written, fatuous, and illogical. To be candid, the book is awful."

Her growing audience of readers disagreed. They loved her wholesome approach.

Grace herself had no illusions about her literary ability. She jokingly remarked that it was her quantity, not her quality that she would be known for.

And once she got started writing, she couldn't stop. The publisher was always asking for another novel from Grace Livingston Hill, because readers across the country had started going into the bookstores to ask if the next Grace Livingston Hill novel had been published.

To Flavius Lutz, it was the last straw. Why was she known as Grace Livingston Hill? Why wasn't his wife known to the world as Grace Livingston Lutz?

Grace said that since she had begun her career as Grace Livingston Hill that was the way her readers knew her. Flavius was vehement that since she was Mrs. Lutz, she shouldn't be ashamed to put it on her books.

Finally, Grace gave in to please her husband. After eight years of marriage and several books, she became known as Grace Livingston Hill Lutz. The name of Lutz appeared on most of her books between 1913 and 1918.

Grace tried to cover up the unpleasant home situation, but it wasn't always possible. When Flavius unexpectedly missed Sunday morning services at church, Grace sent her daughter Margaret to pinch-hit for him on the organ. Eventually, however, when Grace was wondering how much more of Flavius' irrational behavior she could take, he walked out of their stone house and never returned.

Grace never made much of an effort to look for him, either.

Raising her two girls was easier when Flavius wasn't around.

"Mother screened our friends very carefully," her daughter Ruth recalled. "I mildly resented it at the time, but since then I have been very grateful." From their mother and grandmother the two girls learned "reams of Bible verses and Psalms." And Ruth says, "That was the best thing that ever happened to me."

As soon as she could, Grace laid out a tennis court in her backyard and soon all the Christian Endeavor young people from the church were finding their way to the Hill house.

Grace enjoyed young people, and young people enjoyed her. For years she took an active leadership role in the church's Christian Endeavor Society. She could always be counted on to develop a special game or contest. Once she wrote an oratorio on the Old Testament character Naaman that the young people staged for neighboring churches, and when they had polished their performance they put it on in Atlantic City's Steel Pier.

Although her standards were high ("Strict but loving" is how her daughter put it), young people, sometimes as many as a hundred, flocked to the C. E. group. "She planned lots of fun," is the way one of them put it.

What impressed people was her indefatigable energy. She made the children's clothes, did housework, worked with the church's Christian Endeavor, taught a Sunday school class; and then after the children were put to bed, she went to her room to write—sometimes until three or four in the morning. "She never knew when to go to bed," a neighbor reported.

Grace wrote some lines about her Auntie Belle that might just as well have applied to herself: "All these things she did—and yet wrote books. . . . Perhaps she wrote more and better because she was doing so eagerly in every direction: her public, her church, her family, her home."

Grace was a doer. When she felt that the biblical instruction she was receiving from her church's pulpit was inadequate, she rented a meeting hall and invited outstanding Bible teachers to come to Swarthmore and speak. This developed into a community Bible class which she continued to sponsor for fifteen years.

Outside Swarthmore near an old stone quarry was an Italian settlement about which Grace was concerned. In her novel *The Witness*, the hero of the novel purchases and renovates an abandoned old church. This is just about what happened when Grace started a mission Sunday school among the Italian immigrants and then renovated the Leiper Presbyterian Church which had been abandoned for several years.

Another of her pet projects was to find needy young people and send them to a Christian camp during the summer.

"All these things she did—and yet wrote books."

After a few historical books and mystery novels,

she found herself more at home with the genre of romantic fiction, and between age sixty-five and eighty she wrote forty-three novels, nearly three per year.

A few of her earlier books also display her strong social concern for the underprivileged. But in all her books, her Christian commitment is obvious. At one point her publisher, J. B. Lippincott of Philadelphia, asked her to eliminate some of the religious passages which they thought might offend some of their reading audience. Grace flatly refused. She did what her father would have done: she left the publisher and sought another. Harper and Brothers was glad to have her on any terms.

Before long, Lippincott asked her to come back. She consented and J. B. Lippincott never blue-penciled a line of her manuscripts after that.

"I am not writing just for the sake of writing. I have attempted to convey in my own way, and through my novels, a message which God has given and to convey that message with whatever abilities were given to me. . . . Whatever I've been able to accomplish has been God's doing."

Her writing style was unorthodox. In an article in *The Writer*, she explained: "It often amuses me to have eager young writers ask me to give them the inside story about my methods of work. For the truth is I never did conscientiously prepare for my literary career and furthermore I have no method at all. . . . I just sit down at my typewriter and go ahead. Sometimes a sentence just pops into my head and that starts me off. . . . Until the book is finished, I have no idea how the story is going to be worked out myself. I almost never rewrite a story."

At another time, she said, "My working hours? I work whenever I can find the time. . . . I can't say that I shut myself up in a room. My door is open at all times. The telephone constantly interrupts and then I go back to my writing. Friends drop in on me or members of the family hold a conclave in the next room. If I'm busy, I simply disconnect my mind and keep working."

She joked once about never reading a novel by Steinbeck or Hemingway because she said she was afraid that "they might influence my style too drastically."

She shunned the realism of modern writers and was criticized for it, but she never lived her life in a garret. "I've refused to consider my career separate from my daily life," she once said.

To her, teaching a Sunday school class among Italian immigrants was every bit as important as grinding out another manuscript for her publisher.

Her first true success as a novelist came with the publication of *Marcia Schuyler* when she was forty-three years old. She died at the age of eighty-two, leaving a half-finished novel on her desk.

During her lifetime four million copies of her books were sold. Since her death in 1947, another four million have been sold.

Did success come easy for Grace Livingston Hill?

Perhaps it did for her as a writer, but the more important aspects of her life were strewn with problems.

She has been criticized for her idealistic novels, yet she saw two marriages end in different kinds of tragedy. She valued family ties deeply, yet she had to pick up the pieces and hold her family together without a man in the house.

Could Grace have made her second marriage work? The fact is that Flavius Lutz was unable to cope with Grace's strength. He was too weak a man. When he flailed out in his frustration, she appeared stronger than ever. If she had minimized her personal strength, if she had been willing to sacrifice her family, perhaps some semblance of a marriage might have been preserved. But the price was more than she was willing to pay.

In the process, she lost a husband, but kept her daughters. Her two daughters grew up, had happy marriages, and both became deeply involved in Christian ministries.

What would have happened if Frank Hill had lived a long life? And what would have happened if Flavius Lutz had not walked out on her? Would Grace have been a best-selling novelist? Would she have gone on to be described as "America's most beloved author"? Probably not.

Out of the dual crucibles of bereavement and marital disappointment came the works of a writer known for romance and idealism, a novelist who has directed millions of impressionable lives toward wholesome family relationships and solid Christian values.

CHAPTER
FIVE

Meet
Jack
(C.S.)
and
Joy
Lewis

WHAT made a nice Jewish girl like Joy Davidman marry an Oxford professor like C. S. Lewis?

Why would a confirmed bachelor in his late fifties marry a divorcée when he was so vehemently opposed to divorce? Or was he, to put it bluntly, trapped into marriage?

If you count the months that they lived together as man and wife, it was a short marriage indeed. But it was a surprisingly good one, one that endured suffering and pain, miracles and joy.

It taught both of them how good marriage could be, and both of them were caught by surprise. In fact, you might even say that they were "surprised by Joy."

You have to admit, however, that the first announcement of the marriage was hardly romantic: "You may as well know (but don't talk of it, for all is still uncertain) that I may soon be, in rapid succession, a bridegroom and a widower. There may, in fact, be a deathbed marriage." That was the way the marriage of Jack and Joy Lewis began.

In 1925, Helen Joy Davidman (her friends called her Joy) was a little ten-year-old Jewish girl attending grade school in the Bronx.

In 1925, Clive Staples Lewis (his friends called him Jack) was a young don teaching English literature at Oxford University. He was a "determined atheist."

By 1937, Joy Davidman had graduated from college, had become a card-carrying Communist, and had ventured to Hollywood to write movie scripts for MGM.

By 1937, Jack Lewis had become a convert to Christianity, had become a recognized classical scholar, and was beginning to think about writing a book about the devil to be called *The Screwtape Letters.*

By 1943, Joy Davidman—now associate editor of the Communist *New Masses* and a "confirmed atheist"—was married to a fellow Communist, an alcoholic who was a freelance writer.

By 1943, Jack Lewis was broadcasting a series of talks called *Mere Christianity* for the British Broadcasting Corporation.

Jack Lewis, the dignified Oxford don, and Joy Davidman, the feisty Jewish Communist from the Bronx, seemed farther apart than ever.

The story of how they got together—and their brief but unusual marriage—is just as unlikely as any of the science fiction that C. S. Lewis penned.

C. S. Lewis, of course, became famous in many areas. He earned a scholarly reputation in language and letters. His *Chronicles of Narnia* are beloved by children (as well as their parents). His science fiction is read and admired by many. His apologetics (*Mere Christianity, Pilgrim's Regress, Miracles*) have wooed many (including Charles Colson) to Christ. Other books (*Screwtape Letters, The Problem of Pain, The Great Divorce*) have become Christian classics. He is regarded as the premier Christian writer of the twentieth century.

But who was Joy Davidman? For C. S. Lewis-watchers (and his fan club was growing rapidly in the 1950s), she seemed to erupt into his life suddenly and then was wrenched away from him in death almost before they knew her.

But Joy Davidman was more than a shadowy figure, a mysterious woman in black, a blip on the screen of C. S. Lewis' life.

A poet who had her efforts published in the prestigious Yale Younger Poets series when she was only twenty-three, and a novelist whose first work

Anya (published when she was twenty-five) was acclaimed by *The New York Times* and *Saturday Review of Literature*, Joy Davidman exuded writing talent.

She was born in 1915. Her parents, both educators in the New York City school system, saw that she was raised a good atheist. "[We] sucked in atheism with [our] canned milk," she said later. By the time she was eight years old, she delighted her father by announcing that, following in his footsteps, she had become an atheist. By the time she was twenty, she had a master's degree from Columbia University.

In her early twenties she drifted into Communism. "My motives were a mixed lot. Youthful rebelliousness, youthful vanity, youthful contempt of the stupid people who seemed to be running society, all these played a part."

Having gotten her Communist card, she joined the staff of the semiofficial party magazine, *New Masses*.

Her excursion to Hollywood as a film writer was brief. MGM apparently didn't like her scripts and she responded by calling the movie moguls a bunch of buffoons.

Back in New York she plunged into Communist party concerns. "She worked very hard to convert her friends," one of them reported. As associate editor of *New Masses*, she concentrated on book and movie reviews and also served as poetry editor.

One acquaintance described her as "unattractive

physically, not particularly ugly or interesting, but rather dumpy and though obviously female, rather unfeminine. Her manner and mannerisms were almost a stereotype of the 1930s radical. She was aggressive, impatient, and intolerant."

At twenty-seven, she was charmed by fellow Communist Bill Gresham, a folk singer, storyteller, and writer, who had fought in the Spanish Civil War. He had been married before, but the marriage had been ruined by his alcoholism and his inability to settle down. He was a wanderer.

Joy overlooked his problems and married him in the summer of 1942.

In the next three years, Joy and Bill had two boys, several cats—Joy loved cats—and three residences from Manhattan to Queens to Ossining. Joy always had the notion that a change of residence would solve the problems of her marriage, but it never did. Bill kept on drinking, kept playing around with other women, and could never provide a suitable income for a family to live on.

Joy, who always prided herself on being in control of things, was at her wits' end. It all came to a climax when "one day he telephoned me . . . to tell me he was having a nervous breakdown. He felt his mind going, he couldn't stay where he was and he couldn't bring himself to come home." Frantically, she phoned every haunt and den which she thought he might frequent, but without success. "There was nothing left to do," she said, "but wait and see if he turned up alive or dead. I put the babies to sleep and waited. For the first time in my life I felt helpless.

"My pride was forced to admit," she says, "that I was not, after all, the 'master of my fate' and 'the captain of my soul.' All my defenses—the walls of arrogance and cocksureness and self-love, behind which I had hid from God—went down momentarily, and God came in."

To her own amazement she found herself on her knees praying. "I must say, I was the world's most surprised atheist."

Joy didn't arise from her knees with a full-blown theology, but from then on she had no doubt in her mind that there was a living God.

She began reading literature from a fresh viewpoint. Francis Thompson's "The Hound of Heaven" ("I fled Him down the night and down the days; I fled Him down the arches of the years") caused her to break into tears. C. S. Lewis' works were now devoured ("I snatched at books I had despised before"). But most of all, she began reading the Bible and there she met the Redeemer. "When I read the New Testament, I recognized Him. He was Jesus."

When Bill came back home, he was so impressed with the change he saw in his wife that he began attending church with her. Soon he made a profession of faith as well.

Joy became as ardent a Christian as she had been a Communist. One friend wrote that Joy "was sure of what she believed, and she loved to take people on in debates. She was argumentative, and she spoke with contempt for those she felt were superficial thinkers."

One Christian writer whose thinking she admired was C. S. Lewis, and because she admired his thinking, she wrote a letter to him early in 1950. She took exception to a point he made in one of his books; Lewis responded quickly and decimated her arguments. She was amazed. "Lord, he knocked my props out from under me unerringly, one shot to a pigeon. . . . Being disposed of so neatly by a master of debate, all fair and square—it seems to be one of the great pleasures of life. . . . What I feel is a craftman's joy at the sight of a superior performance."

Though her husband, Bill, had made a Christian profession, he soon began dabbling in cults and other religions. Then he returned to his alcoholic patterns.

But as Lyle Dorsett says in *And God Came In*, "The most devastating blow to the marriage came with Bill Gresham's continuing infidelity. . . . The hard-drinking novelist, trying to fill the empty space inside himself with liquor . . . sought satisfaction in a string of extramarital liaisons—short-lived affairs and one-night stands. Bill never tried to hide these indiscretions, and he could not understand why Joy was hurt by them."

Early in 1952 Joy's cousin Renee Pierce came to live with the Greshams. Separated from her husband, Renee needed lodging for herself and her two children. In the arrangement, Joy got a good housekeeper. Joy loved writing and gardening, not cleaning the house, as anyone who set foot in her house could immediately recognize.

Throughout the first half of 1952 she became more and more confused about her relationship with Bill. As a Christian she wanted to preserve the marriage, but she had lost all respect for him. Preserving the marriage seemed to be a losing battle. Because of his infidelity, she no longer wanted to sleep with him. And yet she felt sorry for him. He was psychologically troubled and insecure. She didn't know what to do, where to turn.

Finally she decided she needed to get away, "to run away from him physically" in order to clarify her thinking. She needed to talk with someone, someone she could respect, so she turned to the man whom she regarded as "one of the clearest thinkers of our time," C. S. Lewis.

Joy had other reasons for going to England. As a student of English literature, she could enjoy the visit for educational reasons; and because she was recovering from a recent flare-up of jaundice, she would profit physically from the time abroad. She also had a book manuscript to complete. But her main reason for going was to meet the man she idolized, C. S. Lewis, and to see if he could give her some spiritual understanding regarding her muddled matrimony.

So in early September 1952, Joy left her children

in the care of her cousin Renee and sailed to England to meet the confirmed bachelor C. S. Lewis.

Born near Belfast, Ireland, in November 1898, C. S. Lewis grew up, he says, with "good parents, good food and a garden . . . to play in." His only brother Warren ("Warnie"), three years older, was what Lewis termed "a confederate from the first." A nurse enthralled him with tales of leprechauns and buried treasures, and his parents surrounded him with books.

Before he was ten, however, his mother died of cancer, and in reaction his father's behavior became alternately depressed and erratic. "All that was tranquil and reliable," C. S. Lewis wrote, "disappeared from my life." Warren and Jack grew closer; "two frightened urchins huddled for warmth in a bleak world," is the way Lewis puts it in *Surprised by Joy*.

For the next eight years Warren and Jack were enrolled in a variety of educational experiences (Jack attended five schools in eight years) before World War I.

In 1917 he joined the army, and late that year he was ordered to the military front in France. He wired his father to come and see him off. His father responded, "Don't understand telegram. Please write." Jack Lewis shot back another wire, but his father still didn't come.

In April 1918, the Germans launched their second putsch. It was a time Lewis never forgot: "the cold, the frights . . . the horribly smashed men still moving like half-crushed beetles, the sitting or standing corpses, the landscape of sheer earth without a blade of grass, the boots worn day and night until they seemed to grow to your feet."

On April 15, Jack Lewis was wounded. Shrapnel from an exploding shell lodged in his chest. "The one under my arm," he wrote a month later," is worse than a flesh wound, as the bit of metal which went in there is now in my chest."

As Jack Lewis returned to civilian life and to Oxford University, there is a mysterious gap in his autobiography, *Surprised by Joy.* He writes. "One huge and complex episode will be omitted. I have no choice about this reticence. All I can or need say is that my earlier hostility to the emotions was very fully and variously avenged."

Green and Hooper in *C. S. Lewis: A Biography* suggest that "the only really overwhelming 'love-affair' of his early life" took place in this mysterious gap.

The situation seems to have begun when Jack was recuperating from his war injuries in a London hospital. He begged his father in Ireland to visit him: "Come and see me. I am homesick," he wrote. His father didn't respond.

A month later Jack was moved to a convalescent center in Bristol, near the home of an army buddy and former school friend, Paddy Moore. Previously Jack had visited in Paddy's home and had enjoyed his brief stays. Now Jack, motherless since ten and feeling psychologically fatherless, turned to Paddy's mother, Janie Moore.

Paddy had asked Jack to look after his mother in case he didn't return from France, and about the time that Jack arrived in Bristol, Janie Moore received official word that her son had been killed in action.

The developing relationship between Jack Lewis and Janie Moore is hard to describe because Jack did not want to talk to anyone else about it and also because he hinted that Janie had been more to him than a foster mother. Janie was attracted to him, not only because she had lost a husband and a son, but also because, as she wrote, "he possesses such a wonderful power of understanding and sympathy."

The following year, when Jack was enrolled in Oxford, his father started showing some concern that his son was spending his vacations in Bristol with Janie Moore rather than in Belfast with him. He wrote to his other son, Warren, "I confess I do not know what to do about Jack's affair. It worries and depresses me greatly. All I know about the lady is that she is old enough to be his mother, and that she is in poor circumstances." He was also concerned because Jack was "an impetuous, kind-hearted creature who could be cajoled by any woman who had been through the mill."

In 1920, Janie Moore and her daughter Maureen moved from Bristol to Oxford, renting a small house there. Jack helped with the rent, though he himself was continuing to receive financial aid from his father. A few months later Jack, still an undergraduate himself, found larger accommodations, rented them, and invited the Moores to move in with him.

He was twenty-two at the time; Janie Moore was forty-eight. He wrote to a friend: "I combine the life of an Oxford undergraduate with that of a country householder—a feat which I imagine is seldom performed."

His father didn't like it at all; he described himself as "estranged from his son."

Even his brother Warren couldn't understand it. "What actually happened," he wrote, "was that Jack had set up a joint establishment with Mrs. Moore, an arrangement which bound him to her service for the next thirty years and ended only with her death in January 1951. How the arrangement came into being no one will ever know, for it was perhaps the only subject which Jack never mentioned to me, more than never mentioned, for on the only occasion when I hinted at my curiosity he silenced me with an abruptness which was sufficient warning never to re-open the subject."

Between 1930 and 1950, Warren lived with Jack Lewis and Janie Moore. During that period the relationship seemed to be that of an overly possessive and selfish mother to her son. "I do not think I ever saw Jack at his desk for more than half an hour without Mrs. Moore calling for him. 'Coming,' Jack would roar, down would go his pen, and he would be away perhaps five minutes, perhaps half an hour, and then return and calmly resume work on a half-finished sentence."

Jack Lewis and Janie Moore lived together not as man and wife, but as son and mother. Yet the relationship was shrouded in mystery and suspicion. Granted, Jack had vowed to Paddy Moore that he would look after his mother, but he wasn't obligated to live with her. A psychological dependency obviously had developed.

Later in life, Jack referred to her as "Mother," and there was a sense in which they had adopted each other after Paddy Moore died on the battlefield in France.

Jack Lewis, of course, went on to become an Oxford don and literary scholar; in those early years he was also a convinced atheist. Janie Moore, bitter about her lot in life, no doubt fed his atheism.

Little in Christianity attracted him. "Christianity," he writes in *Surprised by Joy*, "was mainly associated for me with ugly architecture, ugly music, and bad poetry." But what bothered him most was "my deep-seated hatred of authority. No word in my vocabulary expressed deeper hatred than the word 'interference.' But Christianity placed at the center what then seemed to me a transcendental Interferer."

Gradually, Jack's atheism crumbled, no thanks to Janie Moore, who remained an atheist till death. At first Jack began to realize that atheism didn't make good sense philosophically. He thought he

157

could accept a universal Absolute, an impersonal, uncaring, abstract Principle. "We could talk religiously about the Absolute; there was no danger of Its doing anything about us. . . . There was nothing to fear; better still, nothing to obey."

It was, however, one step closer to truth. "And so," he says, "the great Angler played His fish, and I never dreamed that the hook was in my tongue."

Reading George Herbert, George MacDonald, and G. K. Chesterton unnerved him. They were unabashed Christians who were good writers—and their Christianity made surprisingly good sense. "A young atheist," Lewis says coyly, "cannot guard his faith too carefully. Dangers lie in wait for him on every side."

Lewis liked to engage in philosophical argument, and he was ready to discuss whether the Infinite could be a personal being. But soon he realized that if he lost the argument and had to believe in God as a personal being, it was a new ball game. "I was to be allowed to play at philosophy no longer. . . . My Adversary . . . would not argue about it. He only said, 'I am the Lord.' "

Later he said that his conversion did not result from his search for God. For him it was more like "the mouse's search for a cat."

And then he tells of that night in Oxford in 1929 when "I gave in, and admitted that God was God, and knelt and prayed; perhaps, that night, the most dejected and reluctant convert in all England." He described himself as "a prodigal who is brought in kicking, struggling, resentful, and darting his eyes in every direction for a chance to escape."

Once he was in the fold, however, his writings brought many other prodigals, also struggling and resentful, into the kingdom of God.

As a scholar, Lewis specialized in Medieval and Renaissance English literature; but as a Christian he soon branched out into other areas, including science fiction, with *Out of the Silent Planet* in 1938, various types of theological and apologetic works (*The Great Divorce, The Screwtape Letters, The Problem of Pain, Miracles*) and children's works (the Narnia series).

Perhaps his best known and most quoted work is *The Screwtape Letters,* fictional correspondence from an experienced devil named Screwtape, who was high in the Infernal Civil Service, to a junior colleague, who happened to be his nephew, named Wormwood. Wormwood had been sent on assignment to earth to secure the damnation of a young man who lived with a very trying mother. (Some Lewis buffs have thought the "very trying mother" resembles Janie Moore.)

During World War II he was asked to give a restatement of Christian doctrine in lay language over the British Broadcasting Corporation. The talks were later brought together in one volume called *Mere Christianity.* Along with his restatement of orthodox Christian doctrine, Lewis took a strong position for Christian marriage. "The Christian rule is: Either marriage, with complete faithfulness to your partner, or else total abstinence." Marriage between Christians is for life, he taught.

In 1948, Janie Moore, having lost the use of her legs, and with her mind slipping away as well, had to be placed in a nursing home. Jack continued to visit her every day. When she died in 1951, it seemed a great weight had been lifted from Jack's shoulders.

He never thought of himself as much of a letter writer, but his output of correspondence multiplied after 1950. The first letter in his *Letters to an American Lady* (an anonymous woman) is dated only shortly before Janie's death, about the same time Joy Davidman began her correspondence with Jack Lewis.

He couldn't reply to all the letters he received, but Joy's letters to him "stood out from the ruck" because they were "amusing and well-written."

Two years later, Joy Davidman came to England. Accompanied by a friend from London, she visited Oxford and asked Jack Lewis to have luncheon with them. (Curiously, when Joy walked into his life, he was working on his autobiography, entitled *Surprised by Joy.*) Evidently Jack, now fifty-four and still shy among women, enjoyed the luncheon, for shortly afterward he reciprocated, inviting Joy and her friend along with a fellow professor to lunch at his place.

A few weeks later, Jack's brother, Warren, was included in another luncheon engagement. In his diary, Warren described Joy as of "medium height, good figure, horn-rimmed specs, quite extraordinarily uninhibited."

While in England, Joy completed her manuscript on the Ten Commandments, *Smoke on the Mountain*, dedicating it to C. S. Lewis. He agreed to write the introduction. In it, he said, "Joy Davidman is one who comes to us from the second generation of unbelief; her parents, Jewish by blood, rationalists by conviction. This makes her approach extremely interesting to the reclaimed apostates of my own generation; the daring paradoxes of our youth were the stale platitudes of hers."

For Joy, England was delightful. "I've never felt at home anywhere as I do in London or Oxford," she wrote during her stay.

But back in the States there was trouble awaiting her. Instead of diminishing in her absence, her marital problems were becoming more complicated. Shortly after Christmas and only a few days before her scheduled return, Joy received a letter from her husband, Bill. "I didn't want to cloud your holiday with things that would upset you," he told her, but "Renee and I are in love."

He said that he appreciated "what resolutions you have made about coming home and trying to make a go of our marriage." But it wasn't worth it, he said, to sacrifice human life "on the altar of will power." His four-page, single-spaced letter concluded by suggesting that the "optimum solution would be for you to be married to some really swell guy, Renee and I to be married, and both families to live in easy calling distance so that the Gresham kids could have Mommy and Daddy on hand." Obviously, Bill Gresham had it all worked out.

Only with Jack Lewis did Joy share the letter. He expressed his strong feelings against divorce; but he admitted that he saw no way that the marriage could be saved.

Joy didn't know what to expect when she arrived back in the States. But as soon as she arrived in New York, she found out. "Bill greeted me by knocking me about a bit and half choking me." He had been drinking again.

Before long, she resigned herself to the divorce. She wrote to a friend, "I always took it that divorce was only the last possible resort, and felt I ought to put up with anything I could bear for the children's sake. And I hoped that Bill's adulteries, irresponsibilities, etc., would end, if he ever recovered from his various neuroses; also that his becoming a Christian would make a difference."

But Bill's previous Christian profession had now been forgotten; he had renounced Christianity.

So Joy despaired of seeing any change in him and she didn't fight it when Bill followed Renee to Florida. In Florida he filed for divorce on the grounds of desertion and incompatibility.

It didn't take Joy very long to decide what to do next. There was nothing to keep her in America any longer. And in November 1953, eleven months after she had left, she was back in England, this time with her two boys. David was nine; Douglas was eight.

With little money but with confidence that she was in God's will, she found a two-room apartment in a section of London where several other writers lived. From intermittent alimony checks and equally intermittent royalty checks for freelance writing, she struggled to pay the rent. Nevertheless, she faced her challenges positively. "The Lord really is my Shepherd, by gum," she wrote in a letter back to the States.

Occasionally, she took her two boys to visit Jack Lewis in Oxford. Warren and Jack taught the boys how to play chess; they also took frequent walks in the woods together.

Joy had talked so much about Jack to her sons and had built up his reputation to such a degree that the boys were disappointed upon meeting him. Later, one of the sons said, "Heroes were supposed to be dressed in knight's armor, but this man looked so ordinary."

Joy's first eighteen months back in England were difficult. Not only were finances tight, but her brash personality didn't win any friends for her. As Lyle Dorsett says, "Joy's aggressive attitude and facial expressions, her sharp language and love of argument for the challenge of it . . . were viewed as rudeness and vulgarity. . . . Joy's status as a divorced . . . woman made things worse. . . . Her obviously brilliant mind, the breadth of her reading, and her nearly photographic memory intimidated still others."

Dorsett also points out that Joy had a bad temper and "could be nastily censorious. . . . She caustically punctured sham and pomposity wherever she saw them." She also had a tendency to lecture people.

Little wonder that she had trouble winning friends.

The one friend she could count on was Jack Lewis, though she hesitated to presume on his friendship. She restrained herself from visiting Oxford as often as she wanted to, because she felt her two active sons might be too much of a strain on the two bachelor professors.

But when Lewis became aware of her financial needs, he volunteered to help. One of the ways he did this was by paying the tuition for the boys' schooling.

In 1955 Joy moved to Oxford to a duplex apartment about a mile from the residence of the Lewis brothers. It was Jack himself who had encouraged Joy's move and had found the house for her.

In the beginning, Jack was undeniably the pursued, not the pursuer. According to the Hooper-Green biography, he was even known to hide when he saw Joy coming to visit him. No doubt this was due to several factors: his shyness, his fear of developing a relationship with a divorced woman, and his desire to preserve his life-long independence.

But that changed. Though Jack continued to hold that he could not marry a divorced woman (the Church of England contended that remarriage after divorce constituted adultery), he soon was walking to her house every day to see her. And Joy wrote that "the most wonderful ecstasy came from just holding hands and walking on the heather."

Brother Warren wrote in his diary that Jack and Joy "began to see each other every day. It was obvious what was going to happen."

For Joy, at the beginning, it was hero-worship. Quickly it moved toward genuine love. For Jack it started as intellectual stimulation, then a compatible friendship. Love may not have blossomed for him until after marriage.

Warren said as much in his diary: "For Jack the attraction was at first intellectual." Her mind matched his "in width of interest, in analytical grasp, and above all in humor and sense of fun."

But still it is doubtful whether Jack would ever have married Joy had he not felt obligated to do so.

It all happened after the British Home Office decided not to renew Joy's permit to remain in England. After all, she had been a card-carrying Communist a dozen years earlier. Lewis, who did not cherish any fondness for the United States, could not bear to think of Joy being forced to return "to that dreadful place."

The only way to keep her in England was to marry her. Yet his church opposed marriage to a divorced woman, and Jack was a loyal churchman.

To get around the problem, he decided to marry Joy in a civil ceremony, but not to seek permission for a religious ceremony from the Church of England. In addition, they would not live together as man and wife.

Jack told his brother Warren that nothing would change. Joy would continue to live in her house with her two boys and he would continue to live in The Kilns with Warren. "The marriage," he told Warren, "was a pure formality designed to give Joy the right to go on living in England."

The fact that Joy consented to such an arrangement is even more amazing than the fact that Jack had proposed it. Moreover, both of them agreed to keep the civil marriage as secret as possible.

In *A Severe Mercy* Sheldon Van Auken tells of a meeting he had with Lewis: "He told me of marrying Joy in a civil ceremony simply as an act of friendship to prevent the Government deporting her to America as a Communist, despite her being a lapsed Communist, and, in fact, a Jewish Christian. He and she had even drawn up a paper stating that the marriage was not a real one."

Jack told biographer Roger Green that it was "a pure matter of friendship and expediency."

But a few months later there was a complication. Joy complained of pain, especially in her left hip. At first it was diagnosed as acute rheumatism; but it was much worse.

Meanwhile, Jack was increasingly uncomfortable

about the marriage arrangement. He visited her every evening, and with each visit his love for Joy seemed to be strengthened.

Eventually he decided to ask permission for a religious ceremony. He thought that the church might grant permission because Joy's first husband had been divorced prior to his marriage to Joy. Jack argued that this would invalidate Joy's first marriage and so she should be declared free to marry again. The church authorities did not buy his reasoning.

In October, Joy was taken to a hospital "in excruciating pain." The diagnosis was now changed to cancer in an advanced stage. It had already eroded her left femur.

There seemed to be little hope. In November three operations were performed, but they seemed merely to delay the inevitable.

By now, Jack was conscience-stricken about hiding the fact of his civil marriage to Joy. In December, with Joy in the hospital, he brought her boys to live in his home and told Joy to write to her friends in America and announce the marriage. On Christmas Eve, Jack placed an announcement in *The Times*, London's prestigious paper: "A marriage has taken place between Professor C. S. Lewis . . . and Mrs. Joy Gresham, now a patient in the Churchill Hospital, Oxford. It is requested that no letters be sent."

Joy's case seemed terminal. She could live a few weeks, perhaps a few months.

She handled her plight surprisingly well. Warren wrote, "Her pluck and cheerfulness are beyond praise."

She spoke of her physical agony being "combined with a strange spiritual ecstasy. I think I know now how the martyrs felt. All of this has strengthened my faith and brought me very close to God."

But as the pain continued, day in and day out, Joy became discouraged. She was not getting better; she was only lingering. The radiation therapy merely seemed to be prolonging her misery. In one letter she confessed, "I am trying very hard to hold on to my faith, but I find it very difficult; there seems such a gratuitous and merciless cruelty in this."

A week later, however, she seemed more positive. "I feel now that I can bear, not too unhappily, whatever is to come."

While she prayed for "grace to accept her condition," many were praying for her recovery. Her husband was actually praying that God might allow him to bear her pain so that she might have relief from it.

The following March, Jack called in a minister to come and pray for her. He had been successful in other cases in which he had laid hands on the sick.

When he arrived and saw Joy's desperate physical condition—she was far worse than he had imagined—he laid his hands on her and prayed for her. But unexpectedly, he also consented to perform an ecclesiastical ceremony so that Jack and Joy could have their union solemnized by the church. It was, in Warren's words, "a notable act of charity" for the Anglican cleric to perform the wedding.

After the ceremony, Joy was signed out of the hospital, placed in an ambulance, and driven to The Kilns, where Jack and Warren lived. There they expected she would soon die; doctors had given her only a limited time to live.

But surprisingly—perhaps miraculously—she didn't die. Instead, she began to improve. Pain in her hip gradually disappeared. Her health steadily improved. As Chad Walsh wrote, "The expert on miracles [C. S. Lewis had written a book on the subject] began to witness one before his very eyes."

Just as surprisingly, Jack Lewis was beginning to notice a problem in his own bones. He had asked the Lord to allow him to take Joy's pain; now it seemed that was literally happening. While Joy was gaining calcium in her bones, he was losing it in his. His disease was diagnosed as osteoporosis.

In September, Lewis wrote, "My wife's condition . . . has improved, if not miraculously (but who knows?) at any rate wonderfully."

In October, Joy wrote, "I am slowly learning to walk again." The following month she was riding in a car and even going up and down steps. By January, doctors had to acknowledge it: Joy's cancer had been amazingly arrested.

Six months later, Joy was still exuberant: "Jack and I are managing to be surprisingly happy, considering the circumstances; you'd think we were a honeymoon couple in our early twenties, rather than our middle-aged selves."

As more strength returned, she directed the redecorating of The Kilns. It hadn't been decorated for thirty years. "The walls and carpets are full of holes," Joy wrote; "the carpets are tattered rags." She also said facetiously that she was afraid to move the bookcases lest the walls should fall down.

She also began to manage Jack's finances. Money had always been a nuisance to him. Until Joy took over, he never even had a savings account.

In August they vacationed in Ireland. Jack called it a "belated honeymoon." Four months earlier when he and Joy had stayed at a country hotel he wrote, "I'm such a confirmed old bachelor that I couldn't help feeling I was being rather naughty staying with a woman at a hotel. Just like people in the newspapers."

It was a joyful year. "I never expected to have in my sixties the happiness that passed me by in my twenties," he told a friend.

Joy resumed work again, assisting both Jack and Warren with their manuscripts. In spare time, they did crossword puzzles and played Scrabble together.

It was Jack's pattern to arise early in the morning; Joy slept later. "I'm a barbarously early riser and have usually got my breakfast and dealt with my letters before the rest of the house is astir. . . . I love the empty, silent, dewy, cobwebby hours."

Joy liked walking, though she now had one thigh

three inches shorter than the other and had gained weight since the radiation therapy had begun.

And Jack knew very well that cancer's sword of Damocles still hung over them.

Then in October 1959, the grim news came. Jack wrote, "We are in retreat. The tide has turned. Apparently, the wonderful recovery Joy made in 1957 was only a reprieve, not a pardon."

This time, however, they faced the outlook differently. At Christmas 1959 he wrote, "We hobble along wonderfully well. I am ashamed . . . to tell you that it is Joy who supports me, rather than I her."

In March, Joy wrote, "I've got so many cancers at work on me that I expect them to start organizing a union."

Joy still had one unfulfilled dream. She had always wanted to visit Greece. Though a classical scholar, Jack had never been there. In fact, he had never been out of the British Isles except for his World War I experience in France. He hesitated to visit Greece because he feared that the reality might disillusion him; the mental images that he had inflated through the decades might be punctured.

For Joy's sake, he consented to take the trip. It was admittedly risky, because Joy's pain was increasing steadily. But she was insistent. "I'd rather go out with a bang than a whimper," Joy said, "particularly on the steps of the Parthenon."

So they went. Joy exerted all her strength to

limp to the top of the Acropolis and through the Lion Gate of Mycenae.

"From one point of view," Jack wrote a month later, "it was madness, but neither of us regrets it."

He also wrote, "Joy knew she was dying. I knew she was dying, and she knew I knew she was dying—but when we heard the shepherds playing their flutes in the hills it seemed to make no difference."

Shortly after their return to England, Joy was taken again to the hospital. This time there was no reprieve.

By July she was on her deathbed and knew it. "Don't get me a posh coffin," she said to her husband. "Posh coffins are rot."

"It is incredible how much happiness, even how much gaiety, we sometimes had together after all hope was gone," Jack wrote. "How long, how tranquilly, how nourishingly, we talked together that last night."

Two of her last remarks to Jack were, "You have made me so happy," and "I am at peace with God."

Though Joy's passing was calm, Jack was crushed by the loss. His two years of married life had been his happiest and most relaxed. Now he had lost the catalyst. He had written books on pain and had counseled people on suffering and bereavement, but now he himself was the victim.

His book *A Grief Observed* grew out of this period of despair. In the book he grappled with the doubt and depression into which his bereavement had plunged him. He spoke of "the agonies, the mad midnight moments." He complained, "I have no photograph of her that's any good. I cannot even see her face distinctly in my imagination." God seemed far away. He asked for divine comfort and all he got was "A door slammed in your face, and a sound of bolting and double bolting on the inside. After that, silence."

He couldn't understand what God was doing. God seemed cruel; could God at the same time be good? Was God only a Cosmic Sadist? He wrote his true feelings; he hid nothing.

Then gradually he saw his grief from a better perspective. "What sort of a lover am I to think so much about my affliction and so much less about hers? Even the insane call 'Come back' is all for my sake. I never even raised the question whether such a return, if it were possible, would be good for her. . . . Could I have wished her anything worse? Having got once through death to come back and then, at some later date, have all her dying to do over again? They call Stephen the first martyr. Hadn't Lazarus the rawer deal?"

Then suddenly after his long bout with depression he records: "Something quite unexpected has happened. It came early this morning. For various reasons, not in themselves at all mysterious, my heart was lighter than it had been for many weeks. For one thing I suppose I am recovering physically from a good deal of mere exhaustion."

But Jack Lewis never completely recovered from

the passing of Joy. He plunged himself into his work, no longer teaching at Oxford, but now at Cambridge. Then his own body began to fail. It was a combination of physical ailments.

He continued writing, finishing his book on prayer, *Letters to Malcolm,* and an article, a few months before his death, on the right to happiness. He told his brother Warren, "I have done all I wanted to do and am ready to go."

On November 22, 1963, the day that President John F. Kennedy was assassinated, C. S. Lewis died; it was only a few days before his sixty-fifth birthday.

Though his brief marriage to Joy was not a long segment of those sixty-five years, it was an extremely significant time.

Between the time of the civil ceremony and the religious ceremony, C. S. Lewis was working on a manuscript which later evolved into his book *The Four Loves.* The book traces the meaning of the four Greek words for love—affection, friendship, eros, and charity.

In *A Grief Observed,* Lewis tells how Joy and he "feasted on love; every mode of it—solemn and merry, romantic and realistic, sometimes as dramatic as a thunderstorm, sometimes as comfortable and unemphatic as putting on your soft slippers. No cranny of heart or body remained unsatisfied."

He spoke of her as "my daughter, and my mother, my pupil and my teacher, my subject and my sovereign . . . my trusty comrade, friend, shipmate, fellow-soldier. My mistress, but at the same time all that any man friend has ever been to me."

His views of women were incomplete until he married Joy. After all, his mother had died when he was only a lad. From the time he was ten to the time he was twenty-two, he was in male company almost constantly. Janie Moore was the first woman who showed him compassion, but her love was so needy that it was apparently warped psychologically.

In his early books Lewis concentrated on "the legalities of sexual love," but in *The Four Loves* he did not depreciate Eros, as long as it is not "honored without reservation and obeyed unconditionally."

Despite the backgrounds that both Joy and Jack brought into their marriage, and despite the cultural differences that could have driven a gulf between them, their marriage did what any good marriage should do—it made each of them into stronger, more complete human beings. It may have begun as a friendship, but as it grew it eventually explored all of the "four loves." For Professor Lewis, theory became reality; for ex-Communist Joy Davidman, she discovered a true comrade in arms.

BIBLIOGRAPHY

Grateful acknowledgment is given to authors J. C. Pollock and Lyle Dorsett, whose books *Hudson Taylor and Maria* (McGraw Hill) and *And God Came In* (Macmillan) deal in noteworthy detail with the marriages of Hudson and Maria Taylor and Jack and Joy Lewis.

THE KNOXES

McCrie, Thomas, *The Life of John Knox*. London: Thomas Nelson. 1847.

Ridley, Jasper, *John Knox*. New York: Oxford University Press. 1968.

MacGregor, Geddes, *The Thundering Scot*. Philadelphia: Westminster Press. 1957.

Reid, W. Stanford, *Trumpeter of God*. New York: Scribner's. 1974.

Brown, Hume, *John Knox*. London: A. and C. Black. 1895.

Perry, Eustace. *John Knox*. London: Hodder and Stoughton. 1937.

THE TAYLORS

Pollock, J. C., *Hudson Taylor and Maria*. New York: McGraw Hill. 1962.

Taylor, Dr. and Mrs. Howard, *Hudson Taylor's Spiritual Secret*. Chicago: Moody Press. 1950.

Taylor, Dr. and Mrs. Howard, *Hudson Taylor and the China Inland Mission*. Philadelphia: China Inland Mission. 1918.

THE SUNDAYS

Ellis, William T., *Billy Sunday: The Man and His Message*. Philadelphia: John C. Winston. 1936.

McLaughlin, W. G., Jr., *Billy Sunday Was His Real Name*. Chicago: University of Chicago Press. 1955.

Lockerbie, D. Bruce, *Billy Sunday*. Waco, Texas: Word Books. 1965.

THE HILLS

Karr, Jean, *Grace Livingston Hill*. New York: Greenburg. 1948.

THE LEWISES

Van Auken, Sheldon, *A Severe Mercy*. San Francisco: Harper and Row. 1977.

Lewis, C. S., *Surprised by Joy*. New York: Harcourt, Brace. 1956.

Lewis, C. S., *A Grief Observed*. New York: Seabury. 1961.

Lewis, C. S., *Letters*. New York: Harcourt, Brace. 1966.

Dorsett, Lyle, *And God Came In*. New York: Macmillan. 1983.

Soper, David Wesley, ed., *These Found the Way*. Philadelphia: Westminster Press. 1951.

Kilby, Clyde S., and Mead, Marjorie Lamp, eds., *Brothers and Friends*. San Francisco: Harper and Row. 1982.

Green, Roger Lancelot, and Hooper, Walter. *C. S. Lewis: A Biography*. New York: Harcourt, Brace, Jovanovich. 1974.

Kilby, Clyde S., ed., *Letters to an American Lady*. Grand Rapids: Eerdmans Publishing Company. 1961.

Catherine Marshall had a husband

WILLIAM J. PETERSEN

LIVING BOOKS
Tyndale House Publishers, Inc.
Wheaton, Illinois

First printing, October 1986

Library of Congress Catalog Card Number 86-50455
ISBN 0-8423-0204-2
Copyright © 1986 by William J. Petersen
All rights reserved
Printed in the United States of America

CONTENTS

We early discovered
that the important thing
was not the differences between us,
but the will,
the determination
to work them out.
After all,
every couple has difficulties.
No two lives are fused
into perfect oneness
without a certain amount
of painful adjustment.

CATHERINE
MARSHALL

INTRODUCTION

"Husbands and wives are basically incompatible," Catherine Marshall once wrote. But a little thing like incompatibility hasn't always stood in the way of a good marriage. God has a knack for using the struggles of married life and the tensions of raising a family to make us moldable (and, in many cases, more Christlike). This is discernible in most Christian marriages.

But the marriages of Christian leaders seem to be even more fraught with clogs and bogs than the average Christian marriage. Catherine Marshall, for example, never understood why her husband had to travel so much. Mary Livingstone, Susie Spurgeon, and Mary Bryan were also bothered by the extensive travels of their celebrated husbands.

Sometimes Christian leaders are so single-minded that it seems as if they would be better off single. That's what some biographers have said about David Livingstone. And that's what Peter Marshall's biographer once thought about him (and his biographer, incidentally, was his wife). But the marriage of the Marshalls, like many Christian marriages that seem destined to fail, came through with flying colors. Why? What makes the union of two very different personalities succeed?

One answer is that sometimes a husband or wife brings a special ingredient into a marriage that makes it hum. Can you imagine how drab John Bunyan's life might have been without Elizabeth? And where would William Jennings Bryan have been if he didn't have a wife to keep his pockets filled with radishes? Mary, of course, was much more than a pocket-stuffer.

Another answer is that, in spite of obstacles and pain, romance can and does endure. One of the pleasant surprises in the marriages of Christian leaders is the prevalence of romance. Who would have guessed that the great Baptist preacher, Charles Haddon Spurgeon, was a very loving husband or that the Bryans kept a very romantic relationship throughout their lives?

Another answer is that each couple finds, through trial and error, a pattern of living that works. No one set pattern makes a marriage good. William and Mary Bryan were a team of equals; John and Elizabeth Bunyan were not. Even when one person—Catherine Marshall, for instance—

has two marriages, the patterns for the two may not be similar. Good marriages are not shaped by a cookie cutter; they are shaped by people.

I trust that you will come to know and enjoy these Christian leaders as I have, and I trust that you will also learn from their marriages.

Catherine Marshall once wrote that problems in the home provide God with teaching opportunities. "What's required of us," she said, "is the open-mindedness of an eager learner."

So first enjoy and then eagerly learn.

William J. Petersen

Meet
John
and
Elizabeth
Bunyan

J ohn Bunyan, a seventeenth-century English Baptist, is best known for his classic allegory, *The Pilgrim's Progress*, which has outsold every Christian book except the Bible and has been translated into scores of languages. Unfortunately, not too many people know of its sequel, which tells of the pilgrimage of Christian's wife.

But that is to be expected. After all, not too many people know about Elizabeth Bunyan either. And that's a pity, for her influence on the famous author was great. And the story of their marriage is a tale as engaging as anything Bunyan wrote.

As far as his married life was concerned, John Bunyan was a pilgrim who made progress. But, admittedly, a lot of progress needed to be made.

His married life—and he was married twice—was not a continual Celestial City. In fact, it started in a Slough of Despond and wallowed at times in a Valley of Humiliation.

John was one of those husbands who was never home. During the first thirteen years of married life with Elizabeth (his second wife), John was home for less than two years. Most of the time he spent in the county jail, not a very good way to maintain a marriage.

Yet the marriage turned out well, and was certainly far more happy than his first marriage.

It is not surprising that his first marriage was not particularly happy, for there was little in his upbringing that gave promise that he would amount to much. His father was a tinker who pushed his noisy cart along Bedfordshire's dusty roads and banged his kettle in front of prospective customers' doors. He was illiterate, his vocabulary pockmarked with curse words.

John called his father's house "the meanest and most despised of all families in the land," which was probably a slight exaggeration. It was a little thatched-roof cottage on the outskirts of the half-timbered hamlet of Elstow, a mile south of Bedford.

It was probably his mother who encouraged him to trudge to school at Bedford, where he learned "to read and write according to the rate of other poor men's children." But then his father called upon him to learn the tinkering trade and to help put food on the table for the family. John says he "almost utterly" forgot all he had learned in his school primer.

An active child, a British version of Huck Finn, he was addicted to athletics and curious about nature. His mother seemed delighted with his questioning mind.

Then when he was fifteen his mother died. She was only forty. For the sensitive teenager, it was a crushing loss. A month later, perhaps from the same epidemic, his sister suddenly passed away. Only a year younger than John, Margaret had been his closest playmate and his best friend.

Less than a month later, John's father remarried. For John, a sensitive boy still grief-stricken by the sudden deaths of his mother and sister, the sudden marriage must have cut like a knife.

He tried not to let his hurt show. He swore more and didn't let anyone know that he was crying on the inside. And three months later, on the day he turned sixteen and became eligible to join the army, he became a soldier.

It was the time of England's Civil War, with the

king and his Royalists battling against the Parliamentary army and its rising star, Oliver Cromwell. John Bunyan never said what side he fought on, and his biographers have debated the issue ever since. But probably he was in the Parliamentary army, since the residents of Bedfordshire were anti-Royalist. (Two years earlier they had petitioned the king, "Many are the miseries your subjects suffer and our fears are beyond our miseries.")

No doubt John took part in a couple of small skirmishes, although one that he didn't take part in was the one he remembered the longest. "When I was just ready to go, one of the company desired to go in my room. . . . He took my place, and coming to the siege, as he stood sentinel, he was shot in the head with a musket bullet and died." He later felt he had been preserved by God's providence.

In 1647, after thirty-two months of military duty, he returned to Elstow and became an apprentice tinker. Unhappy living in the same house with his stepmother, John wanted to move out. And the best way to do that was to get married.

Very little is known about his first wife. She was not a local girl. John may have met her when he was in the army, but more possibly he met her when he began his travels from town to town as a tinker. Because their first daughter was named Mary, biographers conclude that her first name may also have been Mary.

Basically, three things are known about Mary: She was just as poor as John was, if not poorer; she had a very religious father from whom she inherited two religious books; and she had a tendency to nag.

"We came together," recalls John, "as poor as poor might be, not having so much household stuff as a dish or spoon betwixt us both."

Her father, whom she idolized, had recently died. John could sincerely sympathize with Mary. He knew what it was to grieve over a departed parent. Perhaps that, more than anything else, is what attracted Mary to John. She needed sympathy and a masculine image in her life. John could provide both. On John's part, he needed someone to care for, a bird with a broken wing, someone who would look up to him.

Married at nineteen, John was one part little boy, one part rebellious adolescent, and one part big man.

But it didn't take Mary long to realize that John wasn't the spitting image of her father. She wanted to remake him, to reprogram him. "She would often tell me what a godly man her father was, and how he would reprove and correct vice, both in his house and amongst his neighbors; what a strict and holy life he lived in his day, both in word and deed."

John tried to be as virtuous as her father had been. He read to her—because she herself couldn't read—the two religious books her father had bequeathed her, *The Plain Man's Pathway to Heaven* and *The Practice of Piety*. He also became a good churchman.

"I fell in very eagerly with the religious practices of the times, to wit, to go to church twice a day . . . and there very devoutly both say and sing as others did, yet retaining my wicked life."

His wicked life consisted of his addiction to swearing and to Sunday sports. Neither of these bothered him until he read in one of his wife's books that swearing is "an evident demonstration of a reprobate" and until his minister preached one Sunday morning on the ungodliness of Sabbath amusements.

That afternoon John went out to play his usual Sunday afternoon game of tipcat (an early form of baseball) on the village green. As John took his turn at bat, "a voice did suddenly dart from heaven into my soul, which said, 'Wilt thou leave thy sins and go to Heaven, or have thy sins and go to Hell?'"

John stopped, looked up to heaven, and thought he saw Jesus looking down in displeasure on him. At first, he was stunned. But then, reckoning it was too late for him to change his ways, he picked up his bat again and returned to the game. "I resolved . . . to go on in sin. . . . I had as good be damned for many sins, as to be damned for few."

So John decided "to take my fill of sin, still studying what sin was yet to be committed, that I might taste the sweetness of it."

The sin in which John was most proficient was cursing, a habit picked up from his father. "One day as I was standing at a neighbor's shop window and there cursing and swearing, . . . there sat within the woman of the house, and heard me, who though she was a very loose and ungodly wretch, yet protested that I swore and cursed at that most fearful rate, that she was made to tremble to hear me. . . ."

He says that he hung his head "and wished with all my heart that I might be a little child again" and learn to speak without swearing.

John did make an attempt at reform. Now twenty-one, he had just become a father for the first time, and little Mary had been born blind. John was deeply affected. He began to take life more seriously again. He did quite well at clearing up his speech. In fact, as he recalled, "I fell to some outward reformation."

His neighbors were impressed. "I loved to be talked of as one that was truly godly," he says, but "I was nothing but a poor painted hypocrite."

One day as he was peddling his wares through the streets of Bedford, he noticed "three or four poor women sitting . . . talking about the things of God." John, who was now priding himself on his new religious image, began chatting with them about his new hobby, religion, but when they referred to a new birth and the work of God in their hearts, John didn't know what they were talking about. Yet he saw that they had a contentment that he had never possessed.

He began attending the Baptist meeting in Bedford where these humble women went. "I could not stay away; and the more I went, the more I did question my condition."

John struggled. He felt there was a wall that he could not get through. He wondered if the day of grace had passed for him or if he was not among the elect. He could not imagine that God loved him.

His sinfulness loomed like a monster over him. "I was more loathsome in my own eyes than was a toad. . . . I fell deeply into despair."

The pastor of the church, John Gifford, tried to help him, but Bunyan wallowed in his Slough of Despond. He would have times of spiritual insight into God's mercy, but then he would fall back into depression.

One Sunday, Gifford spoke on a text from the Song of Solomon: "Behold, thou art . . . my love." The text stuck with John. The next morning he felt like telling the verse "to the very crows that eat upon the plowed lands before me."

Then came another low period. "All my comfort was taken from me; darkness seized upon me, after which whole floods of blasphemies, both against God, Christ and the Scriptures, were poured upon my spirit, to my great confusion and astonishment."

John thought he must be possessed of the devil

or else crazy. Every time he thought of God, some blasphemous thought would come into his mind.

Pastor Gifford suggested that he read Martin Luther's commentary on Galatians. As John began reading, he was amazed. Luther seemed to have written the commentary directly to him. "This made me marvel," he said. Luther too had faced enormous temptations from Satan and had struggled with blasphemies.

It was a turning point for Bunyan.

He still had his ups and downs, but gradually Scripture, Luther's commentary, and Pastor Gifford's patient counsel began to bear fruit. "Mr. Gifford's doctrine was much for my stability," wrote John.

And then there were the Bible verses that kept coming into his mind as he plodded the streets. Sometimes they were a bit jumbled, and when he returned home, he couldn't find them in his Bible, but they gave him much to meditate on. "My grace is sufficient for thee. . . . Thy righteousness is in heaven. . . . Jesus Christ is my righteousness. . . . I will never leave thee nor forsake thee. . . . Him that cometh to me I will in no wise cast out."

Though his wife Mary knew her Bible fairly well, she wasn't much help to John in his spiritual wrestling. The established church had been good enough for her father; why wasn't it good enough for John?

It is significant that *Pilgrim's Progress* begins with Christian expressing his spiritual concerns to his family. In response, his wife and relatives tell him to go to bed, get a good night's sleep, and perhaps he will feel better in the morning. No doubt the same thing had happened in the Bunyan household.

In *Pilgrim's Progress* when Christian continued to talk with his family about his struggles, "sometimes they would deride, and sometimes they would chide, and sometimes they would quite neglect him. Wherefore he began to retire himself to his chamber to pray for and pity them, and also to condole his own misery; he would also walk solitarily in the fields, sometimes reading, and sometimes praying, and thus for some days he spent his time." That was probably autobiographical as well.

Undoubtedly, John and Mary cared deeply for each other, but they weren't on the same wavelength during John's spiritual struggles. Mary simply couldn't understand what all the fuss was about. Her father never agonized about his religion that way.

Besides, Mary had problems of her own. Not only was she experiencing a difficult second pregnancy, but Mary, their blind daughter, was toddling now. That made life nerve-wracking.

For most of the past two years, John, now twenty-four, had been preoccupied with his sinful state. He had been walking to the Baptist church in Bedford every Sunday, while his wife and daughter continued to attend the Anglican church in Elstow where they lived.

Eventually, however, Mary's anguish broke through to him. She was in great pain; in fact, he feared that her life was in danger. He tells about it in *Grace Abounding*: "Her pangs . . . were fierce and strong upon her, even as if she would immediately have fallen in labor."

At the time John was questioning whether God existed, and, if he did, whether he cared for John and realized the turmoil he was now undergoing. As his wife lay groaning in pain, John prayed, "Lord, if thou wilt now remove this sad affliction from my wife, and cause her to be troubled no more this night, then I shall know that Thou canst discern the secret thoughts of my heart."

No sooner had the prayer gone through his mind than Mary's pains were eased and she fell into a deep sleep. Once again John was assured that God existed and that he cared.

"At this time also," John writes, "I saw more in those words 'heirs of God' than ever I shall be able to express while I live in this world." Gradually he was getting his spiritual equilibrium.

By the time the second child, Elizabeth, was born in 1654, John had been baptized into the Baptist church in Bedford. Later the family moved to Bedford.

Why the Bunyans moved from Elstow to a small house on St. Cuthbert Street in Bedford in 1655 is not certain. John's business had been growing despite his personal turmoils, and

Bedford would certainly have provided more opportunity for growth than Elstow. But John's move was probably prompted by spiritual concerns. No doubt he thought that by living in Bedford, Mary and the children might be influenced by John Gifford's preaching. Besides that, he himself had been spending an increasing amount of time counseling with Pastor Gifford, who had much to teach him, and a move would make such meetings easier. In addition, and John couldn't understand why, the church was calling on him to take more responsibility, including preaching on occasion.

The first time he was asked to speak in public "it did much dash and abash my spirit." He was amazed when the congregation asked him to speak again. But soon he was in demand as a speaker, and he preached in woods, in barns, on village greens, and in town chapels.

It was quite a novelty to hear a tinker preach, so crowds flocked whenever a meeting was announced.

Though he was a lay preacher, some of his nagging temptations clung to him. He was sometimes tempted to pour out blasphemies in the middle of a sermon. But he had many other things besides spiritual concerns to occupy his mind.

Two sons—John and Thomas—were born during those busy years. And it may have been shortly after Thomas was born that John's wife became ill and died. The exact time or cause of her death

24

is unknown, but since it is known that she had difficulty with her pregnancies, it is probable that after her fourth child she was too weak to withstand infection.

Mary's death left John with four small children, ranging from Mary, the blind daughter who was now eight, to Thomas, still a babe-in-arms.

The congregation, closely knit and caring, assisted John with his family. Doubtless they also let him know that it was his duty to find a wife without too much delay.

John describes himself as "shy" toward women. In fact, he says that he did not allow himself to "so much as touch a woman's hand." John never denied his vices, but being overly bold to the opposite sex was not one of them.

One of the younger church members to babysit for John was Elizabeth, still a teenager herself. There were several things about Elizabeth that interested John: She was a believer, she handled his children well, and, though she was young, she enjoyed talking with him about spiritual matters.

When John Bunyan married Elizabeth, she was only sixteen or seventeen. John was thirty-one. The wedding, simple as it was, took place late in 1659. That was also the year of the crackdown, the year when Englishmen were ordered to worship only in the Church of England, the established church; all other religious services were illegal. (Non-Anglican Protestants were known as Dissenters or Nonconformists.)

John Bunyan had already seen turbulent times. In 1658 his first wife had died; so had Oliver Cromwell, England's Lord Protector. Cromwell had extended toleration for Nonconformists, and when he died, it signaled the end of religious freedom for Baptists like John Bunyan. So the prospects for 1659 didn't look good. England was preparing for the return of a Stuart king, Charles II, to the throne. And the Stuarts had been notoriously hostile to Nonconformists.

But the bright spot in 1659, which made the year glow for the Bedford tinker, was Elizabeth.

Elizabeth was young, but she wasn't stupid. As a member of the Baptist church, she must have known what the probabilities were for her as the wife of a tinker who moonlighted as a Baptist preacher. And she knew what kind of man she was marrying.

Outwardly, he was a rather typical working-class Englishman. A contemporary describes him as "tall of stature, strong-boned though not corpulent, somewhat of a ruddy face with sparkling eyes, wearing his hair on his upper lip after the old British fashion; his hair reddish . . . his nose well-set . . . and his mouth moderately large."

Yet inwardly, he was far from typical—and far from being well-adjusted. At times he was morbidly introspective. He was extremely sensitive because his mind was so burdened with fears and guilt. And he was a preacher associated with an outlawed religion.

But Elizabeth cared deeply for the man she married. She was, apparently, well prepared to be the wife of a man whose work kept him away from home. During the week, he carried a heavy anvil on his back, traveling to nearby villages and hamlets, mending pots, pans, and lanterns, and occasionally selling one as well. When he came home at night, he was weary.

On weekends he was on call as a lay preacher, even though it had now become illegal to preach to more than five people at a time, except in the established church. For John, weekends brought an exciting change of pace; for teenaged Elizabeth, weekends meant being alone with her four stepchildren in the two-room cottage they called home.

Despite the hardships for both of them, the first year of marriage was a happy one. He enjoyed sharing spiritual matters with his wife, and he was relieved to have found a good mother for his children.

But the following year was different. The Baptists in Bedford lost their minister by death and their property by confiscation, and it looked as if they would lose a lot more if Judge Francis Wingate had anything to do with it. (Apparently Judge Wingate had lost part of his estate when Oliver Cromwell was in power, and he seemed eager for revenge upon any Cromwell sympathizers.)

John was aware that his movements, especially

on Sunday, were being watched. "I saw what was a-coming," he wrote.

On November 12, 1660, he was asked to preach in a house in Lower Samsell, about twelve miles from Bedford. Judge Wingate found out about it and issued a warrant for Bunyan's arrest.

"I could have escaped," John said, "and kept out of his hands." In fact, some of his friends had suggested that the meeting be cancelled or at least that Bunyan flee before the constable came.

For John, the decision wasn't easy. He had been telling congregations to be strong even in persecution. If he should run away and play the coward, how would other Christians respond?

Yet at the same time John knew that imprisonment would mean separation from his young wife. "I was as a man pulling down his house upon the head of his wife and children. . . ." After wrestling with all the options, he concluded, "I must do it, I must do it." So he walked to the front of his small congregation and opened the meeting in prayer.

That was as far as John got. The constable entered and placed him under arrest.

John was taken to the Bedford jail, and Elizabeth, who was pregnant at the time, was so shocked by the event that she had a miscarriage. After one year of marriage, she was left as a virtual widow with four children.

John's imprisonment was to last for three months. At the end of that time, he was to be released if he agreed to conform to the laws of the land. If he wouldn't conform, harsher punishment would be exacted. John feared hanging, but deportation was also a possibility.

Elizabeth and his children visited him every day. According to one tradition, his blind daughter brought him a jug of soup daily.

John agonized over whether he should continue to preach. Family visits did not make his decision any easier. Every time Elizabeth and the children closed the cell door and left him behind in prison, he agonized more. But how could he stop preaching?

He wrote, "The parting with my wife and poor children has often been to me in this place as the pulling of my flesh from my bones." He imagined "the hardships, miseries and wants my poor family was like to meet with should I be taken from them, especially my poor blind child, who lay nearer my heart than all I had besides. Poor child, thought I, what sorrow art thou like to have for thy portion in this world. . . . But yet I must venture all with God, though it goeth to the quick to leave you."

So when his first three months were completed, John refused to agree to stop preaching, and as a result he was imprisoned indefinitely. He had no desire to be a martyr—his family meant too much to him—but what choice did he have? He felt compelled to preach the Word of God.

A few weeks later the new king, Charles II, was

crowned. In honor of the occasion, it was announced that hundreds of prisoners throughout England would be released.

As soon as the news got to Bedford, Elizabeth made plans to go to London to make an appeal for her husband. Still a teenager, she probably had never been to London before, but that didn't seem to daunt her. In London she presented her petition to the Earl of Bedford, asking for her husband's release. In turn, he brought the matter to the House of Lords, which quickly passed the buck to the Judges of Assize, who were scheduled to meet in Bedford later in the summer.

She must have grown impatient waiting for her chance to petition the judges. She had no knowledge of proper protocol, but she had heard that one of the judges, Matthew Hale, was known to be more lenient in his attitudes towards Nonconformists.

Hesitantly, she approached him. He answered that he was afraid he couldn't help her, although he would see if anything were possible.

The next day, she tried another angle, presenting her petition to a different judge as he rode by her in his coach. His response was cold and direct: John Bunyan had been convicted of a crime and could not be released until he promised to stop preaching.

Each rejection made Elizabeth more desperate in her attempts. She was just about ready to give up when a sheriff encouraged her to try one more time. The judges were scheduled to meet in the Swan Chamber of Bedford along with several other justices and leading gentry of the area. It would be her last chance.

She entered, she said, "with trembling heart." At first, she addressed Judge Hale, who she thought might be willing to listen to her. "My lord, I make bold to come once again to your lordship, to know what may be done with my husband." Hale answered that he couldn't do anything for John Bunyan. She tried to argue that her husband had been unlawfully convicted. But it was useless for a teenaged housewife to lecture judges about the law.

She told her story about how she had gone to London and had presented her petition to a member of the House of Lords and how he had told her that the judges would give it consideration. She begged them at least to consider the matter. They realized that she wouldn't be put off easily. One judge asked, "Will your husband stop preaching if he is released?"

They had not been married long, but Elizabeth knew what her husband's answer would be. "No," she answered, "he dare not, as long as he can speak."

"Then he is a peacebreaker."

"No, he is a peaceable man," she responded quickly. "He simply wants to pursue his calling so that he can feed and clothe his family." She paused and then began talking about the family. "My lord, I have four small children that cannot help themselves. One of them is blind. We have nothing to live on but the charity of good people."

"You have four children?" one judge asked incredulously. "You're too young to have four children."

She explained to the judges that she really was the stepmother to the children. Then she also added, "I was with child when my husband was arrested. . . . But I was so distressed at the news that I fell into labor and continued in labor for eight days. Then the baby was delivered, but it died."

It was a touching story, and a couple of the judges began to soften. Others said she was merely trying to sway them by pretending she was poverty-stricken. They charged that Bunyan made more money as a preacher than as a tinker.

When his occupation of tinker was mentioned, Elizabeth was defensive. "And because he is a tinker and a poor man, he is despised and cannot have justice."

They didn't answer her strong charge. Instead they pointed out again that if they released him, he would immediately start preaching again.

"He preaches nothing but the Word of God," Elizabeth interjected.

One of the justices scoffed, "He preaches the Word of God?" He moved toward her almost as if he were going to strike her.

Elizabeth took a step back and then begged

them to send for her husband and let him answer for himself. "He can answer you better than I can. I've forgotten so many things."

During the entire time she had held up extremely well; finally she broke into tears. It was not, she says, "because they were so hard-hearted against me and my husband, but to think what a sad account such poor creatures will have to give at the coming of the Lord."

Slowly, she moved out of the judicial chambers. Her efforts had been fruitless. But they were efforts that her husband would never forget.

"So far as marriage is concerned," writes biographer Monica Furlong, "he seems to have been particularly fortunate in his second marriage to Elizabeth. He writes with obvious love of the pain of being separated from her, of the joy of sharing his religious ideas with her, and she in turn obviously recognized what was important to him in his life and work, and supported him, even when, as during his imprisonment, it involved her in considerable suffering and hardship."

For most of the next twelve years John was in jail. During this time, "the family must have been very poor," writes Ola Winslow. "The cruelest aspect of an imprisonment like Bunyan's was that it made an entire family destitute. The friends of the Bedford Meeting kept the Bunyan family out of a sense of religious duty, but the congregation was a poor one, and charity is a chancy sort of income; the hardships must have been considerable."

To provide some income for his family, John made bootlaces in jail, but the income it provided was meager indeed. He also preached to the other prisoners and managed to write ten works, including his autobiographical *Grace Abounding*.

Released finally in 1672 under Charles II's Declaration of Indulgence (a general pardon for religious prisoners), John became pastor of the local church. He was now forty-three and Elizabeth was nearly thirty. He opened up his tinker's shop again because "his temporal affairs had gone to wreck," but more and more he was in demand as a preacher. He was playfully called "Bishop Bunyan," and his stand for principle had made him a folk hero throughout England's Midlands.

Four years later, his preaching got him into trouble again. He was returned to prison for six months. But what an eventful imprisonment that was! During that time he wrote much of *Pilgrim's Progress*, which was published two years later and which made him a household name throughout the country. The two parts of this classic show how much Bunyan had learned to appreciate women and marriage.

In his writings John doesn't speak much about his marriage, but as he grew older, women and children become increasingly more prominent in them. John's earlier works, including Part I of *Pilgrim's Progress*, focus on men. In Part I,

Christian leaves his wife and children behind. The women who are depicted in it are incidental characters. Though John's sense of humor peeks through repeatedly, Part I is still a grim journey, filled with ominous people and places like Doubting Castle and the Giant Despair, the Valley of Humiliation and Apollyon, and the Slough of Despond.

But in Part II, written about nine years later, Christian's wife begins her journey to the Celestial City, and it has been termed "a smiling journey." In it the Valley of the Shadow is passed in the daytime.

The focus is now on Christiana, who is modeled after Elizabeth. "Christiana is not a dream woman," writes Monica Furlong. She is "believable." She does not battle monsters and ogres. She meets fascinating people like Mrs. Bats-Eyes, Mrs. Light-Mind, and Madam Bubble.

Part I is a solitary pilgrimage. Part II is a family walking tour. It may seem humdrum compared to Part I, but it is gracious and good-humored. Part I shows John's own spiritual struggles and answers the question, "What must I do to be saved?" Part II shows Elizabeth's characteristics of determination, grace, and tenderness and answers the question, "How do I grow as a Christian?"

At times there is a gaiety, almost a frivolity in Part II, although Christiana's journey is taken just as seriously as her husband's was previously.

When John writes about women in Part II, there is more refinement, as if in his mind women were associated with refinement.

Perhaps it is not strange at all that John should treat women so sympathetically. The poor women of Bedford had played a key role in his conversion when they engaged him in spiritual conversation, and women continued to be prominent in the church when he served it as pastor. His mother and sister were noble figures in his early years, and Elizabeth had been a tower of strength for him during his imprisonment.

John taught that a wife "is to be subject to her husband, but she is not to be her husband's slave; she is his yoke-fellow, his flesh and bones. The wife is master next to her husband, and is to rule in his absence; and even in his presence she is to guide the house and to bring up the children. The husband, if his wife is a believer, should so love her that their life together may preach the marriage of Christ to his Church." According to his contemporaries, that was a fair description of the relationship of John and Elizabeth.

John's marriage brought him much satisfaction. So did the forward movement of the Nonconformist congregations. As pastor of the Bedford church and as an evangelist throughout the Midlands (even in places as far away as London), John saw the numbers of Baptists grow rapidly. It was said that when he went to preach in London "if there was one day's notice, the meeting house was crowded to overflowing."

But when King Charles II died in 1685, and his brother King James II took the throne, Nonconformists like Bunyan experienced another reign of terror. Once again, non-Anglican worshipers were hauled off to jail, and Baptists and others took special precautions to keep their meeting places unknown. Places of meeting were changed every few weeks; sentinels were posted to give warning; hymns were no longer sung because congregational singing would attract attention; more services were held in the evening.

For John, it looked as if another prison stay was inevitable. So John transferred all his property to his "well-beloved wife, Elizabeth."

To avoid detection as he traveled he disguised himself, once pretending to be a professional wagon driver, wearing a smock and carrying a whip in his hand. Stopped by a constable who asked if he knew "that devil of a fellow Bunyan," John replied: "Know him? You might call him a devil if you knew him as well as I once did."

But the persecution under James was short-lived. After 1688, the year Bunyan died, the new rulers, William III and Mary II, did their best to promote religious toleration. John was in no more danger of being imprisoned. He continued to preach often.

When John was almost sixty, he was asked by a young man to see if he could mend the relationship between him and his father in the town of

Reading. Doubtless remembering the problems that he had had with his own father, John went out of his way to make the journey on horseback. On his return he was caught in a driving rainstorm. He caught a cold, began running a high fever, and a few days later he died.

Elizabeth, who had inherited John's entire estate (which was worth only forty-two pounds), died less than three years later. She was only forty-six.

It is difficult to assess Elizabeth's influence on John, but undoubtedly she played a major factor in his maturing. At the age of twenty, John had not been a strong personality. As one biographer put it, Mary (his first wife) seemed to have the stronger personality because John "was not yet sure where he wanted to go." His "daily conduct was observed and measured by the recording angel at home and to his humiliation he found that the standards admired in Elstow seemed tawdry and contemptible in the eyes of his wife."

The Apostle Paul speaks of the law as a schoolmaster that brings us to Christ. Mary functioned as the law for John, but it was Elizabeth who helped him to mature in the grace of God.

The character of his preaching and writing changed because of Elizabeth's influence. Previously he had preached "against man's sins and their fearful state because of them." But about the time of his marriage to Elizabeth, "I altered in my preaching" because "the Lord came in upon my own soul with some staid peace and comfort through Christ, for he did give me many sweet discoveries of his blessed grace." Just before he met Elizabeth, he published a tract called, "A Few Sighs from Hell, or The Groans of a Damned Soul." His first sermon published after he met Elizabeth was on the text, "Ye are not under the law, but under grace."

Of course, God was doing much in the heart of John Bunyan apart from Elizabeth's influence, but God's timing of bringing Elizabeth into John's life was remarkably effective. John found in her a strength and consistent support that he had not known before.

In his twenties, he may have been mentally disturbed. Certainly he was self-centered and morbid. But in his forties and fifties, he became a well-balanced man with humor and grace, purpose and confidence, and he was sought out for his wise counsel.

Too little is known of Elizabeth. But one thing is sure: when she came into John's life, heavenly music started playing, and even twelve years of separation, while he was in prison, couldn't put a stop to it.

CHAPTER
TWO

Meet David and Mary Livingstone

I t would not have been easy for anyone to have been married to David
Livingstone. He was a loner, he was intensely driven, and he found it difficult
to work closely with people.

In fact, some of his biographers say
that he should never have married.

Fortunately, Mary was not hard to get along
with—at least at first. David himself described her
as "amiable and good tempered." He also described her as "a matter-of-fact lady, a little, thick,
black-haired girl, sturdy and all I want."

It was not what you would call a romantic marriage, but it certainly was not without love. It was
a marriage full of frustration for both of them,
especially for Mary. It was also a marriage that
provided plenty of ammunition for gossips,

second-guessers, and various critics, including Mary's parents as well as David's. There were so many questions the critics wanted answered. Why did David take Mary and the children on dangerous African expeditions? What drove Mary to drink? Is it possible to be unhappy when you're married to the most popular man in the world? What fascinating questions! What a fascinating couple! After all, they were involved in a lover's triangle, and the third party was named Africa.

David Livingstone was a confirmed bachelor when he first volunteered for missionary service. In answer to the simple question "Are you married?" he wrote on his application form: "Unmarried; under no engagement relating to marriage, never made proposals of marriage, nor conducted myself to any woman as to cause her to suspect that I intended anything relating to marriage."

But during the next couple of years he was frequently reminded that he would be sorry if he didn't get married soon. People told him that a missionary's life is a lonely one.

Missionary life can be wretched without a partner. Livingstone feared that missionary life might be even more wretched with the wrong partner.

But after he had spent three years in lonely

missionary service in Africa, Livingstone reluctantly admitted that maybe his advisors had been right after all. By this time he was begging parents and friends to write him more often, but because letters sometimes took half a year to arrive, it was difficult to carry on a meaningful dialogue. He was lonely, and he needed a close companion.

But where would he find a wife in the middle of Bechuanaland in the 1840s? The only eligible candidates in all of South Africa were daughters of missionaries and daughters of government servants. And according to Livingstone, who usually expressed his opinions bluntly, "Daughters of missionaries have miserably contracted minds; colonial ladies worse and worse." Prospects didn't look good.

But then, after some hand-to-paw combat with a lion, he was convalescing at the Kuruman mission station where Robert and Mary Moffat had been serving as missionaries for a score of years. Strolling under the syringa trees with Mary, the eldest daughter of the Moffats, David experienced some emotions that he had thought were deeply buried.

"In love!" he wrote to his old bachelor friends in London. "Words, yea thoughts fail, so I leave it to your imagination."

She was twenty-three, and he was thirty. One biographer states, "She happened to be the first young woman that he had met since he had left England." Three months later, they were engaged.

He wrote a friend, "After nearly four years of African life as a bachelor, I screwed up my courage to put a question beneath one of the fruit trees."

From his standpoint, she would make an ideal wife for him. The daughter of pioneer missionaries six hundred miles inland from Cape Town, South Africa, Mary had been raised in a mud hut. She knew how to make her own clothes, bread, candles, and soap. She was hardy, knew what missionary life was all about, and was "good-tempered." She wouldn't win any beauty contests, but David didn't care about that.

Her parents were both strong-minded and strong-willed. Her mother—outspoken, pious, and often domineering—bore ten children and raised three native children in addition. Her father had risen from Scottish poverty to dominate South Africa's missionary landscape. He had what one writer called "a smothering effect on his colleagues."

And except for his wife, who was the power behind the throne, his family was smothered too. The children grew up with inferiority feelings—especially Mary, who was neither attractive physically nor brilliant mentally.

Standards in the Moffat home were high, and anyone who didn't meet those standards could expect criticism. Younger missionaries were made to feel like teenagers who weren't allowed to grow up. That's the way Mary felt too.

But David didn't respond to her father as other

missionaries did. Though he was new on the field and was nearly twenty years younger than her father, he talked to him as an equal.

What Mary saw in Livingstone was a man with the same strength of character that her father possessed, but a man who, unlike her father, had a basic modesty, a sense of humor, and a deep regard for honesty. Not only was he unlike her father, but his background was very different from hers.

While Mary was living in a mud hut in Africa, David had been growing up in a one-room tenement in a factory town outside Glasgow, Scotland. The Livingstone parents and their five children were squeezed into a ten-by-fourteen foot room, which was their kitchen, bedroom, and living room combined. Biographer Tim Jeal writes, "Truckle beds were pulled out at night to cover the whole floorspace. Cooking, eating, reading, washing and mending all went on in the one room."

When he was ten, David went to work in the mill that controlled life in Blantyre. He became a "piecer," piecing together threads on the spinning frames. Like everyone else, he worked six days a week from eight in the morning until eight at night, with a half hour for breakfast and an hour for lunch.

Somehow David forced himself to go to the company school from eight to ten every evening. There he not only managed to keep his eyes open, but he also got his education. Often he returned home and read until midnight, when his mother made him blow out the candle. His sister recalled that he was "determined to learn."

David's father abhorred alcohol and "trashy novels," which were how he classified all books that weren't religious. David refused to read the religious books that his father set in front of him. He preferred scientific works and travel books. It "reached the point of open rebellion on my part," David admitted later, "and his last application of the rod was on my refusal to peruse Wilberforce's *Practical Christianity*." David said he hated "dry doctrinal books."

When he was twenty, however, against the wishes of his father, he read a book by an amateur astronomer and minister who was seeking to reconcile science with Christianity. David was fascinated, and concluded that "religion and science are not hostile, but friendly to each other." Once that intellectual hurdle was crossed, he was able, as he put it, to make "a personal application" of Christ's atonement.

The Independent church in Hamilton to which he applied for membership was not so sure. The Scottish elders "dooted if Dauvit was soun' " and gave him personal instruction for the next five months.

The following year, after reading a tract by a missionary to China calling for missionary doctors, David had a direction in life. And when David started moving in a direction, nothing deterred him. Two years later, he left the mill at which he had worked for the previous twelve years and entered medical school in Glasgow.

Then he applied to the London Missionary Society for overseas service with China in mind. The society did not seem too impressed with his credentials but accepted him on probation.

Because he was "hardly ready" for theological college, he was given private tutoring. The society's directors spoke negatively about his rusticity (meaning he was a country bumpkin from Scotland) and his heaviness of manner (meaning that he took himself too seriously).

They tried him out as a preacher in a church, but he failed at that. As he stood before the congregation, his mind went blank. He read his text, repeated it slowly, swallowed deeply, and then said, "Friends, I have forgotten all I had to say." He left the church as quickly as he could. (A couple of years later he was able to preach a sermon, but afterwards several members of the congregation told him if "they knew he was to preach again they would not enter the chapel.")

Another problem for the directors was David's praying. When he led in prayer, he seemed to pause interminably while thinking what he should pray for next.

Instead of rejecting him, however, the directors decided to extend his probation. After a few more months they approved him as a missionary candidate because of his good sense and quiet vigor.

While awaiting the decision of the directors, he began courting a girl from a middle-class family. It was apparently his first serious courtship. Feeling awkward in her presence, he confessed to her that he was "not very well acquainted with the feelings of those who had been ladies all their lives."

He was twenty-six now, but David Livingstone was considered no great catch for a young woman. A friend said, "I have to admit he was no bonny. His face wore at all times the strongly marked lines of potent will." Another friend remarked that "by no means did he have a winning face," though he did have "an indescribable charm."

When his first love rejected him, David—with a bit of a sour grapes reaction—commented that she was probably too much of a lady to become a good wife for a missionary.

In 1839 the Opium War between China and England broke out, and that changed the thinking of the London Missionary Society about sending more missionaries to China. The directors then suggested that Livingstone think of the West Indies. David didn't like the idea. The West Indies were too civilized. The dark continent of Africa would be more of a challenge.

Then he happened to bump into Robert Moffat, home in England after a score of years in the interior of South Africa. Said Moffat to David, "At dawn I can look out and see the smoke of a thousand villages where the gospel has not been preached." From then on David aimed at Africa, regardless of what the board of directors said.

His fellow missionary candidates liked David. He had "a certain roughness or bluntness of manner," and there was a "great persistence in holding to his own ideas," but there was also a "great kindliness" about him.

David's persistence in holding to his own ideas frequently got him into trouble. With the mission directors, he seemed to wage a continuing debate. He did not like the idea of taking orders from anyone.

Just before going to Africa, he took his finals with the Glasgow medical facility, and he almost had to forfeit his degree because of his outspoken disagreement with them regarding the value of a stethoscope. He didn't think it had the potential that they said it had.

On board ship to Africa, David, one of the few passengers who didn't get seasick, tended medically to those that did. Arriving in Africa, he was assigned to work out of the Moffat's mission station at Kuruman, six hundred miles inland from Cape Town. The Moffats were still on furlough in England, and the station needed the services of a doctor. David was told to think about establishing a station farther inland, but any action would have to wait until the Moffats returned to the field.

That opened the door a crack for David. Though Kuruman was the farthest inland of any mission station, it was still too civilized for him. He wrote letters to the directors in London, requesting that they allow him to do more than just think about a new station. David had been in Africa only five months, and already he was convinced that missionary strategy was either too conservative or simply misguided.

He explored the interior; that was the necessary research for a later decision. When he returned to Kuruman, he wrote, "I did not come to Africa to be suspended on the tail of anyone. What is of infinitely more importance [is that] souls are perishing while I have no power to point them to the Cross. I could not settle down at Kuruman."

His research took him further inland than any white man had ever been before, although he had been in Africa for less than a year and was still struggling to pick up the African languages.

Then in 1843, when Roger Edwards and his wife left Kuruman to begin a new station, David eagerly accompanied them. The spot they selected was Mabotsa, about 220 miles from Kuruman. "A lovelier spot you never saw," David wrote.

It was here where David felt his loneliness more than ever before. The fact that Roger Edwards kept telling him that he needed to get married didn't help matters any.

And it was in Mabotsa where David had his wrestling match with a lion. Lions had been marauding the cattle pens of the Africans, and the villagers were reluctant to do anything about it.

David told them that if they would kill one lion, the other lions would get the idea that they weren't welcome and would leave the area. The Africans weren't so sure that this newcomer knew what he was talking about.

David accompanied the Africans as they stalked the lions. Spotting several of them, he took aim and fired both barrels of his rifle; then he stopped to reload. Suddenly he heard a shout. "Looking half round, I saw the lion just in the act of springing upon me. . . . He caught my shoulder as he sprang, and we both came to the ground together. Growling horribly close to my ear, he shook me as a terrier dog does a rat."

An African, coming to David's rescue, fired at the lion. He missed, but the lion turned his attention to his new assailant. Another African then speared the lion, and soon the beast, wounded previously by David's bullets and then by the spear, fell down dead.

David's upper arm was splintered, and the lion's teeth made a series of gashes. Never again was he able to lift his left arm above his shoulder.

Later David was asked what his thoughts were as he lay on the ground wrestling with the lion. He responded, "I was wondering which part of me he would eat first."

For weeks he was extremely ill, but then he recovered enough to be taken to Kuruman where he could receive better assistance. The Moffats had just returned to the station after four years on furlough. And the Moffat's daughter Mary became his nurse.

Before long, Mary the nurse became Mary the fiancée.

After he sufficiently recovered from his lion wounds and received Mary's consent to become his wife, he headed back to Mabotsa to build a house.

On his way he stopped to write Mary a letter. In it he reminded her to get a marriage license and to order some household goods for their Mabotsa home. He closed the letter with the words, "Let your affection be towards Him much more than towards me."

His letter to the mission board, informing them of his proposed marriage, appears as if he had simply made a cold business decision: "Various considerations connected with this new sphere of labor, and which to you need not be specified in detail, having led me to the conclusion that it was my duty to enter into the marriage relation, I have made the necessary arrangements for union with Mary, the eldest daughter of Mr. Moffat, in the beginning of January 1845. . . . And if I have not deceived myself I was in some measure guided by a desire that the divine glory might be promoted in my increased usefulness."

But that was the kind of King's English that he normally used when he wrote to his directors. Only to some personal friends and to Mary did his letters convey warmth, humor, and informality.

The home he built for Mary in Mabotsa was fifty-two feet by twenty feet, with walls a foot thick: "It is pretty hard work," he wrote Mary, "and almost enough to drive love out of my head, but it is not situated there; it is in my heart, and won't come out unless you behave so as to quench it. . . ."

He also put in a couple of lines for Mary's mother, who had her opinions on everything and was seldom bashful about expressing them. She had apparently told Livingstone (whom she always called by his last name) not to put too many windows in the house. David wrote to Mary that if her mother "thinks there are too many she can just let me know. I can build them all up in two days and let the light come down the chimney if that would please."

In David's mind was the notion that he could build Mabotsa into a mission station similar to the one that Mary's parents had built at Kuruman. At the same time he wanted to incorporate some new ideas, like using African evangelists and starting a seminary to train African pastors. But there was a hitch in that plan: David already had had a taste of exploration, and he was on the verge of becoming addicted.

For now, he wanted to get something started at Mabotsa, "whence the rays of divine light might radiate far and wide." When he wasn't constructing his house, he was trying to get a school started for African children. It was rather frustrating because on some days he might have fifty youngsters but on other days he would have only five.

"If I can get them on a little," he wrote to his bride-to-be, "I shall translate some of your infant-school hymns into Sechuana rhyme, and you may yet, if you have time, teach them the tunes to them. I, poor mortal, am as mute as a fish in regard to singing."

Wedding day was January 2, 1845, in Kuruman, with Robert and Mary Moffat looking on. David and Mary honeymooned in Mabotsa, which name, incidentally, means "wedding feast." If David hoped that it would prove to be one for Mary and himself, he soon had to face reality.

The probem was his colleague in Mabotsa, Roger Edwards. "We parted in apparent harmony when I went to get married," said David, "and when I returned, a storm burst on my head such as I had never had before." David spoke of him as being "a fiery old gent."

Livingstone was too much of a go-getter for Edwards, and the older missionary couldn't handle it. Edwards felt that he had been a "lackey" for Moffat in his first ten years of missionary service, and now for the first time he had a chance to do something on his own without Patriarch Moffat looking over his shoulder. But when he set up his new base at Mabotsa, Livingstone was with him. It was Livingstone who came up with new ideas and pushed them through. The junior partner in the operation was taking over, and Edwards strongly resented being "a mere appendix to this young man."

To top it off, Livingstone married Moffat's daughter. Edwards must have felt that even in Mabotsa, 220 miles from Kuruman, he couldn't get away from the eyes of the Moffat family.

Edwards wasn't the only missionary with whom Livingstone had disagreements. David was impatient and aggressive, and older missionaries resented a newcomer telling them how to run things.

David did not feel he could speak with Mary about these disagreements. He wrote to a friend, "I tell you my sorrows although I have a wife," indicating that he did not feel he could share some of his deeper problems with her. It may have been, as some biographers have suggested, that he lacked confidence in her mental ability. More probably, however, it was because Mary didn't have a philosophical mind. She had more the soul of an artist than a scholar.

Problems between the Edwardses and the Livingstones continued to mount. Mrs. Edwards called David "shabby, ungentlemanly and un-christian" and Edwards called him "dishonest, dishonorable and mischievous."

Obviously, Mabotsa was not big enough for both couples. So, before the year was over, David and Mary Livingstone packed their bags and left their honeymoon cottage, heading farther north-ward into the African interior.

David halted his caravan at a spot he called "a blank on the map" and wrote friends that he was now the "most remotely situated missionary in southern Africa." The "blank on the map" was called Chinuone. A severe drought had begun to envelop the area even before David and Mary arrived, and during their twenty-month stay the famine got even worse. In those months, Mary bore two children and tried to get a school started for African children in her spare time.

Eventually, David realized that if Mary and the children didn't get some decent food, the results would be disastrous. So he sent them to his in-laws in Kuruman. When Mary arrived there the Africans hardly recognized her, because she had lost considerable weight. A few days later David arrived and they taunted him, "How lean she is! Have you starved her?"

David decided he had better seek a new site for missionary endeavors. So shortly after they returned to Chinuone, he went with several Africans to seek a better location. Mary and the two children stayed behind in what was now a virtual ghost town.

She sent David a note. Life among the ruins of Chinuone was a bit dreary in the daytime, she wrote, but at least the nights wouldn't be boring. The lions were moving in to resume possession.

A month later, David finally returned to take her and the children to their new home in Kolobeng. The new home was actually not as good as the old one. It was a drafty, fly-infested hut of poles and reeds, insufferably hot in the daytime and amazingly cold at night.

Kolobeng was home for David and Mary for the next four years, their longest sojourn in any one spot. With all its problems and frustrations, it was probably the happiest time in Mary's life.

David describes an ordinary day: "The daily routine; up with the sun, family worship, breakfast, school, then manual work as required—ploughing, sowing, smythying, and every other sort. Mary, busy all the morning with culinary and other work; a rest of two hours after dinner; then she goes to the infant school with an attendance of from 60 to 80. Manual work for him again till 5 o'clock; then lessons in the town and talk to such as are disposed to listen. The cows are milked; then a meeting; followed by a prayer meeting in Sechele's house (the village chief) which brings him home about 8:30 too tired for any mental exertions. I do not enumerate these duties by way of telling you how much we do, but to let you know a cause of sorrow I have that so little of my time is devoted to real missionary work."

Mary had to make her own candles, soap, and butter. She ground her own meal and baked bread in ant-mud covered with hot ashes. When meat was scarce, they lived on caterpillars or roast locusts. David didn't like boiled locusts, "but when they are roasted, I should much prefer them to shrimp," and then he adds, "though I would avoid both if possible."

Often the local chief sent them zebra meat—too often, according to David. The real delicacy was a species of frog, "nearly as large as a chicken," and just about as good.

Their permanent home was finished after a year of living in their drafty hut. Actually, it wasn't quite completed, because David hadn't installed an outer door as yet. A buffalo skin hung over the opening. Once, however, David says, "A big wolf came and took away the buffalo skin. Mary wanted me to go and see whether the room door was fastened, but . . . I advised her to take a fork in her hand and go herself, as I was too comfortably situated to go myself." David seemed to have remarkable confidence in Mary's ability to take care of herself.

David had more confidence in Mary than he did in the missionary enterprise. Missionary work had been discouraging to him partly because he did not see results quickly enough. Only one African had declared his faith in Christ during David's six years as a missionary. And when he looked at the efforts of other missionaries, it didn't seem as if they had much more to show for their labors. Even his in-laws, after thirty years of service, had not seen great success.

Only a small part of Africa had been touched by missionary endeavors. What about the rest?

He looked northward. "I cannot help earnestly coveting the privilege of introducing the gospel into a new people. . . . Perhaps it arises from ambition, but it is not of an ignoble sort."

At another time he wrote, "God had an only Son, and He was a missionary and a physician. A poor, poor imitation of Him I am, or wish to be."

While David was having second thoughts about his aptitude as a missionary, he began to realize that perhaps his greatest contribution to the missionary cause would be to open up Africa's interior for other missionaries.

Three months after Mary gave birth to their third child, David took her to stay with her parents in Kolobeng while he went on a four-month six-hundred-mile trek to find a legendary lake, Lake Ngami, about which the Africans had told him. Several Europeans had previously tried to find it, but none had succeeded.

David Livingstone found it. He was more interested in what might lie on the other side of the lake, however. So the following year David was eager to make the trip again, this time going beyond the lake, and this time going with his family.

Taking his wife and children caused the tongue of almost every missionary in Africa to wag. On this extremely hazardous journey across a desert, a wide river infested with crocodiles, disease-ridden swamps, and unpredictable African tribesmen, David dared to take his family. Mary was five months pregnant, and she had three small children with her.

But the options were for Mary to stay with her

mother again or for her to go exploring with David. She chose to go with David.

The trip was beset with problems, not the least of which were the malaria-carrying mosquitoes which ravaged the children. Soon the children began to run high fevers, and though the Livingstone family had made it to legendary Lake Ngami, they could not go further. They returned to Kolobeng as soon as possible.

They arrived none too soon. A week later, Mary delivered her fourth child. The child, however, lived only a few weeks before succumbing to an infection.

Mary too became ill. She suffered from paralysis for several weeks. David wrote, "The right side of her face became motionless" and "the pain continually recurs and affects the right side and leg."

To give her time to recuperate, David took her to Kuruman, where they stayed with the Moffats for three months. Physically, it was a restful time for Mary. Emotionally, there was an air of an uneasy truce. As biographer Tim Jeal states, "It was a tense and disagreeable time."

The news leaked out that David was planning still another trip to Lake Ngami and beyond. Nobody wanted to talk about it or even to think the unthinkable—that David would want Mary and the children to go with him again.

Mrs. Moffat struggled to contain herself, and that wasn't easy. She normally spoke her mind on any subject. Three months later, she could restrain herself no longer. The Livingstones had returned to their station in Kolobeng. Mary was expecting another child. That was the good news. The bad news was that David still planned to have her accompany him on the next expedition.

Mrs. Moffat wrote a letter to her son-in-law as soon as she got the news. "My dear Livingstone," it began, and any letter that started like that sounded ominous. She warmed to her subject by stating that she should have had the courage to have a candid discussion when they had been together at Kuruman. Then she tackled it head-on. "Mary had told me all along that should she be pregnant you would not take her." Instead, Mary would let David go exploring by himself and she would bring the children with her to Kuruman. "But to my dismay I now get a letter in which she writes: 'I must again wend my way to the far interior.' . . . O Livingstone, what do you mean? Was it not enough that you lost one lovely babe, and scarcely saved the other, while the mother came home threatened with paralysis? . . . A pregnant woman with three children trailing about with a company of the other sex, through the wilds of Africa, among savage men and beasts. . . . The thing is preposterous."

Even if her daughter had not been involved, Mrs. Moffat would have questioned the expedition. If David were going farther inland to set up a new mission station, she would have understood, but she couldn't understand why a missionary would spend so much time exploring.

Mrs. Moffat wasn't simply an overly protective mother. She had given birth to ten children in Africa, and she knew what it was like to live in primitive and hazardous conditions. She knew that God would protect his children if they were doing his will. But she was afraid that David and Mary weren't doing God's will when they were exploring instead of evangelizing.

In David's mind, however, was the notion that he could open up a continent for hundreds of new missionaries. Besides, he never liked people telling him what to do—least of all a mother-in-law. As one observer described him, he was "unaggressively obstinate."

Mrs. Moffat didn't realize that Mary agreed with David's thinking. At first, Mary thought she might remain at Kolobeng while David explored. But since Kolobeng was being threatened by the Boers and was still drought-stricken, the family was no longer safe there.

Should she return to Kuruman and stay with her parents again? Neither Mary nor David liked that option. Biographer George Seaver writes: "Mary could no longer feel happy in her parents' home; she would be subject to their whim and treated as she had always been from childhood—as a child; but she was a child no longer; she was a wife and mother. And her husband was a human being with a sense of humor, a freedom-loving fellow-mortal, and she loved him."

And David loved Mary, too, though he often didn't express it. He enjoyed her company; she was a good traveler; and he would miss her if she weren't with him.

Staying at Kuruman would have presented other problems. If Mary were in Kuruman, she would be hearing all those breezes of gossip: "Why is he always leaving her? Can't they get along? Something must be wrong with their marriage." Mary had many reasons to leave Kuruman.

Besides, David was a physician. Where else should a pregnant woman be but at the side of her husband the doctor?

Seaver comments on this stage of Livingstone's life: "This journey was to prove the crux of his career. It forced upon him the realization that his aims as an active missionary and his duties as a husband were two things incompatible, and that one or the other must be sacrificed."

But why couldn't he wait another year or two for his exploration, at least until Mary had regained more strength? Livingstone was concerned that if slave traders reached Africa's interior before missionaries, the Africans would never again be open to the gospel message; instead they would fear anything that came from the white man. But if a missionary would come to them with his wife and children, they would recognize him as a man of peace. David was determined to be that man.

Soon David, Mary, and the children were leading a small caravan, exploring once again the interior of Africa. They investigated the wilds for the next seven months. For some of the time water was extremely scarce. David wrote, "No one knows the value of water till he is deprived of it. . . . I have drunk water with rhinoceros urine and buffaloes' dung." So had Mary and the children.

Their most significant discovery was the upper Zambezi River, which, if it proved to be navigable to the Indian Ocean, would provide missionaries an easy way to get to central Africa.

Returning, they stopped the caravan for eight days along the banks of the Chobe River. There, Mary gave birth to her fifth child. Then they moved on. This time the baby survived. Mary, however, once again suffered from paralysis, and it was more severe than before.

This frightened David. But it also confirmed a difficult decision. David had unfinished business in Africa. Until he found a better way for missionaries to reach the interior, he would not know if his exploration had accomplished anything for the cause of Christ. "I view the end of the geographical feat as the beginning of the missionary enterprise," he had written, but until he had crossed Africa from coast to coast he couldn't write *Finis* above the geographical feat.

Yet that was a trip that would take two years.

Since Mary's paralysis had returned, it was obvious that she couldn't accompany him. Besides, their oldest son Robert would soon be six years old, and David wanted him to get some proper education.

To the mission board David wrote a long letter telling them his plans. What he needed, he said, were "two years devoid of family cares. . . . As we must send our children to England soon, it would be no great additional expense to send them now along with their mother. This arrangement would enable me to proceed alone and devote about two, perhaps three, years to this new region."

He added that this really wasn't his personal preference. What he would like to do, he said, was to settle down on a mission station where he could devote time to the children. "But Providence seems to call me to the regions beyond."

It wouldn't be easy to say good-bye to his wife and children and he knew it. He said that he felt as if he were "orphanizing" his children. He said that it hurt as if he were tearing out his insides.

Criticism was bound to come, no matter what he did. He admitted that "there is much impurity in my motives," but yet "they are in the main for the glory of Him to whom I have dedicated my all."

At another time he wrote, "Some of the brethren do not hesistate to tell the natives that my object is to obtain the applause of men. This bothers me, for sometimes I suspect my own motives."

Doubting his motives was not the only problem. He had no money to support his family while they lived in England. He told the mission board that they must find a way to provide for his family in England. Without waiting for the board to approve his plan to explore the Zambezi or to confirm their willingness to look after Mary and the children, he decided to go ahead anyway.

"So powerfully convinced am I that it is the will of our Lord I should, I will go, no matter who opposes. . . . I will open a way to the interior or perish."

It was a tearful parting at Cape Town, South Africa. David told his children to consider Jesus, rather than himself, as their father from then on. "I have given you back to Him and you are in His care." He wasn't sure that the mission board could provide for the family, but he was sure that Jesus could.

For a few weeks David stayed in Cape Town to get supplies. Almost every day he wrote to Mary.

In one letter he wrote,

"My dearest Mary:

"How I miss you now, and the children. My heart yearns incessantly over you. How many thoughts of the past crowd into my mind. I feel as if I would treat you all much more tenderly and lovingly than ever.

"You have been a great blessing to me. You attended to my comfort in many, many ways. May God bless you for all your kindnesses. I see no face now to be compared with that sunburnt one which has so often greeted me with its kind looks. Let us do our duty to our Savior, and we shall meet again. I wish that time were now."

A few days later he wrote to his oldest daughter, just five years old: "My dearest Agnes, This is your own little letter. Mamma will read it to you. . . . I shall not see you again for a long time, and I am very sorry."

With his supplies purchased, David began his trek back into the interior. It was a difficult time for him emotionally and he shared his feelings in his journal: "28th September 1852—Have I seen the end of my wife and children? . . . O Jesus, use me a little for thy glory. I have done nothing for thee yet, and I would like to do something."

While David battled loneliness, disease, drought, wild animals, and hostile tribesmen, Mary had battles of her own when she arrived in England. With four children in tow, she was a stranger in her own country. Africa was much more her home than England. Her first residence in Great Britain was with David's parents in Scotland. It was a small home to begin with, and David's two unmarried sisters were living there, but that wasn't the heart of the problem.

David's parents were strict and orderly, prim and precise. Mary's lifestyle and background were far different from theirs. Writes Jeal, "It is not hard to imagine the impact of the arrival of a strange daughter-in-law and four children, none of them older than seven, on a religious and meticulously ordered Scottish household."

She arrived in poor physical health, and before long her mental health was ailing.

She stayed with the Livingstones less than half a year, but for both parties it must have seemed far longer than that. She left in a huff, telling her in-laws that she didn't want to see them again, didn't want them running her life, and didn't want them telling her how to raise her children.

After that she wandered around England, living what Jeal terms "a wretched nomadic existence," staying sometimes in rented rooms and sometimes with some of David's old friends whom she knew only by name. It was a humiliating existence for her, and not always a happy one for David's old friends upon whose doors she unexpectedly knocked.

Her in-laws lost contact with her and didn't know if they should try to find her or not. David's father eventually wrote to the mission board:

"Mrs. L. does not write to us, nor are we anxious that she should, neither do we wish her to know that we are enquiring about them. Yet we do love the children much. . . . Their mother was pleased to forbid all communication with us no less than three different times. . . . Owing to her strange behavior ever since we became acquainted with her, we have resolved to have no more intercourse with her until there is evidence that she is a changed person."

Mary was never reconciled to her in-laws, but a year later she felt that she had seen enough of

England and resolved to go back to Africa. David was scheduled to return soon, and she wanted to go to Cape Town to meet him. But the leaders of the mission board refused to advance her money for the trip, and she was unable to go.

Things kept deteriorating for Mary. She became physically ill again and could not afford medical treatment. Unhappy with the mission board's lack of concern, she became bitter and started to spread scandalous rumors about the mission. She wrote an urgent letter to David, begging him to return, but she never knew whether he got the letter or not.

She began drinking, and this made her pleas to the mission board for money more desperate: "Be lenient with me. I don't attempt to justify myself. I may not have been so discreet in the use of my money."

Time dragged. David was supposed to have returned to England after a two-year expedition, but two years passed and he was still exploring Africa. Two years, then three, then four years.

His initial intention had been to go from the center of Africa westward to the Atlantic Ocean, but after he had been successful in that venture, he felt he needed to go eastward to the Indian Ocean, following the Zambezi River.

In Africa's interior, David wondered why Mary didn't write more often. "I get no letters from my wife," he complained in 1855. "Cannot account for it no way."

But Mary had nothing to say. She was not proud of the fact that she had been unable to cope in England. And if she had written, her bitterness would have run all over the paper.

David's letters to her, unfortunately, tended to be sermonic. "Hope you give much of your time to the children," he wrote to his wife who had been cooped up with them in one rooming house after another. "You will be sorry for it if you don't."

"Patience is a virtue," he wrote on another occasion, reminding her that some husbands had to stay away from their wives for five or six years. His sermonic letters did not ease her mind.

While Mary was sinking in despair, her husband was being hailed in absentia as a national hero. The Royal Geographical Society hailed his travel across Africa as "the greatest triumph in geographical research . . . in our times."

And when he finally returned to England in mid-December 1856, he received a festive welcome. It had been four and a half years since Mary had seen him.

When Mary got the official word that he would be landing in a few weeks, her clouds began to lift; her depression soon disappeared.

For the next six months, Mary and David were together in London, except for the week that David took to visit his recently widowed mother in Scotland. (For obvious reasons, Mary and the children stayed in London.) Even though David spent most of his waking hours penning his *Missionary Travels*, Mary was recovering her spirit again. It was a happy time for the Livingstone family. As David wrote, the children milled around, but he had the knack of shutting out all distractions, including children, while he was working. On weekends, David, Mary, and the children went on long walks in the woods together.

Published that fall, *Missionary Travels* was an overnight best-seller and added to Livingstone's stature as an international celebrity. Soon he was acclaimed as a saint as well as an explorer-scientist. He received honorary degrees from Oxford and was proposed to be a Fellow of the Royal Society.

London feted David with one banquet after another, and Mary usually accompanied him. Sometimes honor was showered upon Mary as well. In fact, she heard Lord Shaftesbury (who no doubt didn't know her too well) praise "her spirit and her counsel" and also how she had endured her time in England "with patience and resignation, and even joy."

Few people knew the depths to which Mary had plunged only a year before. Now she seemed like a model wife, and David a model husband. One person in whose home they stayed said, "The doctor was sportive and fond of a joke and Mrs. Livingstone entered into his humor. Dr. and Mrs. Livingstone were much attached, and thoroughly understood each other. In society both were reserved and quiet. Neither of them cared for grandeur. It was a great trial to Dr. Livingstone to go to a grand dinner."

David said that he was uncomfortable with "lionizing"; along with Mary he looked forward to the day when they could return to Africa together.

When David spoke, he publicly thanked his wife for forgiving him for staying in Africa four and a half years instead of the two which he had promised. He spoke of how useful she would be on his next exploration. "She is familiar with the languages; she is able to work; she is willing to endure. . . . Glad am I indeed to be accompanied by my guardian angel."

And glad was Mary indeed to be going with him.

While in England, David severed his official ties with the mission. The mission directors tended to consider his explorations as secular rather than missionary. David was convinced that exploration was the only way to open Africa up for further Christian outreach. So he accepted a formal commission from the British government to serve as government consul and to command an expedition to central Africa, and in particular, the Zambezi River area.

David chose his own team, and it was understood that Mary would be a part of it. So after a whirlwind furlough in England of only fifteen months, he made arrangements to return to Africa.

When they embarked in February 1858, three of their children stayed behind for education; only the youngest, not yet seven, accompanied them. It seemed almost like a long delayed honeymoon for David and Mary.

But it didn't work out. On board the ship, Mary became seasick. At least, that is what David assumed at first. Soon they both realized that it was not seasickness; it was morning sickness. Mary was pregnant again. It was the worst news that Mary could imagine. It meant that she and David would be separated again. It meant returning to the tormented life that she had been living in England.

As soon as they arrived in Africa, Mary was detoured to Kuruman where she would stay with her parents until the baby arrived. Then it would be back to England again, because Mary could not endure living with her mother indefinitely.

"It was a bitter parting with my wife, like tearing the heart out of one. It was so unexpected," David wrote. At another time he wrote that if he could have what he wanted most, it would be simply this: "I would like to be alone with my wife." Instead, he was alone with Africa, his second wife.

The baby, Anna Marie, was born that November; shortly afterward, Mary returned to England to be with her other children. Her departure from Kuruman was hastened by the gossip of the other missionaries. "Her husband cannot live with her. That is why they are separated." It didn't take long for some of Mary's bitterness to return.

This separation from David proved no more pleasant than the previous one. The older children were now teenagers, and Mary was unable to cope with them. She wanted to leave them and join David, but that was impossible. Again, she felt trapped. W. Garden Blaikie writes simply, "Her letters to her husband tell of much spiritual darkness." Once again she was drinking heavily. She was given to "queer and disagreeable moods."

In 1861 a letter finally came from David, asking her to come and meet him in Africa. She didn't need to be coaxed. Her youngest child, only three, was left with David's sisters; the others were in school.

Escorting her on the trip was James Stewart, a handsome young Scottish cleric. Before long, gossip started spreading that the two were having an affair.

It was no affair; the problem was simply that Mary was drinking too much, so much that she was "utterly besotted at times."

A contemporary writer says that Mary, now forty, had become "a coarse, vulgar woman" and extremely overweight.

Without David, she was nothing; with him she was a queen. She needed to be with him. She felt she had failed with the children; she felt she had failed spiritually. David was always steady, always sure. She needed him desperately.

But David was having problems of his own. As a lone explorer, he had been eminently successful; as a leader of an exploring team, he was a flop. The crew was almost mutinous. After four years, his Zambezi River expedition was an expensive fiasco. It had shown his weaknesses as a leader.

So he looked forward to Mary's arrival. As he made his way to the mouth of the Zambezi to meet the ship, he encountered one disastrous delay after another. "Always too late," he wrote sadly in his journal.

That's what Mary must have thought too when her ship arrived at the Zambezi and David was nowhere to be seen. In poor emotional health already, she didn't need another disappointment.

Not finding Livingstone, the captain of Mary's ship turned his craft around and headed for Mozambique, planning to return to the Zambezi a week later. But when the ship was caught in a tornado, its return was delayed for three weeks.

By this time, both Mary and David were distressed. But finally on February 1, 1862, the captain of the vessel spotted the hull of a small paddle steamer near the mouth of the Zambezi.

Stewart tells the story: "I could make out with a glass a firmly built man of about middle height, standing on the port paddle-box and directing the ship's course. He was not exactly dressed as a naval officer, but he wore that gold-laced cap which has since become so well known both at home and in Africa. This was Dr. Livingstone, and I said to his wife, 'There he is at last.' She looked brighter at this announcement than I had seen her do any day for seven months before."

Despite the momentary joy of reunion after years of separation, there were problems. Mary wasn't the same woman David had known before.

At first she seemed the same. She could joke as she used to do when she was able to cheer him up regardless of the circumstances. In fact, once when he thought that others wouldn't understand their lighthearted jesting, he told her, "We old bodies ought now to be more sober, and not play so much."

But underneath her sometimes carefree exterior, David detected something that troubled him. Her bitterness was deeper now; her Christian faith was shaky. Once amiable, she now found it difficult to get along with anyone.

David faced other problems too. Because of the delays, they seemed likely to spend the malarial season in the lower Zambezi area, a notorious region for the disease. David wanted to get Mary off to a nearby island to escape the danger. Once again, delays prevented them from leaving.

It was about this time that Mary discovered the gossip that had been circulating aboard ship regarding James Stewart and herself. Gossip always ruffled Mary, but this seemed especially disturbing to her. Depression set in again. She told David that she "would never have a house in this country." He tried to joke with her to break her despondency, but nothing altered her mood. The following week, she began running a high fever.

A member of Livingstone's party commented, "The state of her mind has been such as to predispose her to any disease, while her indiscretions in eating and drinking previously have been such as to undermine her health."

According to David, she lost her will to live. He tried what he could to reduce her fever, but even massive doses of quinine were ineffective. Her mind wandered; she rambled on about her children.

David stayed by her bedside. It was a "rude bed formed of boxes, but covered with a soft mattress."

Stewart described the scene: "The man who had faced so many deaths, and braved so many dangers, was now utterly broken down and weeping like a child."

Mary's breathing became labored, then irregular. He took her in his arms. "Are you resting in Jesus?" he asked, realizing that she probably couldn't understand what he was saying. Within a few hours, she breathed her last.

Though weary, David went through Mary's possessions to search for answers; he sought to be consoled about her spiritual condition. Recently, all he heard from her was bitterness and despair. When she emerged from gloom, she would joke and laugh. But he hadn't seen any evidence of spirituality since she had returned to Africa.

Then he discovered a prayer she had written. It was short, simple, and plaintive. "Accept me, Lord, as I am, and make me such as Thou wouldst have me to be." He also came across a letter on which she had written: "Let others plead for pensions; I give my services in the world from uninterested motives. I have motives for my own conduct I would not exchange for a hundred pensions."

Under a large baobab tree in Shupanga, Africa, Mary Moffat Livingstone was buried. She was only forty-one years old.

David mourned deeply.

His journal entries display his grief: "It is the first heavy stroke I have suffered. . . . I loved her when I married her, and the longer I lived with her I loved her the more. Oh Mary, my Mary. How often we have longed for a quiet home. . . . Surely He has rewarded you by taking you to the best home."

Two weeks later he wrote, "For the first time in my life I feel willing to die."

In the following months he sought for ways to understand what had happened to Mary emotionally. He recalled that great Christians in church history often "tell of religious gloom, or of paroxysms of opposition and fierce rebellion against God, which found vent in terrible expressions. These were followed by great elevations of faith and reactions of confiding love, the results of divine influence which carried the soul far above the region of the intellect."

He wrote to his mother-in-law and then to his children in England. "A right straightforward woman was she. No crooked way was ever hers, and she could act with decision and energy when required."

"Everything else that happened in my career," he wrote in another letter, "made the mind rise to overcome it, but with this sad stroke I feel crushed and void of strength. I try to bow to the stroke as from the Lord . . . but there are regrets that will follow me to my dying day. If I had only done so and so. . . ."

Mrs. Moffat penned a very understanding and insightful letter to David, in which she admitted that her daughter Mary could not be termed "eminently pious" (a remarkable understatement), but she went on to add that "the Lord knew that her heart was right. And while her life's voyage had been difficult and stormy, God had not allowed her to become a wreck."

Later David, with clearer vision, described Mary as a "sincere if somewhat dejected Christian."

David never remarried. For another eleven years he explored Africa, most of the time as a solitary figure, accompanied only by native Africans.

But like Mary, his life was beset by disappointments.

Says biographer Seaver: "It must have seemed

that all he had striven for had been failure; that over it all might be written one word: Disillusion. In everything he had failed; he had failed as a husband; he had failed as a father; he had failed as a missionary; he had failed as a geographer; he had failed most of all as a liberator. It was through his fault that his wife had died untimely, through his neglect that his children were orphaned." Indeed, he had failed to end the slave trade and failed to establish permanent Christian missions. He was painfully aware that he had not reached his goals.

All that is true. And yet it was through his death that Africa became such a focus of missionary activity that today Africa south of the Sahara is turning to Christianity. His efforts were not, in the long run, fruitless.

David was an intensely driven man who could push himself to superhuman limits. Goal-oriented, he ventured all no matter how others viewed it. "He that loveth father or mother more than me is not worthy of me; and he that loveth son or daughter more than me is not worthy of me" (Matt. 10:37) was a verse he took seriously.

Mary too could push herself to surprising limits—when she had support. She needed approval; she required a place where she could be herself, a place where she could contribute meaningfully, a place where she was safe from the barbs of others. She found that place at David's side. David was her lord and protector.

CHAPTER THREE

Meet William and Mary Bryan

O n his wife's wedding ring he had inscribed "Won, 1880/One, 1884." The first year was their engagement, the second was their marriage.

But William Jennings Bryan isn't known today for winning anything. He ran for president three times on the Democratic ticket and lost each time. He served as President Wilson's secretary of state and resigned just prior to the outbreak of World War I. He argued the Scopes "Monkey Trial" against Clarence Darrow, and though court records indicate he won, the verdict of modern society is that he lost.

An orator, he is caricatured today as a pompous windbag, conceited and narrow-minded. His sharp-tongued contemporary, H. L. Mencken, called Bryan "a charlatan, a mountebank, a zany without sense or dignity . . . a peasant come home to the barnyard." Obviously, Will wasn't universally loved. But admirers called him the greatest lay preacher in American history.

And his wife Mary? What was it like to be married to a politician who lost more often than he won, and who was booed by his own party at the last convention he attended?

Like the trainer-manager of a prizefighter, Mary was always in his corner, encouraging him, advising him what to do in the next round, and dressing his wounds when he returned to his corner.

Mary accepted him as he was: a political progressive and theological conservative. He was a hard man for most people to figure out, but Mary, of course, wasn't like most people. She had him all figured out. After all, she had helped make him. And she worked with him to preserve their storybook romance, which began in their college days.

They were both in college when they first met; he was nineteen, she was eighteen. The year was 1879 and the occasion was an open house at the Jacksonville Female Academy, which the fellows at neighboring Illinois College (now Illinois State University) dubbed "the Jail for Angels."

On one side of the room were the coeds in

crinolines and upswept hairdoes; on the other side were the boys. In between the two factions, which were nervously eyeing each other, were the refreshments—several plates of cookies and a giant urn of tea.

As the two sides edged toward the center, Will Bryan noticed a girl with large gray-brown eyes. Over one of the plates of cookies—and Will was often captivated by cookies—he began talking with her. He liked her sense of humor. He liked the way she looked. In fact, he liked everything about her. In a word, he was smitten.

Mary was not. She had to admit that Will was "a handsome, broad-shouldered six-footer," but his nose was prominent, "too large to look well," and his black hair "was parted with distressing straightness." Yet, she had never seen such a smile. It was the broadest she had ever seen. Someone said later, "That man can whisper into his own ear."

But what bothered Mary about Will was that he seemed "too good." One biographer says he "oozed rectitude." Mary thought so too, but then decided it is better to have a man who is "too good" than one who is "not good enough," and so she decided to see him again.

Will was rooming at the home of a local physician whose wife had become an incurable matchmaker. Convinced that Mary Baird would be the ideal catch for Will Bryan, she praised each of them to the other and set up a neutral meeting place at the home of Will's Latin professor.

When Mary's mother became ill and was hospitalized in a Jacksonville sanatorium, Will had an even better excuse to be with her. From the sanatorium, they took buggy rides together, and that got them into trouble. Though they had her mother's permission, Mary's school did not allow such unchaperoned excursions. So Mary was suspended for the rest of the semester.

To make sure that Mary would not have another secret rendezvous with Will Bryan before she returned home, the principal personally escorted her to the train and waited until the train left the depot before he returned to school. What he didn't know was that Will was hiding in the baggage car. As soon as the train was in motion, he found his way to Mary's side.

The train ride was a turning point for Mary. Earlier, she had been uneasy about Will. Though he had a sense of humor, he wasn't carefree. He seemed too serious about life. He was goal-oriented. The questions he asked her were serious questions, questions about what she wanted to be in life, how important Jesus Christ was to her, and what her devotional practices were. No one had ever pinned her down on such matters before. At first, the questioning seemed almost like an invasion of privacy. But then she began to value a person who was interested in what was really important in life and was also interested in her personally.

On the train, Mary realized that she and Will were going the same direction in life.

The following fall, when Mary was allowed to return to school, Will wasted no time. With fifty dollars he won in a speaking contest, he bought a ring, and on Thanksgiving Day he traveled to Mary's home to ask her father's approval.

Her father, Mary says, was "a gentleman of the old school, tall, dignified and very reserved." He was enough to scare any twenty-year-old.

"Hope you will not be frightened," Mary wrote Will before his mission, "though I imagine it would be a rather disagreeable task." Her father could be rather stubborn, she warned, but even if he said no the first time, his mind could be changed. "There is a party concerned who can and will manage him," Mary wrote confidently.

Will guessed that the best way to approach his father-in-law would be to quote some Scripture. "Mr. Baird, I have been reading Proverbs a good deal lately, and I find that Solomon said, 'Whoso findeth a wife, findeth a good thing, and obtaineth the favor of the Lord.'"

Baird knew where the young man was headed and after a moment responded slowly, "Yes, I believe that Solomon did say that; but Paul suggests that while he that marrieth doeth well, he that marrieth not doeth better."

Bryan's college debate training had prepared him well. He cleared his throat and then responded: "Yes, Paul did say that, but we should consider whenever there is a disagreement on a subject, who is the greater authority. It seems to me, sir, that Solomon would have to be regarded as the greater authority on the subject of marriage. After all, Paul was never married, but Solomon had many wives."

Will won Mr. Baird's consent, but it took four more years before he and Mary said their vows.

Much of their courtship was done by correspondence, though Mary was less than happy about Will as a letter writer. It wasn't that he didn't write frequently; it was rather that he tended to be pontifical, didactic, and absent-minded when he wrote. Too often, he sounded like a lawyer or a minister rather than a suitor. Mary simply expressed herself honestly. If she was angry, she would say so. If she felt he was cold and stiff, she would say so. Fortunately, Will accepted her refreshing honesty, and he also had the grace to be able to laugh at himself.

Occasionally his letters show his sense of humor. Once he wrote, "How do you think I look without my mustache? As I shaved off that long-petted and delicately fondled evidence of manhood, I was deeply impressed with that awful truth that it is easier to destroy than to create. The result of weeks of patient, weary watching gone in a moment."

Will the suitor had more serious concerns than his mustache. Courtship was only one of three crucial matters on the docket during his college years. The other two were spiritual and vocational decisions.

Since his father was a Baptist and his mother a dedicated Methodist, Will as a child had decided to go to a Baptist church on Sunday mornings and to a Methodist church on Sunday evenings. But when the Presbyterians in town had revival meetings, he went to the Presbyterian church, and it was there at age fourteen that he had his conversion experience. Although it was a serious commitment to Jesus Christ, it did not greatly alter his life-style. "Having been brought up in a Christian home, conversion did not mean a change in my habits of life or habits of thought. I do not know of a virtue that came into my life as a result . . . because all the virtues had been taught me by my parents."

At college, however, Will was introduced to some thorny religious issues: the theory of evolution, whether the Flood really happened, whether the Scriptures were scientifically reliable, and others. Once he even wrote to Robert Ingersoll, the noted agnostic, to get input from him.

But the internal struggle didn't last long, and Will, believing there must be "a Designer back of the Design, a Creator behind the Creation," committed himself increasingly to the authority of the Bible.

Vocationally, too, Will vacillated for awhile. When he was eight, he had thought he might become a Baptist preacher. He changed his mind when he realized that he would have to be immersed first. As a ten-year-old he thought about becoming a pumpkin farmer, but pumpkins failed to keep him excited. However, when he was twelve his father ran for a seat in the House of Representatives and lost by only 240 votes. The excitement of the campaign was enough to make Will resolve to become a politician. Committing his life to Jesus Christ at age fourteen didn't change his commitment to politics: it only meant that henceforth he resolved to become a *Christian* politician.

At college Will distinguished himself as valedictorian of his class and as the best backward broad jumper in the area. He also became increasingly adept at speechmaking.

After college, Will enrolled in law school in Chicago, causing a two-year separation from Mary. He wrote her prolifically and begged her for patience regarding marriage. Before getting married he wanted to finish law school and get settled as a lawyer. He said that as soon as he made as much as five hundred dollars a year as a lawyer, he would make Mary his bride.

While at law school, he became a notary public. On his first official document, he penned: "I, W. J. Bryan, a notary public in and for the County of Cook, State of Illinois, do hereby certify that I this day appeared before myself and being duly sworn, deposed and said that I loved and do love Mary E. Baird better than I do anyone else in the world and further that I always will love her, will be good to her and contribute as largely as possible to her happiness and usefulness." Though the document was playful, Will meant the sentiment.

After law school, returning to his college town of Jacksonville, Will joined a law firm. On July 4, 1883, he hung out his shingle. (Will always enjoyed doing memorable things on special days.)

In his first month of practice he earned only nine dollars and sixty cents.

Later, he recalled those early days: "I remember with what anxious expectation I nailed up my modest sign, 'W. J. Bryan, Lawyer,' on the doorpost and awaited the rush of clients. I use the word 'awaited' advisedly, because waiting was the word. . . . The days passed wearily. There was a continuing tread upon the stairs leading up to the second floor where the firm's offices were and I would turn to the door each time I heard a hand upon the knob, only to find that the visitor had turned into the office of Mr. Brown, Mr. Kirby, or Mr. Russell."

Will briefly entertained the notion of moving to Kansas or New Mexico, where there were fewer lawyers and more opportunities to earn enough income to support a wife. But Mary was patient and hopeful, "as she would be in all dark hours," according to one biographer. "Don't be discouraged," she wrote him as their engagement was completing its third year. "You're going through the narrows now."

The following year, 1884, was a bit more rewarding for Will, and by summer they were making wedding plans. "I am practicing on 'and with all my worldly goods I thee endow' so as to make it duly impressive," Will wrote. "If you dare laugh when I say that, I won't kiss you when he tells me to salute the bride."

On October 1, 1884, four years after their engagement, they exchanged their vows. On Mary's wedding band, Will inscribed, "Won, 1880/ One, 1884."

Though Will had started building a house in Jacksonville for his bride, he hadn't been able to complete it by their wedding day—even after a four-year engagement. So, after their honeymoon, they had no place to live. Will's solution? He would return to his law practice in Jacksonville, while Mary would return temporarily to her parents' home 140 miles south. Since they both prided themselves in practicality, they agreed on the arrangement.

But it didn't work.

Mary had endured a four-year long-distance engagement with patience, but she didn't want to suffer through a separation after marriage. Consequently, a couple of weeks later, she packed her suitcase and went to Jacksonville to be with her husband. Their home still wasn't completed, but they lived with friends until it was.

Mary had a mind of her own. She let Will chart the course, but if the ship seemed to be headed towards the rocks, she took over as copilot. Will really didn't mind. His mother had been the same kind of woman.

Mary was more than an assistant; she was a full partner. Plans were made cooperatively. For instance, one of the first matters they discussed was what to do with their leisure time. Their friends had urged them to take up tennis and join some social groups. But Will and Mary decided to devote their spare time to study. Will resolved to read books on the economy; as a romantic birthday present Mary would give him a book on railroad legislation. Mary meanwhile joined a German conversation club, took a course in early English, and began reading her husband's law books.

According to one biographer, Mary "did not take eagerly to housework." Instead, she enjoyed stretching her mind and interacting with her husband on legal issues. But life wasn't merely intellectual in the Bryan household. At least it wasn't after their first child was born, which happened one day short of their first wedding anniversary. And then Mary's parents moved in. They needed Mary's care. Her mother had been chronically ill, and her father was going blind.

To outsiders it may have looked as if Will and Mary Bryan were settling in for a long stay in Jacksonville, Illinois. Not so. Will was restless. He felt there was more for him to do than practice law and raise a family in a small midwestern town. Though he was serving as president of the local YMCA and teaching a Sunday school class, he felt confined. He wanted to become involved in politics, but the political bosses of downstate Illinois did not look kindly on young upstarts like Bryan.

So in 1887, on his return from a business trip to Lincoln, Nebraska, Will asked Mary if she would consider a move there. "You know Jacksonville," she responded. "You have seen Lincoln. If you think that a change is for the best, I am willing to go." So were the in-laws. (It was important that the in-laws also be willing to move, because Will and Mary needed a down payment for a new home in Lincoln, and Mary's father could provide one interest-free.)

On October 1, their wedding anniversary, Will went to Lincoln, leaving Mary, their two-year-old daughter, and his in-laws temporarily behind. He promised to send for them as soon as he had built a house. (Leaving his wife behind while he looked for housing developed into a habit.) In Lincoln, he slept on a folding cot in his office and lived on a diet of apples and gingersnaps.

When they were all reunited in Lincoln, the Bryans picked up where they had left off in Jacksonville. Once again he began teaching Sunday school and leading the YMCA. Mary wasn't too happy about Will's YMCA involvement. The YMCA's men's meeting was held each Sunday afternoon at 4:00, a time when Mary thought Will should be home with his family. "The men's meeting would break up the afternoon and take him from us," Mary lamented. "We laid this sacrifice on the altar, but with unwilling hands, and I doubt if the recording angel gave us any credit."

Will did find time, however, to lead his family in daily devotions, consisting of Scripture reading, prayer, and singing a hymn.

Both Mary and Will, now in their late twenties, started men's and women's discussion groups that soon involved the city's leadership. In a few months, Will became chairman of the city's Democratic committee. As he began making political speeches throughout the area, his oratory captivated the crowds.

He even astonished himself. The morning after one political speech, he told his wife, "I have had a strange experience. Last night I found that I had power over the audience. I could move them as I chose. I have more than usual power as a speaker. I know it. God grant that I may use it wisely." On their knees they prayed together, committing this talent to God.

Meanwhile, Mary continued to pore over Will's law books. After taking the necessary courses at law school, the only woman in her class of seventeen, she passed the bar examination and finished third in her class.

Why did she study law? She wanted to share as much as possible in her husband's life. "If a wife does not show an interest in her husband's work and does not go with him when he asks her, the time may come when he will cease to ask her."

Studying law was simply one way to share Will's interest.

In 1890 Will, now thirty, ran for U.S. Congress. Because the area was strongly Republican, Mary thought it might be a waste of time for him to run as a Democrat. Besides, his opponents ridiculed him as "effervescent as a bottle of soda pop" and as a "calamity howler." But he waged an effective campaign and won easily.

Winning that election was only one hurdle. At times, rough political criticism bothered Mary. She knew Will better than the critics, and she knew that 99 percent of what they said of him wasn't true. He was nicknamed the "Boy Orator of the Platte." True, said an opponent, for "at its mouth the Platte is six miles wide and six inches deep." Such statements bothered Mary at first, but after a few political campaigns she understood that she couldn't take campaign oratory too seriously.

The next move was to Washington, D.C., though once again Will left Mary behind while finding a home. Then with three children and Mary's father (Mary's mother had died shortly before the election), Will and Mary went East for his two terms as a U.S. Congressman.

According to Louis Koenig, "Bryan was a latter-day Jeffersonian, jealous of liberty, confident of local government, suspicious of distant Washington, and respectful of the virtues of the small farmer." And his convictions made him bold. Despite his youth and freshman status, Will was not bashful in Congress. He quickly gained a reputation for his debating skills. And when Will spoke on the floor of Congress, Mary was often seen in the gallery, nodding, frowning, and making other signs for Will's benefit. Mary memorized Will's first major Congressional speech and, as he was delivering it on the floor, her lips were moving in the gallery in unison with his.

Mary was also his research assistant. When a major issue was scheduled to be discussed, Mary went to the Library of Congress to get as much background as she could for her husband. They worked together on answering his mail and frequently collaborated on his speeches.

As far as housework was concerned, Mary was pleased to be able to hire girls to handle it. She was a better executive assistant than she was a maid. She and Will shunned the Washington social whirl, but their youth and exuberance made them popular figures anyway.

Their oldest daughter, Ruth, a precocious child, was often asked questions by reporters. Once a reporter during a national election asked her whether she thought her father would be elected. She responded, "I don't know about the rest of the nation, but I think he will get a lot of votes on our street."

Their second child was a boy. William was described by his father as a "regular boy." His father also said, "How a boy like that ever lives through childhood is a mystery." One day Mary looked out the window and saw young William working his way along the telephone wires, hand over hand. Frequently, when Will and Mary went visiting, they would have their conversation interrupted by a shriek when someone spotted William on top of a roof or hanging precariously from a slender limb of a tree.

Their third child, Grace, was quiet and studious, often in poor health.

Mary, busy as a mother and as a political aide to Will, adapted well to Washington. Though she enjoyed Lincoln and Jacksonville more, she liked challenges, and Washington politics was certainly a challenge. Koenig says, "A woman of intellect, she handled easily the current topics of political debate, knew the political personalities Bryan dealt with, and was shrewder than he in assessing them. Her chief indulgence was a Wednesday morning swim with the ladies. She gave little attention to dress, for which the Eastern press one day criticized her."

Apart from Mary, Will didn't make close friends. He loved people collectively, but "kept them at arm's length individually."

Still in his early thirties, he didn't hesitate to contradict the party bosses and even President Grover Cleveland when he felt it necessary, even though he was a member of the same political party.

After two terms in the House, he ran for the

Senate in 1894 and easily won Nebraska's popular election, capturing 75 percent of the votes. But in the 1890s senators were chosen by the state legislature. The legislators snubbed Bryan and chose a man who received only 2 percent of the popular vote.

Rejection like this bothered Mary more than it did Will. After the loss, Mary came to him and said, "Will, do a favor for me."

"As long as it's not the impossible," he responded.

She asked him to give up politics and devote himself to his law practice.

"Mary," Will answered, "you have asked the impossible."

What Mary didn't realize then was that Will was almost on the verge of an even more demanding political race: the campaign for president.

The financial depression of 1893 made the economy the major issue of the day, and Will felt strongly that the answer to the nation's woes was the free coinage of silver and a graduated income tax. On behalf of these issues and others as well, Will was invited to speak throughout the West and South. He also was named editor-in-chief of the *Omaha World-Herald*, a title which required him to write editorials and shape the paper's editorial policy.

When the Democratic party seemed to be bewildered and unable to find a candidate to succeed Grover Cleveland, Will volunteered a solution. He dashed off letters to the party chiefs declaring that he would consent to be the nominee for the nation's highest office if they couldn't find anyone else.

The thought was ridiculous. One said, "Here was a man barely thirty-six, living in a comparatively unimportant Republican state west of the Mississippi River, audaciously announcing his probable candidacy for the presidential nomination. . . . Absurdity!"

So Will was certainly the darkest of the dark horses at the national convention in Chicago in 1896. But during the meeting, he stepped to the podium and delivered his famous "Cross of Gold" address. Though he had not even been officially listed as a candidate, his dramatic oration catapulted him to the forefront. On the fifth ballot, the young nobody from Nebraska won the nomination.

Though Bryan won the nomination, he had split the party. New York's Tammany Hall politicians refused to support him and sat on the sidelines during most of the campaign.

Will had a chance to win some of them over when he opened his Eastern campaign in New York's Madison Square Garden. Only a few of the party bosses showed up, but twenty thousand New Yorkers didn't want to miss it. Knowing the importance of the occasion and fearing that he might be misquoted by the Eastern press, Will decided to read his speech rather than present it in his usual dramatic style. When Mary found out, she was horrified. She begged him not to be foolish enough to change his usual style. But Will felt it was more important to impress the reporters with a solid, substantial address.

It was a hot, sultry evening. Will's message was ninety minutes long, and many of the bored New Yorkers walked out before the speech was one hour through.

Mary had been right, and Will's chance to be president of the United States may have been lost by his refusal to heed his wife's advice.

After that, the campaign was uphill all the way. Mary campaigned at Will's side, coaching him with his speeches, helping him conserve his strength, explaining his positions to reporters, and making arrangements with reception committees at various whistle-stops.

A decided underdog, Will started climbing week by week. During the four month campaign, he made 3,000 speeches and traveled 18,000 miles.

When the ballots were counted, he lost the election by 500,000 votes to William McKinley. A shift of only 20,000 votes in a few key states would have won him the presidency.

Whether any Democrat could have won after the economic recession of Cleveland's term in office is questionable, for the unemployed and hard-pressed had switched to the Republican side. But Bryan's vigorous campaign made it surprisingly close.

Back home in Lincoln, Will began to write a book. It was entitled *The First Battle*. For the thirty-six year old politician there were more battles to come.

As usual, Mary was at his side in the battles. Up at five each morning, she began to open the mail, which sometimes totaled 2,500 pieces a day. At seven, she woke the children and Will. Since Will, when he was home, liked a hearty breakfast, she usually prepared eggs, sausages, and waffles to start the day. Will especially liked waffles, but his favorite food was radishes. He could eat radishes day or night. When he traveled, he carried a package of radishes with him on the train. The way he stuffed radishes into the pockets of his suit coats ruined the shape of his clothes.

Radishes weren't the only items in his pockets, however. He frequently crumpled up telegrams and letters and stashed them into his pockets as well. It was up to Mary to unload his pockets when he returned home.

"What if he did fill his pockets with wadded-up telegrams?" Mary once said somewhat defensively. "He never lost any."

Traveling was a problem for Will in another way. His suitcases were never big enough. Biographer J. C. Long writes: "No matter how large his suitcase, he couldn't seem to make his things fit into it. Unless Mrs. Bryan was at hand to pack it for him, he would pile in the articles and then step on them until they were sufficiently mashed down to permit the closing of the lid."

Will never changed his style of clothes in forty years. He wore a black frock alpaca coat, a black string tie, and a broadbrimmed hat. His clothes were a trademark that he never changed.

His desk, disorderly in the extreme, was another trademark. Mary likened Will to a squirrel, hiding things in various places in his desk. It may have looked helter-skelter, but when he needed something "he seemed to know exactly where to dig. His eye would roam over the different piles. Then suddenly he would dig down and he very seldom failed to bring up the required document."

Mary said that as disorderly as his desk was, his mind was a neat filing cabinet. Items filed into his mind were retained for years and could be brought out again at a moment's notice during a critical debate.

But it was up to Mary to do the filing. Will seldom had time for much original research or reading. He depended on Mary. She "plodded through heavy books in order to give him the leading thoughts and help form for him a background of erudition which he was too busy to acquire unaided."

During these years of intense political involvement, the Bryans gave freely and generously to needy causes. One evening, when the doorbell rang at their Lincoln home, Will and Mary were surprised to find a Japanese lad at the door. They asked what he wanted and he responded that he wanted an education. Having read one of Will's spellbinding speeches and convinced that Bryan could do anything, he came to Lincoln to enlist their aid.

Will and Mary agreed to let him stay overnight in their home until they could make other arrangements with the Japanese consul. But the young man stayed in their home for five years and finally graduated from the University of Nebraska, with Will and Mary providing room, board, and tuition.

Mary admitted that Will was often taken in by people. He was too gullible. Mary once wrote, "His universal friendliness implied a trust which was at times misplaced, and his patience and forbearance sometimes tolerated unworthy men about him."

But Mary insisted that though he was sometimes wrong about individuals, he was seldom wrong about the public as a whole. A newspaper editor once told Mary: "I watch which way people are going and run around the corner and get in front of them. Bryan takes a place in advance and the people follow him."

Will discussed most major issues with Mary. They didn't always agree. Sometimes Mary tempered Will's position; at other times, he held it in spite of Mary.

"Isn't that an extreme position?" Mary might

say. "If you stand for that, people will call you a fanatic, a wild-eyed reformer."

"But I must stand there," Will would respond. "All progress comes through compromise, not a compromise of principle, but an adjustment between the more radical and the less radical. If I begin far in advance, when the compromise is made, our position will be much ahead of the place I would have secured by a less radical position."

Many of his positions were radical at the time. He pushed for an income tax, an anti-trust law, women's suffrage, a League of Nations, a minimum wage, and the popular election of senators long before these issues were enacted into law.

Quoting the Bible verse, "The common people heard him [Jesus] gladly" (Mark 12:37) he liked to think of himself as a commoner, championing the rights of the working class. One biographer says, "Bryan, the pioneer, cut down the trees of the political forest, pulled up the stumps, plowed the soil and planted the seed. Others reaped the harvest. . . . Bryan seldom won a battle, but every defeat eventually turned into a triumph." Franklin Roosevelt said that Bryan was the embodiment of the man who would rather be right than president. "He did not have to dare to do what to him seemed right," Roosevelt said. "He could not do otherwise."

When the Spanish-American War broke out, Will volunteered his services and was made a colonel, leading a regiment from Nebraska. Politically, it was a gamble, but Will didn't join the army for political reasons. He simply felt that during a time of war it was the duty of a thirty-eight-year-old man to be in uniform. As soon as the war ended, Will returned to become, for the second time, the Democratic candidate for president. This was 1900. Once again, he lost to William McKinley.

Mary's political role had been increasing. Frequently, she wrote the editorials for the Omaha newspaper. During the campaign she served as Will's press agent, handling reporters with grace and quiet humor.

In 1905, the year after Mary's father died, she and Will embarked on a round-the-world trip. Financed by the Hearst newspaper chain, the tour cost Will and Mary nothing.

In Japan, Will and Mary were warmly welcomed, partly because people had heard of the way they had "adopted" a Japanese student in their home. While there, they received letters from thirty-two other Japanese youths wishing to be "adopted."

However, the Bryans had some awkward moments in Japan. At a banquet honoring Admiral Togo for his naval victory over the Russians, Will toasted him with water instead of champagne. At first the Japanese were offended, but Will, always quick with a response, said, "Admiral Togo, you have won your great naval victory on water, so I drink to you in water. When you win a great victory on champagne, I will drink to you in champagne."

Will and Mary followed the customs of taking off their shoes whenever they entered a Japanese home. But there were no slippers in Japan big enough to accommodate Will's feet. He endured several days in his stocking feet before buying the biggest slippers he could find and then cutting away the toes to make room for his large feet.

In Russia, they met with the czar and novelist Leo Tolstoy. They struck up a friendship with Tolstoy that lasted several years.

When they returned to America, it was time for Will to plunge into yet another political campaign. After gaining his third presidential nomination, he campaigned against William Howard Taft. The year was 1908. For the third time Will lost, and this loss was the most decisive of his three attempts. "My only regret," he told his daughter Grace, "is that your mother will never be the First Lady of the Land to the nation, as she has always been to me."

Four years later, Will had another opportunity to run. This time, Mary urged him to do so, and her reasoning was sound. The Republican party was divided, and this was an opportune time for the Democrats to win. Besides, "I wanted him to take the nomination," she said. "I wanted him to be president. I wanted him to conquer his enemies. We had worked so long and so hard."

But Will, now fifty-two, felt that someone else

should be the candidate this time, and he backed Woodrow Wilson. His backing insured Wilson's nomination.

Will campaigned almost as hard for Wilson as he had previously campaigned for himself. Running against both Taft and Teddy Roosevelt, Wilson won the election, but his total popular vote was less than Bryan had received four years earlier.

Shortly after the election, Will was offered the position of secretary of state, a job he accepted with the provision that he would not have to serve intoxicating liquors at their table during official state functions. (Though Will and Mary had not before been crusading Prohibitionists, they were lifelong abstainers.)

Will's goal as secretary of state was to eliminate war, a rather tall order for anyone. Though not technically a pacifist, he vigorously opposed war as a way for nations to resolve their disputes. Once in office, he wasted no time in getting nations to sign peace treaties with one another. A major accomplishment of his term was the fact that thirty peace treaties were signed within two years.

Will opposed the notion that the way for a nation to fight militarism is to increase its own militancy. Once he said, "Those who advocate the policy of 'fighting the devil with fire' seem to overlook two important factors: (1) the devil is better acquainted with fire than his adversaries; (2) being at no expense for fuel, he has an economic advantage which tells powerfully in any prolonged contest."

Then trouble broke out in Europe. Will worked at being the mediator between Germany and England, trying to maintain neutrality. But his moves were frustrated, sometimes within the president's cabinet itself, but often by German or British diplomats. He watched as the nations drifted toward war and threatened to bring the United States into it.

It was the period of the most intense strain Will had ever faced. He stayed awake nights and then struggled to be ready to face the challenges of the next day. Night after night, Mary stayed up with him, making him tea, soothing him, and trying to get him to rest.

Then when the ship *Lusitania* was sunk by a German submarine, President Wilson drafted a letter to Germany which Will was sure would result in American involvement in the European conflict. It was Will's job to send it. Rather than do so, he offered his resignation.

Before long, America was involved in the war, just as he had feared.

Peacemaking wasn't Will's only concern. No longer officially involved in government, Will and Mary now joined to push for two constitutional amendments. Along with evangelist Billy Sunday, they campaigned for Prohibition, and just as ardently they campaigned for women's suffrage. Said Will, "I shall claim no privileges for myself that I do not ask for my wife." He said he couldn't understand how men could keep women from voting when "most of what men know about government comes from women schoolteachers."

With her children grown, without her father to take care of, and without political responsibilities, Mary seemed to have time, at age fifty-five, to do something she always wanted to do. Back home in Nebraska, she wrote, "On the 25th of June I began my music lessons. I have always wanted to play the pipe organ and this seemed an opportunity. People can always learn the things they really wish to know. If we would only keep alive the ambitions of youth until the opportunity comes."

But physical problems soon beset both her and Will. Diabetes plagued Will, who had a gargantuan appetite and never watched his diet when he traveled. Arthritis bothered Mary. Thus in their late fifties they moved to Florida. There they found more tranquility than they had known previously. They began each day reading a few pages of a secular book; then they read a few pages of Scripture before praying together.

Once again, Will was teaching a Sunday school class. He began as a substitute teacher in a small room in the church. Soon the class grew so large that it had to move to the church auditorium. Then, when the class outgrew the church, Will took his students to a nearby ballpark. The attendance fluctuated between two and five thousand. When Florida vacationers asked to receive copies of his lessons throughout the year, Will began to syndicate them in a hundred newspapers across the nation.

Will also continued to be a popular speaker across the country. Each summer he was on the Chautauqua lecture circuit. He could speak anywhere on almost any subject at the drop of a hat. But Mary said that one of the few times she found him at a loss for words was when he was asked to speak at a rescue mission along New York City's waterfront. Will whispered to Mary, "It takes a man who has been saved from the depths to reach men like these. I cannot do it."

Through the 1920 presidential campaign Will continued to be a force in the Democratic Party. He was present at the 1924 Democratic convention, but because of her poor health, Mary was unable to attend. Will missed her advice, encouragement, and comfort. When a reporter noticed that his wife was not present and asked him about her, Will broke down in tears. Then he told of all that she had meant to him, as a wife, as a friend, and as an advisor. He feared that she would not last long, and he hoped that he would not outlive her.

New York City, the site of the 1924 Democratic convention, had always been a political disaster for Will, and in 1924 he faced humiliation there. When he rose to speak, he was booed by the galleries as well as by many of the delegates. "This is probably the last convention of my party to which

I will be a delegate," Will said, and the crowd cheered and applauded. Still able to respond graciously, Will countered, "Don't applaud. I may change my mind."

His political life was finished, and he knew it. But he also was aware that his physical life was drawing to a close. His father and grandfather had both died before they were sixty. Will, at sixty-four, felt he was living on borrowed time.

He was increasingly concerned about Mary's health. At times she seemed much improved, but when her severe arthritic seizures struck, she experienced great pain and was confined to a wheelchair.

Will began cutting back on his speaking engagements. When asked to take on a speaking crusade to fight the teaching of evolution, Will responded that he did not want to leave Mary again. "I owe it to her to give her such comfort as I can by my presence."

Through the years their love had deepened. Mary wrote a note to him on his sixty-fifth birthday: "I love you better and better each year and have an increasing desire to do all I can for your comfort and happiness. I would not trade you for anything."

The final event in Bryan's declining years and perhaps the event for which he is best known today was the Scopes evolution trial. A young science teacher named John Scopes in the Dayton, Tennessee, high school was arrested for violating the state law which prohibited the teaching of evolution in public school. Well-known lawyer Clarence Darrow was brought in for the defense, and Bryan was asked to serve as counsel for the prosecution. He was glad to do so, since he heartily opposed the teaching of evolution. He saw it as a threat to the nation's faith and ethics, and he believed the trial would help the nation see the danger.

The "Monkey Trial," as it came to be known, lasted nearly two weeks in sultry July weather. The trial, because of the two famous figures involved, received much attention from the media. It became a kind of contest between the liberalism represented by Darrow and the Christian fundamentalism represented by Bryan. Journalists at the trial helped form a lingering stereotype of fundamentalists as bigoted, ignorant, and rural.

At a crucial point, Darrow unexpectedly put Will on the stand and questioned him regarding his belief in the literal interpretation of Scripture. Confident that he could answer all of Darrow's questions, he consented to take the stand. It was a mistake. Although a very knowledgeable layman regarding Scripture, he was not a scientist. Many of Will's responses were brilliant, but Darrow was able to twist other answers for his benefit. In two hours of questioning, Darrow made Bryan look narrow-minded and foolish. Fundamentalism was not dead, but it was, for many Americans, discredited.

Ironically, some of Will's answers alienated him from the fundamentalists. For instance, he did not believe that the Creation necessarily took place in six literal days; the "days" could, he said, have been six periods of time. On the other hand, some of his answers seemed quite naive to progressives.

Scopes was found guilty and fined $100, so it can be said that Will's side won the case. But nevertheless, Will and the cause he represented came out as losers.

After the trial, Mary and Will discussed it and the broader issue of separation of church and state. Religious zeal must not encroach upon individual rights and beliefs, he said. Then he asked her if she thought his religious zeal had gone over the line.

"You are all right so far," she answered. "But will you be able to keep to the narrow path?"

"I think I can."

"But can you control your followers?" Mary asked perceptively.

Will's answer came more slowly this time. "I think I can."

It was only five days later that Will passed away as he took an afternoon nap.

The cause of death? His followers said he died because his heart was broken. Clarence Darrow retorted, "Broken heart, nothing. He died of a busted belly." But according to Dr. J. Thomas Kelly, William Jennings Bryan died of diabetes mellitus.

Confined to a wheelchair for the rest of her life, Mary returned to Florida to complete her husband's memoirs. This was a project she and Will had begun before his death. When the book was finally published, more than half had been written by Mary. Perhaps it was fitting, because probably Will would have accomplished less than 50 percent of his life's work without her.

Mary was a remarkable woman, no doubt about that. The daughter of a prosperous small-town merchant, she had been educated in one of the best finishing schools in Illinois. She earned a law degree while raising a family, taking care of her aged and ailing parents, and being separated often from her busy, politicking husband.

Though Will was loving and caring and though he genuinely wanted to see Mary fulfilled and happy, he was absentminded and self-centered. An optimist and an enthusiast, he was something like a little toy airplane with a wind-up rubber-band-powered propeller. Wind held him up and he would sputter off in surprisingly successful flights. Then he would fall abruptly and unceremoniously in Mary's lap. Undaunted and almost oblivious to his previous collapse, he would wind himself up and take off once again in another direction.

Mary understood him and appreciated his genius. At times she had to bring him down to earth.

About two years before Will's death, a noted

political figure visited them in Florida and congratulated Will on his good fortune in having found such an able and understanding wife.

"Your marriage was a great romance," the visitor said.

"Still is," replied Will.

CHAPTER
FOUR

Meet
Charles
and
Susie
Spurgeon

What did pretty Susie Thompson see in the short, pudgy, awkward young man?

She had culture and class; he was a country bumpkin who didn't know how to dress decently and often was too brash for polite society.

For dates, he invited her to come and hear him preach; once he forgot that she was along. That nearly broke the engagement.

It didn't.

No doubt it helped to prepare her for those times after marriage when, on a Sunday morning, he was so wrapped up in his pastoral duties that he would shake her hand and say, "Good morning, madam, how are you?" as if he had never seen her before in his life.

Charles Haddon Spurgeon, that prince of preachers, that cigar-smoking Calvinist Baptist, that delightfully colorful, cocky character who made the Bible come alive for his congregations, was certainly not regarded as a great "catch" according to London's standards. But Susie loved him and made a splendid marriage out of it.

He called her Susie, and she playfully called him "Tirshatha," the Persian word in Scripture for "the revered one." Since Charles didn't want to be called "Reverend," Susie thought "Tirshatha" would be appropriate.

"Tirshatha" became the greatest preacher of the century. He started a college, an orphanage, and an old people's home, edited a magazine, and penned 140 books and commentaries.

Susie accomplished a few things herself. She started an international Book Fund which distributed thousands of books a year, a Pastor's Aid Fund for needy ministers, and a soup kitchen to aid the poor. She also raised two boys and served as a research assistant to Charles.

Somehow the marriage between these two remarkable—and in some ways very different—individuals flourished.

What made it work?

Charles Spurgeon thought it was a mistake when London's New Park Street Church asked him to be a candidate for the pastorate there. He was only nineteen, and he had never been to seminary, while the New Park Street Church was one of London's most prestigious Nonconformist (non-Anglican) churches.

At least, it *had* been.

Things had been going downhill at the church for the past few years. The church could seat twelve hundred, but on many Sundays only eighty or one hundred attended.

A couple of deacons felt that they needed an energetic young man, someone who could make some changes at New Park Street. That is how they happened to write a letter to Charles.

The young Spurgeon had not had an auspicious beginning, though certainly there was a life-long tie to the ministry. Born in a small rural town about seventy-five miles northeast of London, Charles was the son of a cod yard clerk who served as a Congregational minister on weekends. His mother, only nineteen when Charles was born, bore sixteen other children afterward, only seven of whom survived infancy. Because of the poverty of his parents, Charles spent the first six years of his life with his grandparents.

Since his grandfather was also a Congregational minister, the religious influence in Charles's early years was strong. His grandmother promised him a penny for every hymn by Isaac Watts he could memorize. He memorized so many that she cut the reward to a half-penny.

When Charles returned to his parents' home he was given the best education they could afford, and he made the most of it. His brother said, "Charles never did anything else but study. I kept rabbits, chickens, pigs and a horse; he kept to books."

The serious books he read—Joseph Alleine's *Admonition to Unconverted Sinners* and Richard Baxter's *Call to the Unconverted*—made him agonize internally. For nearly five years he wrestled with questions about his soul's salvation. The sermons that he heard and the prayers of his mother that he overheard only deepened his spiritual struggle.

Later he said, "Children are often very reticent to go to their parents. . . . I know it was so with me. When I was under concern of soul, the last persons I should have elected to speak to upon religion would have been my parents."

And so, he recalled, "It was my sad lot to feel the greatness of my sin without a discovery of the greatness of God's mercy."

Then on the first Sunday in January 1850, he ventured out in a blizzard to go to church. The storm prevented him from attending the church he planned to go to. Instead, he found refuge in a little Primitive Methodist Chapel and went inside.

Only twelve to fifteen people were there; even

the minister didn't show up. So "a shoemaker or tailor or something of the sort went up into the pulpit to preach."

"This man was really stupid," recalls Charles. "His text was 'Look unto me, and be ye saved, all the ends of the earth.' He did not even pronounce the words right."

After ten minutes of repeating himself, the lay preacher realized that he had nothing more to say and was about to conclude when he noticed the teenaged boy who had wandered in out of the snow. "Young man," he said, "you look very miserable, and you always will be miserable if you don't obey my text. But if you do obey now, this moment, you will be saved."

The unexpected shove was what Charles needed. In that moment he looked to Christ for his salvation. "There and then the cloud was gone; the darkness was rolled away." Four months later he was baptized by immersion by a Baptist minister near the school he was attending.

A year and a half later, now seventeen, he accepted a call to be pastor of a forty-member congregation in Waterbeach, a town notorious for drunkenness and profanity. Two years after that he received his call to the church in London.

The night before his preaching debut in New Park Street, he was lodged in a boarding house in London's Bloomsbury district. His fellow boarders were incredulous when he told them where he was going to preach the next day. They told him of the outstanding preachers in all the other London pulpits, and they reminded him of the learned gentlemen who had previously occupied New Park Street's pulpit.

When they looked at Charles, they could hardly keep a straight face. He wore a great black satin stock around his neck and sported a huge blue handkerchief with white polka dots. His hair was unkempt and his manners were proof that he was from the country.

Charles tossed restlessly in his bed all night. As he put it, "I was not in an advantageous condition for pleasant dreams."

The surroundings didn't help. "Pitiless was the grind of the cabs in the street, pitiless the spare room which scarcely afforded me space to kneel, pitiless even the gas lamps which seemed to wink at me as they flickered around the December darkness. I had no friend in all that city full of human beings."

Charles wanted nothing better than to get out of London as quickly as possible. He felt he didn't belong there.

The next morning he got his first look at the church. He described it as "a large, ornate and imposing structure, suggesting an audience wealthy and critical, and far removed from the humble folk to whom my ministry had been sweetness and light."

Charles was very much alone in the big city, and he realized the need for divine help. He reminded himself that he had not sought the speaking assignment. It had been God's doing; therefore it would be up to God to help him in his preaching.

The first morning service had only a fair attendance—about eighty—but the evening service was much better attended.

That was when Susie Thompson caught her first glimpse of Charles.

Although the rest of her family had attended the morning service, the young woman with the long chestnut curls had not gone. During the afternoon, a deacon had visited their home and lamented the fact that there had been so many vacant pews in the morning. "We must get him a better congregation tonight, or else we shall lose him." So the earnest deacon was doing everything he could to drum up a crowd.

"And little Susie must come too," he added.

Little Susie, who looked more like a teenager than a young woman nearly twenty two, didn't like the idea of being called "little." Nor did she like some of the things she had heard about the country preacher. She preferred ministers with some decorum, and she couldn't imagine how she could respect a minister who was younger than she was. However, she reported later, "to please my dear friends, I went with them."

Her first impressions were not at all favorable. "I was not at all fascinated by the young orator's eloquence. . . . His countryfied manner and speech excited more regret than reverence." What stuck in her mind was not the message at all, but "the huge black satin stock, the long, badly trimmed hair, and the blue pocket handkerchief with white spots." As she put it in her cultured way, "these awakened some feelings of amusement." The blue handkerchief was bad enough, but when he took it out and waved it in the middle of the sermon, it was gauche.

But the young preacher made an impression in spite of his gauche behavior. Before too long the New Park Street Chapel officially extended a call to Charles to be their pastor. "No lengthy reply is required," Charles responded. "I ACCEPT IT."

And about the same time, the deacons gave Charles a dozen white pocket handkerchiefs, so he would no longer have to use the dreadful blue handkerchief with white polka dots.

The handkerchiefs didn't transform Charles Haddon Spurgeon into a Beau Brummell. Charles never paid much attention to his clothing; he dressed to be comfortable, and what he wore seemed to accentuate his shape. Charles was built like a tank. His head seemed too large for his body. Until he smiled, his countenance appeared overwhelmingly heavy. Yet when he broke out into a sunny smile, which was never too far beneath the surface, everyone within a hundred yards of him melted.

A fellow minister said, "He had a remarkable face and head. The head was the very image of stubbornness: massive, broad, low, hard; the face was large, rugged, social, brightened by eyes overflowing with humor and softened by a most gracious and sympathetic smile." After a few years he grew a beard and that improved his appearance.

It was more than physical appearance that brought Charles and Susie together. The major factor was Susie's spiritual condition. About a year before she first saw Charles, Susie had made a profession of faith, but since that time, she had become "cold and indifferent to the things of God." Yet there was a spiritual restlessness (she mentions that she was passing through seasons of "despondency and doubt"), and when the nineteen-year-old country preacher was invited back for three Sundays in January, Susie returned to hear him.

The daughter of a prosperous merchant, she was proper and reserved. Her genteel upbringing meant that she was not allowed to read the daily newspapers or discuss world events. And there were certain things that proper people didn't talk about. such as one's spiritual condition.

Yet Susie was becoming "alarmed at my backsliding state" and soon sought counsel from a cousin. It was at this time that the young minister, Charles Spurgeon, gave her a copy of *Pilgrim's Progress*. She was "greatly surprised." On the flyleaf he had written: "Miss Thompson with desires for her progress in the blessed pilgrimage." This was the beginning of a lifelong relationship.

At first, Susie was afraid to talk to Charles. Perhaps it was more reticence on her part than fear. It wasn't easy for Susie to talk to people about spiritual matters, but she was amazed at the interest that he took in her spiritual welfare. He seemed to take delight in counseling her. The counseling paid off. As she put it, "He gently led me . . . to the cross of Christ for the peace and pardon my weary soul was longing for."

Early in June 1854, only six weeks after he had given her *Pilgrim's Progress*, Charles and Susie, along with several other church members, went together to the grand opening of the Crystal Palace, London's new exhibition hall, which was a miniature World's Fair.

Everyone was joking, laughing, and talking so much that they didn't even notice that Charles was talking rather seriously to Susie. If they glanced in their direction, all that they would have noticed was that Charles was showing Susie a book he had brought with him. The book was Martin Tupper's *Proverbial Philosophy*.

"I've been reading this book recently," Charles said in a low voice.

She didn't seem to show much interest. It hardly was the appropriate place to talk about philosophy.

Charles opened the book and pointed to a passage he had previously marked. "What do you think of the writer's suggestion in those verses?"

She looked at where his finger was pointing.

The chapter was entitled "Marriage." She read the passage: "Seek a good wife of thy God, for she is the best gift of His providence. . . . Think of her and pray for her."

She feared to lift her eyes from the text. Then she heard him whispering in her ear: "Do you pray for him who is to be your husband?"

She was blushing and couldn't help it, and she was afraid to say anything for fear that it would be the wrong thing to say. The program soon started, but she didn't take "much note of the glittering pageant before her." Did he really mean what she thought he might mean? Or was she reading too much into it?

After the ceremonies, he asked her, "Would you walk around the Palace with me?"

From that time, she says, "our friendship grew apace and quickly ripened into deepest love."

Two months later, "in a little old-fashioned garden," Charles didn't need a book to declare his love to her. "I thought I knew it already," she said, "but it was a very different matter to hear him say it."

That night she wrote in her diary, "It is impossible to write down all that occurred this morning. I can only adore in silence the mercy of my God, and praise Him for all His benefits."

In January 1855, barely a year after their first meeting, she was baptized by her fiancé. For Susie, who was still shy about sharing her spiritual feelings, it was traumatic, or as she put it, "a somewhat severe ordeal." She had to undergo public questioning about her profession of faith and also to submit a written testimony.

Charles was proud of how well she handled herself. Her written testimony contained some surprises; it displayed a depth that he hadn't realized before.

After that time, Charles usually spent Monday mornings at Susie's house, "bringing his sermon with him to revise for the press; and I learned to be quiet and mind my own business." His sermons were taken down in shorthand as he preached them on Sunday; then early Monday morning, they were set in type, and the proofs were returned to Charles for editing. Charles had the ability to concentrate on the subject at hand, ignoring all his surroundings, even if the surroundings included Susie. Sometimes, as Susie admitted, "I resented this." It was most obvious just before his Sunday morning service when he was preoccupied with the message or the order of service. If Susie would walk into the vestry, he might "rise and greet me with a handshake and a grave 'How are you?' as if I were a strange visitor. . . . This happened not once only, but several times." After the service was over, he joked about it. Susie learned to joke about it too.

One evening he had been invited to a hall near Susie's home, so he and Susie went to the service together. But as soon as he arrived he forgot about her, and Susie was left to fend for herself. "At first,"

Susie recalled, "I was utterly bewildered, and then . . . I was angry." In a huff, she left the hall and went home.

Her mother calmed her down, but Susie went up to her room to have a good cry. After the service was over, Charles came running to the house: "Where's Susie? I have been looking for her everywhere and I can't find her. Did she come home by herself?"

Mrs. Thompson explained what had happened and then got Susie downstairs for a reconciliation. Still indignant at being taken for granted, Susie let Charles know it. And Charles, innocently wondering, "What did I do?" explained that he was simply "putting God first" and that Susie would have to understand if she was going to become the wife of a minister.

Both of them profited from the evening flare-up. Susie learned that "I should never hinder him in his work for the Lord, never try to keep him from fulfilling his engagements, never plead my own ill health as a reason why he should stay home with me." And Charles learned that sometimes it was easy for him to say he was putting God first when actually he was merely displaying poor manners and being self-centered. Susie, fortunately, had much patience.

One of the reasons for their long engagement was that Susie's father was a bit reluctant to bestow his blessing upon Charles. Charles may have been gaining a fantastic reputation as a preacher, but he was still only twenty. Another reason was that there was so much happening at New Park Street that it was difficult to fit a wedding in.

Week after week, the church was crowded, so crowded that it was stifling in the summer months. Charles was concerned that people might stay home because it was so hot in his church. So, since the windows wouldn't open and the deacons wouldn't do anything about it, he took a cane and knocked out every window in the entire sanctuary. He knew that by the following winter a building program would ensure that the church would have new windows "that could be let down."

During the building enlargement, the congregation moved out of the church and rented Exeter Hall, which held 4,500 people.

London was shocked. It was unheard of for a church to rent a public hall for its worship services. Soon the newspapers were castigating the young preacher for his scandalous action.

One newspaper reported, "As his own chapel is under repair, he preaches in Exeter Hall every Sunday, and the place is jammed to suffocation. All his discourses are redolent of bad taste, are vulgar and theatrical, and yet he is so run after that, unless you go half an hour before the time, you will not be able to get in at all."

Another paper described Charles's preaching style as "that of a vulgar colloquial, varied by rant. . . . All the most solemn mysteries of our holy religion are by him rudely, roughly and impiously handled. . . . This is the preaching that 5,000 persons hear."

Charles tried to act as if the criticism didn't faze him. He wrote his father: "For myself, I will rejoice; the devil is roused, the church is awakening, and I am now counted worthy to suffer for Christ's sake." But he also admitted he had trouble sleeping.

Each Saturday he and Susie exchanged letters (no matter how often they had seen each other during the week), and in his letters to Susie he was open about his feelings:

"My Own Doubly-dear Susie:

"I feel very low in spirits, but a sweet promise in Ezekiel cheers me, 'I will give thee the opening of the mouth in the midst of them.' Pray for me, my love."

Susie responded:

"My dearest,

"Words are but cold dishes on which to serve up thoughts and feelings which come warm and glowing from the heart. . . . We know that all is under the control of one of whom Asaph said, 'Surely the wrath of man shall praise Thee; the remainder of wrath shalt Thou restrain.' "

On Sundays he preached to the large congregation without amplification. The strain on him was terrible. Susie wrote, "Sometimes his voice would almost break." His remedy for throat problems was a glass of chili vinegar which he kept on a shelf in the pulpit. (Years later, Charles said that these early challenges "macadamized" his throat.)

He was amazed at the crowds he drew. "I never have an hour to call my own. . . . I believe I could secure a crowded audience at dead of night in a deep snow. . . . Thirteen services are announced for next week. Everywhere, at all hours, places are crammed to the doors."

Renovations to the New Park Street Church didn't solve anything. By the time the building project was completed, the new sanctuary was far too small to house the rapidly growing congregation. One week they met in a field. Charles estimated the crowd at about ten thousand.

That summer Charles went to Scotland on a speaking tour. He needed the change, and he thought it might be a "working vacation." It was his first separation from Susie, and despite the adulation of the Scottish crowds, he missed her. Once he wrote her:

"My Precious Love:

". . . I knew I loved you very much before, but now I feel how necessary you are to me, and you will not lose much by my absence, if you find me, on my return, more attentive to your feelings, as well as equally affectionate."

Thousands had to be turned away from some of the meetings because there was no room, but Charles was not happy with what he felt inside of himself. He wrote Susie: "Pray very earnestly for me. I fear I am not so full of love to God as I used to be. I lament my sad decline in spiritual things. You and others may not have observed it, but I am now conscious of it. . . . What is it to be popular . . . even to have love as sweet as yours if I should be left of God to fall and to depart from His ways? I tremble at the giddy height on which I stand and could wish myself unknown."

When he returned to London, he gave Susie a special project. He asked her to go through an old Puritan book and underline anything that she thought was specially memorable. As a young Christian without much interest in stodgy Puritan sermons she felt unqualified for the task, but she nevertheless agreed to do it if it would help Charles.

He was so impressed with her selections that when she had completed the culling, he turned the excerpts over to a book publisher. The result was a small volume called *Smooth Stones Taken from Ancient Brooks*, since the Puritan author was Thomas Brooks. (Charles enjoyed puns.) Some 140 books in the next 40 years bore the name of Charles Spurgeon, but the one on which Susie and Charles collaborated was the first.

A few months later, the first volume of Charles's sermons was published. He gave a copy to Susie and on the flyleaf he scribbled, "In a few days it will be out of my power to present anything to Miss Thompson."

What he meant was that in only a few days Miss Susannah Thompson would become Mrs. Charles Spurgeon.

Charles, twenty-one, and Susie, nearly twenty-four, were married January 8, 1856. The church was packed; thousands thronged the streets to get a glimpse of the couple; police did their best to keep traffic moving around the church. The ceremony was simple, in keeping with the wishes of both bride and groom.

Afterwards, the newlyweds sailed to France for a ten-day honeymoon in Paris. Not only had Susie previously visited the city many times with her parents, but she had also lived there for several months in order to learn to speak French fluently. So on their honeymoon she served as Charles's guide as they visited Versailles, the Louvre, and the Cathedral of Notre Dame.

In his biography, Russell Conwell wrote, "With a nature like that of Mr. Spurgeon's, with many defects to repair and a lack of general education to be supplied, a cultivated and persevering wife might be considered an unquestioned necessity. . . . She could curb the uncouth eccentricities and correct his mistakes in language or history, and she hesitated not in the most affectionate manner to apply her criticisms when she saw they would do her husband good. He urged her to take the place of a public critic and notice his errors that he might the more readily correct them, and as she was a lady of excellent good sense and of quite extensive reading, she was a far safer critic than any man he could have selected."

Conwell may have slightly overstated the case, but the point is well taken. While Charles was certainly not uneducated, he lacked the refinement and polish that a London minister was expected to have. Susie was a loving guide for him, but most people never saw what went on behind the scenes.

Missionary David Livingstone once asked Charles, "How do you manage to do two men's work in a single day?"

Without a pause, Charles responded, "You have forgotten that there are two of us, and the one you see the least of often does the most work."

Despite the busy schedule that Charles maintained, he and Susie found time to enjoy each other. One of those times was Sunday night after the evening service. Usually when Charles returned from the evening service, he was quite exhausted. He would flop into an easy chair by the fireside, and Susie, sitting on a low cushion by his feet, would read poetry to him. Their favorite poet was George Herbert. Occasionally, however, if Charles felt as if his sermons that day had been ineffectual, he would ask Susie to read Richard Baxter's *Reformed Pastor*. Spurgeon allowed the stern admonitions of Baxter to recharge his spiritual batteries.

Susie tells of a typical reading from Baxter: "I read page after page of such solemn pleadings, interrupted now and again by his stifled heart-sobs, till my voice fails from emotion and sympathy, my eyes grow dim, and my tears mingle with his as we weep together—he from the smitings of a very tender conscience towards God, and I simply and only because I love him and want to share his grief."

On other evenings Susie might read theological books to Charles at his request. There was certainly no shortage of reading materials, for Charles's library rapidly grew to twelve thousand volumes.

Charles seldom prepared his Sunday morning message until Saturday night. (His Sunday evening message was prepared Sunday afternoon.)

On Saturday afternoons, he and Susie would usually have friends in for tea. After tea they would have their time of family worship together. It was understood, however, that all guests would have to leave at seven. That was when Charles began preparing his sermon.

Sometimes the system didn't work too well. "I confess that I frequently sit hour after hour praying and waiting for a subject," Charles admitted. Once he had to make notes for an evening message as he was bouncing over the cobblestones in his carriage on the way to church.

But there was one Saturday evening when Charles was mulling over a text for hours. He had consulted commentaries, praying, jotting down ideas that didn't go anywhere, and becoming increasingly frustrated. "I was as much distressed as he was," Susie said, "but I could not help him. . . . At least, I thought I could not."

Finally, Susie urged him to go to bed and wake up early in the morning. He would be able to think more clearly then. And she promised that she would wake him at dawn.

Early in the morning, however, Susie heard him talking in his sleep. She listened; it wasn't gibberish; it seemed to make sense. "Soon I realized that he was going over the subject . . . and was giving a clear and distinct exposition of its meaning with much force and freshness. . . . If I could but seize and remember the salient points of the discourse, he would have no difficulty in developing and enlarging upon them."

She lay in bed, "repeating over and over again the chief points." Then she herself fell asleep about the time she was supposed to waken Charles.

When he awoke and noticed the time, he was irritated. And Susie was the focus of his irritation. "You promised to waken me very early. See the time! Why did you let me sleep? I don't know what I'm going to do this morning." Facing a large congregation without a message from the Lord was not what Charles enjoyed doing.

Then Susie told him what had happened during the night and repeated to him the main points he had made in his sleep.

"You mean I preached that in my sleep?" He could hardly believe it. "That is just what I wanted. That's the true explanation of the text."

From the explanation Susie had furnished, Charles went into the pulpit and preached a powerful sermon.

Susie the pastor's aide was also Susie the parent. Only nine and half months after she and Charles were married, twin boys were born. They were named Charles and Thomas.

It was a difficult time for Susie. Her delivery had not been easy and she required several weeks of bed rest.

It was also a difficult time for Charles. He couldn't find an auditorium big enough to seat his growing congregation.

Three thousand people were jammed into the 1,500-capacity sanctuary of the New Park Street Chapel and hundreds more were waiting outside. According to biographer Ernest Bacon, "The conductors of the horse-drawn buses on the north side of the Thames used to entice people into their vehicles with the shout, 'Over the water to Charlie.'"

In June evening services were moved back to Exeter Hall, but even 4,500-seat Exeter Hall was too small. The only other possibility was the Surrey Music Hall, which held 12,000 people and was used for exhibitions, circuses, and wild beast shows as well as concerts. If the press had criticized Spurgeon for renting Exeter Hall for a church service, what would they say if he rented the Surrey Music Hall?

On the evening of October 19, 1856, a night

Charles would never forget, he held his first service at Surrey Music Hall. Twelve thousand people packed the hall; another 10,000 were outside.

In the middle of the service as Charles was praying, someone yelled, "FIRE." Someone else shouted, "The galleries are collapsing; the place is falling."

Some of the people panicked and rushed toward the doors. Some leaped from the staircase. Seven died; twenty-eight were seriously injured; many more suffered less severe injuries.

But there was no fire; the galleries weren't collapsing. The instigators of the mischief were never found, but the disruption worked only too well.

Charles tried to quiet the audience. From the pulpit he could see no problem. With considerable poise, the twenty-two-year-old was able to get many in the audience settled. He began his sermon. But then came some more shouts and another disruption. He couldn't continue.

As he turned from the pulpit, he collapsed and had to be carried into a side room.

Susie was home with her twins, not yet a month old. She had been praying for the meeting and praying specifically for Charles. Then she heard a carriage outside. She looked at the time. It was too early for Charles to be returning.

A deacon from the church appeared at the door, informing her of the catastrophe at the Music Hall. A little while later, Charles was brought home. In Susie's words, "he looked a wreck—an hour's agony of mind had changed his whole appearance and bearing."

Charles seemed on the verge of a serious breakdown. "His anguish was so deep and violent . . . that we feared he would never preach again."

The next day he was taken to a deacon's home where there was a large, restful garden, "to restore his mental equilibrium and unloose the bars which had kept his spirit in darkness." At first it didn't seem to help. He continued to be flooded with "tears by day and dreams of terror at night." His Bible didn't help; "prayer yielded no balm to me."

For Susie too it was a confusing time. Would Charles ever return to normalcy again? Even if he did, would he ever preach?

Together they walked slowly through the gardens. Then suddenly he stopped and turned to Susie. "How foolish I have been! What does it matter what becomes of me if the Lord is glorified? If He is exalted, let Him do as He pleases with me. Oh, wifey, I see it all now."

And after missing only one week from his pulpit, he returned again to resume his strenuous preaching load.

The press heaped blame upon Charles for the catastrophe. He was reviled as "a ranting charlatan" and accused of misleading gullible people.

The slander bothered Susie even more than it bothered Charles. She didn't want him to be daunted in his preaching by such attacks. She found a Bible verse and had it printed in Old English type, framed in an Oxford frame, and hung in their bedroom for Charles to see every morning when he woke up. The text was Matthew 5:11,12: "Blessed are ye, when men shall revile you, and persecute you, and shall say all manner of evil against you falsely, for my sake. Rejoice and be exceeding glad; for great is your reward in heaven: for so persecuted they the prophets which were before you."

The crowds continued to come, undaunted by the media. In fact, the tragic incident gave Spurgeon worldwide fame.

Work was progressing slowly on their new church building, to be called the Metropolitan Tabernacle. In the meantime, Charles continued to use the Music Hall for services, but to keep out mischief-makers worshipers had to have tickets to get in. And a ticket to hear Spurgeon was a valuable possession. (The tickets were free, but they served the purpose of keeping out those who wanted to stir up trouble. They also insured that the building would not be overcrowded.) Soon all of London, including lords, earls, mayors, sheriffs, and even royalty, was coming to hear the young preacher.

Before he had turned twenty-five, a vast empire revolved around him. Besides the construction of the huge Metropolitan Tabernacle, he had started a Preachers' College that was growing each year. Most of those who came were poor and could not afford to pay tuition, and that increased the financial burden.

Susie carried the responsibility for managing the family finances. Besides Charles's salary, the sale of his sermons around the world was starting to bring in healthy royalties. With Susie as a shrewd manager, the Spurgeons were able to underwrite the college's expenses in its early years.

For the building of the new sanctuary Charles and Susie were able to contribute five thousand pounds. By sponsoring a church bazaar Susie was able to raise an additional twelve hundred pounds. The total was about 20 percent of the building fund.

Soon an orphanage was started, housing five hundred children. Then a colportage association was launched with nearly one hundred book and Bible salesmen going door to door throughout England selling gospel literature.

Charles kept a heavy schedule of speaking engagements around London, but supplemented them with other assignments throughout the British Isles. Susie enjoyed going with him as frequently as she could. She never liked to see him go without her.

Once when he was about to leave, she broke down in tears. She didn't want him to leave her. He responded, "When any of the Israelites brought a lamb as an offering to the Lord's altar, do you think they stood and wept over it?"

"No, I suppose not."

"Well, don't you see that you are giving me to God as your sacrifice in letting me go and preach the Gospel? Do you think He wants you to cry over your sacrifice?"

In later years they joked about it. Whenever she was on the verge of tears as he was leaving, he would remind her, "Don't cry over your sacrifice."

In 1868, however, when Susie was thirty-six, "her traveling days were done." After that, as she put it, "I was a prisoner in a sick chamber."

But Charles's traveling days were not ended, and the separation was not easy for either of them. Whenever he left home, he would ask, "What can I bring you, wifey?" She would usually say, "Nothing," for as she sincerely felt, "I have all things richly to enjoy except health."

Frequently, though, he would bring her presents anyway, because he liked to surprise her and because he felt a bit guilty about leaving her alone. (And as the manager of the household finances, she would often mildly rebuke him for spending money when he didn't need to.) Once when he left home he asked, "What can I bring you?" She replied, "I should like an opal ring and a piping bullfinch." He knew she was only being playful.

However, not long afterwards he returned home with a tiny box in his hand. He opened the box and took from it a ring. Placing it on her finger, he said, "Here is your opal ring, my darling."

She couldn't believe it. Before she could tell him that he shouldn't have spent his money like that, he told the story: An elderly woman in the congregation had decided to give Susie a present. Not knowing what she had in mind, Charles sent his secretary to the woman's home to receive it. The secretary returned with the tiny box containing the ring.

The bullfinch was another story.

A woman in the congregation owned a pet bird. Unfortunately, the bird's piping aggravated her ailing husband to such an extent that she had to dispose of the bird. She remembered that the Spurgeons liked birds, so she gave it to her pastor saying, "I want you to take my pet bird to Mrs. Spurgeon."

Charles gave it to Susie, shaking his head. "You must be one of your Heavenly Father's spoiled children. He just gives you whatever you ask for."

But not everything. Her health never returned. Despite the joy of an opal ring and a piping bullfinch, those were difficult days for Charles and Susie. She writes, "Dark days those were for both husband and wife for a serious disease had invaded my frame, and little alleviation could be found from the constant, wearying pain it caused."

To convalesce, she went to the seaside resort of Brighton, but her condition worsened. A major operation was required and Sir James Simpson, the discoverer of chloroform, offered his professional services without charge. Though the operation was termed a success in that some of her intense pain was relieved, Susie remained a semi-invalid.

While she remained in Brighton, some of Charles's wealthier friends suggested that they completely rebuild the Spurgeon home, and it was reconstructed from the ground up. Charles took special delight in preparing it for the return of his invalid wife. In one letter he wrote her:

"My Own Dear Sufferer:

"I have been quite a long round today—if a round can be long. First, to Fensbury, to buy a wardrobe—a beauty. . . . Next to Hewlett's, for a chandelier for the dining room. Found one quite to my taste and yours. Then to Negretti and Zambra's, to buy a barometer for my own fancy, for I have long promised to treat myself to one. On the road I obtained the Presburg biscuits, and within their box I send this note, hoping it may reach you the more quickly. They are sweetened with my love and prayers."

Though Charles remained extremely busy, he missed Susie greatly. Once he remarked that "he and the cat (old 'Dick') went up and down the stairs mewing for the mistress."

The load was heavy for Charles. The church, the preachers' college, the orphanage, the satellite churches, his magazine, his books—the pressures kept building. Once he wrote, "I feel as though I had created a great machine and it is ever grinding, grinding, and that I may yet be its victim."

Perhaps he was. A year later, when Susie was home again, the health of Charles, just thirty-five years old, was breaking. His ailment was gout, which is similar to a severe form of rheumatoid arthritis. It was an affliction from which he would never recover. While he would have temporary remissions, in the cold and dampness of the winter the disease would return in all its fury.

He wrote his congregation: "The furnace still glows around me. Since I last preached to you, I have been brought very low, my flesh has been tortured with pain, and my spirit has been prostrate with depression. . . . With some difficulty, I write these lines in my bed, mingling them with the groans of pain and the songs of hope."

For a man who had always been so busy, inactivity brought depression, but even the depression had to give way to the intense pain. Doctors advised Charles to spend some of the winter in the warmth and sunshine of the Mediterranean. Susie knew that there was no other solution, even though, because she could no longer travel, it would mean separation for weeks, sometimes months at a time.

Susie wrote, "These separations were very painful to hearts so tenderly united as were ours."

After several weeks in southern France, Charles recovered sufficiently to resume his pastoral duties in London. These duties didn't diminish. "No one knows the toil and care I have to bear," he wrote once when he felt depressed. "I have to look after the orphanage, have charge of a church with 4,000 members; there is the weekly sermon to be revised, *The Sword and the Trowel* to be edited, and besides all that, a weekly average of five hundred letters to be answered."

Charles did find time to smoke, however.

Despite his health problems, Charles smoked heavily throughout his life. He told the newspapers that "smoking relieved his pain, soothed his brain and helped him to sleep." A London paper described him in his coach as he headed toward the Metropolitan Tabernacle: "Wrapped in a rough blue overcoat, with a species of soft-deerstalking hat on his head, a loose black necktie round his massive throat, and a cigar burning merrily in his mouth, he is surely the most unclerical of all preachers of the Gospel."

This "unclerical preacher" treasured the times when he could enjoy his family, but most of the child-rearing had of necessity been handled by Susie. It was Susie who taught her sons the Scriptures. Son Thomas recalled, "I trace my early conversion directly to her earnest pleading and bright example." On Sunday nights she stayed home, conducting a service for her boys, while her husband preached to six or seven thousand people at the Metropolitan Tabernacle. Both of the boys went into the ministry later in life.

It was a high point of Charles's ministry when he baptized his twin sons by immersion and brought them into church membership when they were eighteen. Recognizing the unique role that Susie played in rearing the boys, the church presented her with a special plaque on the occasion, saying in part that the church elders were grateful to God that "it should have pleased Him to use so greatly the pious teaching and example of our dear sister, Mrs. Spurgeon, to the quickening and fostering of the Divine Life in the hearts of her twin sons . . ."

Charles's absences limited him in his day-to-day influence on his sons. However, he was a loving father. Once he wrote a little couplet about his twin sons:

> *Charlie and Tommy are good little boys.*
> *When they're asleep, they don't make any noise.*

Charles had a playful sense of humor, given to puns. The top shelf of his library was filled with "dummy books" with fake titles. These included *Windows Ventilated* by Stone; Padlock on *The Understanding*; Cuff on *The Head*; Cricket on *The Green*; *Over the Stream* by Bridge; and *Do It Again* by Dunnett.

Charles had more serious connections with books, however. One day after Susie had read the proofs of a new book by Charles called *Lectures to My Students*, he asked her for her opinion of it. She responded, "I wish I could send a copy to every minister in England."

Charles answered, "Why not do it?"

It was a challenge that Susie took seriously. She went upstairs and searched through dresser drawers until she came up with enough money to send out one hundred copies of the book. She sent the books and thought that was the end of it, but when others heard of what she had done, they started sending her money. Soon the Book Fund was started and Susie had her own ministry.

She rejoiced in it. "The mustard seed of my faith grew into a great tree, and sweet birds of hope and expectation sat singing in the branches."

Charles wrote, "You should see her book room, her busy helpers on the parcel-day and the wagon-load of books each fortnight. . . . The loving manager has more than 6,000 names on her lists, and yet she knows every volume that each man has received from the first day until now. The work is not muddled, but done as if by clockwork, yet it is performed with a hearty desire to give pleasure to all receivers."

Charles was pleased that the Book Fund gave Susie a meaningful activity now that the boys were grown: "By this means He called her away from her personal grief, gave tone and concentration to her life, led her in continual dealings with Himself."

Susie enjoyed distributing her husband's books, but she sent out books by many other authors as well. "Solid, old-fashioned, Scriptural,

Puritan theology goes forth." And it went forth around the world to places like Samoa, Russia, Syria, and Timbuktu.

For several years Susie sent out about ten thousand books a year, plus an equal number of her husband's sermons.

As the work grew, Charles became worried; the Book Fund was too much work for her. "The business has overpowered her; the wagon is running over the horse."

Susie, besides her health problems, also struggled at times with fear. With Charles away in the winter and sometimes preaching at a distance in the summers as well, she had to trust the Lord, not her husband, for her safety.

Once when Charles was home, their home had been burglarized. The burglar, after discovering that he had stolen items belonging to the famous preacher, sent Spurgeon a letter which ended, "Why don't you shut your windows and keep a dog?" Charles took the burglar's advice and bought a bulldog named Punch.

Even with "Punchie" there, Susie was uneasy. "I had lately acquired a foolish habit of lying awake in the night with my ear intent to catch the faintest sound." She said that she overcame her fear by concentrating on Bible verses like "What time I am afraid I will trust in Thee."

On the wall of their bedroom was the Bible verse, "I have chosen thee in the furnace of affliction" (Isa. 48:10).

Both of them lived in the furnace for many years. Both of them also faced depressions. Said Charles, "There are dungeons beneath the Castle of Despair."

In 1892, Charles was once again in southern France during January. But this year was different. This year the doctor had given Susie permission to accompany him. He was fifty-seven now, although his illness made him appear older. As his physical condition worsened, Susie was at his bedside.

"Susie," he whispered.

"Yes, dear Tirshatha," she responded, bending over him and clasping his hand in hers.

Then he spoke his last words: "Oh, wifey, I have had such a blessed time with my Lord."

All of England, including the Prince of Wales and the prime minister, mourned his death. A crowd estimated at one hundred thousand came to his funeral.

For another dozen years, Susie continued her work with the Book Fund. She also assisted in preparing Charles's autobiography. She died in 1903 at the age of seventy-one.

In perhaps the first wedding ceremony that he conducted, Charles reminded the bride of the Apostle Paul's admonition, "The husband is the head of the wife." "Don't you try to be the head," he told her, "but you be the neck, then you can turn the head whichever way you like."

In a sermon on marriage Charles mentioned

that a model marriage is "founded on pure love and cemented in mutual esteem." He was describing his own marriage.

"Their object in life is common. There are points where their affections so intimately unite that none could tell which is first and which is second. . . . Their wishes blend, their hearts are indivisible. By degrees, they come to think very much the same thoughts. Intimate association creates conformity; I have known this to become so complete that, at the same moment, the same utterance has leaped to both their lips.

"If Heaven be found on earth, they have it."

CHAPTER
FIVE

Meet
Peter
and
Catherine
Marshall

An eighteen-year-old coed has a crush on a thirty-one-year-old bachelor minister. Puppy love?

He notices her; in fact, he's attracted to her. But what would the people in his fashionable congregation say if they knew their minister was thinking of dating a teenager?

The minister was Peter, the Scottish immigrant, a factory worker turned into a preacher-poet.

The girl was Catherine, or Kate, as he often called her, the minister's daughter from West Virginia, who was trying to get through college on a shoestring and lot of determination.

One thing that they both had in common: They both knew what it was to be poor.

Another thing: They both liked to play

159

games—from Monopoly to Chinese checkers to Parcheesi. In fact, Peter was nicknamed "The G.G.P." or "The Great Game Player" because he played games with a vengeance or, as Catherine put it, "he relaxed hard."

As for Catherine, her college classmates nicknamed her "Calamity Catherine." A debater, she approached the world's problems with intensity and what she termed "blazing indignation."

Catherine didn't like to be taken for granted; Peter had an annoying way of doing just that. Catherine liked to be involved; Peter enjoyed his independence. Catherine was no slave to neatness; Peter was meticulously precise.

Such differences certainly can keep a marriage from becoming dull.

Peter Marshall, of course, became the oft-quoted chaplain of the United States Senate as well as minister of Washington's prestigious New York Avenue Presbyterian Church, where he served until his death at age forty-six.

Then, after Catherine had passed through the valley of the shadow of her husband's death, she emerged from the shadows herself. A widow at thirty-four, Catherine published two best-sellers within three years of Peter's death: *Mr. Jones, Meet the Master,* a collection of her husband's sermons, and *A Man Called Peter,* her husband's biography. Afterwards, she wrote more than a dozen other books, all best-sellers.

Toward the end of her life and a second marriage, Catherine wrote, "Husbands and wives are basically incompatible. . . . That's why the home is His classroom for moulding and shaping us into mature people." Her marriage to Peter Marshall proved this to be true.

In the spring of her freshman year at Atlanta's Agnes Scott College, Catherine first heard of Peter Marshall. He was the new minister in town, having just taken the pulpit of the moldering Westminster Presbyterian Church, an hour's ride away from campus by streetcar, but well worth the trip.

Peter was certainly worth hearing—and, for coeds, worth seeing. A dramatic and poetic preacher, he spoke with a Scottish burr. As a literature major, Catherine was enchanted. But more than that, it was obvious that Peter knew the Lord in a very personal way and had a knack of bringing his congregation with him into a circle of divine friendship. This moved Catherine, who was spiritually restless at the time because her own relationship to Jesus Christ seemed "abstract."

The girls of Agnes Scott were also impressed with the physical aspect of Peter Marshall.

Broad-shouldered, tall, curly-haired, ruggedly handsome—and single—Peter seemed to be the answer to every coed's dream.

Born near Glasgow, Scotland, Peter had lied about his age to join the British Navy. He was only fourteen, and he wanted to fight in World War I. His naval career lasted about forty-eight hours before his fraud was discovered. Too proud to return to his high school and face his classmates, he enrolled in a technical school to study mechanical engineering, and at fifteen, he became a machinist.

But God had other plans for Peter's life.

Major influences on Peter were: (1) a praying mother who reminded him, "Long ago I pit ye in the Lord's hands"; (2) Olympic medalist Eric Liddell (portrayed in the film *Chariots of Fire*), who challenged him to missionary service; and (3) a never-to-be-forgotten incident that took place one jet black night as he was walking across the moors. As the wind howled around him, Peter thought he heard something or someone calling. He slowed his steps to listen more carefully. Suddenly he stumbled and reached out to break his fall. There was nothing there. He had fallen on the edge of an abandoned limestone quarry. One more step would have taken him over the precipice.

Shaken by this experience, he dedicated his life to serve the Lord. In 1927 he emigrated to America in order to study for the ministry. To earn money, he worked at a blast furnace and on a pipeline. Though he had no college degree, he was admitted to seminary and three years later graduated magna cum laude.

Then at the age of thirty-one he accepted the call to the pulpit of Atlanta's Westminster Presbyterian Church. The church services were sparsely attended when he came, but before long his sermons packed the sanctuary, forcing the deacons to stand out on the sidewalks in order to listen through open windows. Students from Georgia Tech, Emory, Oglethorpe, and Agnes Scott flocked to hear him.

From the moment he arrived in town, the matchmakers of Atlanta began working. Some of the young women didn't need any help. The "In" box in his study was often stuffed with letters and anonymous poetry from interested parties. One poem read:

> *What will you do with all of the hearts*
> *That you have pierced or broken?*
> *Will you wear them around your neck on a string*
> *As an ornamental token?*

Meanwhile, Catherine floundered. In her sophomore year she wrote, "I am lazy spiritually. I would like to know God really—not in the abstract. But I don't seem to want to badly enough to do anything about it."

A few weeks later she wrote, "I have had no real, vital religious experience. God does not seem real to me. I believe in God now mostly because of people I know—like Peter to whom religion is a vital, living thing."

As a child she had been profoundly stirred by evangelist Gypsy Smith's preaching, and shortly afterwards, she walked forward as her preacher-father gave a gospel invitation. But now that decision seemed far away.

As she says in *A Man Called Peter*, "I . . . was groping to find my way out of an inherited Christianity into a spiritual experience of my own."

She was now attending Peter's church every Sunday, had shaken hands with him frequently, but had never really talked to him. In her journal she wrote, "I have never met anyone whom I so want to know as Mr. Marshall."

Her letters to her parents in West Virginia started mentioning this young minister: "I have never heard such prayers in my life. It's as if, when he opens his mouth, there is a connected line between you and God. I know this sounds silly, but I've got to meet that man."

In another letter, she pined, "He doesn't even know I exist." After another paragraph, she concluded, "I wish I'd stop thinking about this man."

It was silly, she knew, but during the following summer, she read everything she could about Scottish history, eventually developing a bibliography of thirty-seven books. But by the time she returned for classes in her junior year, she had come to her senses and decided it was ridiculous for her to get moonstruck about a man who didn't even know she existed.

She decided to get interested in some college fellows her own age. In addition, she resolved to dedicate herself to her studies.

She even felt a bit relieved when she heard a rumor that Peter was engaged. That, she thought, would get him off her mind.

But the fellows she dated all seemed so shallow; her mind kept going back to Peter. "Why must the embodiment of all my ideals be twelve years older than I and as remote as the South Pole?"

Then it happened. In the spring of her junior year, she, as a college debater, was asked to join—of all people—Peter Marshall and speak at a Prohibition rally. Her intensity on the platform had earned her the nickname of "Calamity Catherine," and she had debated subjects from Nazism to America's economic collapse. It wasn't hard for her to become intense on the subject of Prohibition.

On the way to the rally, Peter assured her that he definitely was not engaged. "Don't believe everything you hear, my dear girl." But on the way back, he said that he would like to take her bowling sometime. "I've wanted to know you for a long time."

It was more than Catherine had dreamed. She had simply wanted to get to know him better. Now he had actually asked her for a date.

But the date didn't materialize.

165

She saw him at church socials and "he overflowed with warmth toward me," and frequently he would drive her back to school afterwards. After one such get-together, he said, "I'll be in touch with you this week."

But he didn't get in touch. And a few weeks later, when summer vacation began, Catherine went home to West Virginia, more puzzled than ever about her dream man. She asked herself, "Why did he always seem so interested in me when I was with him, but then never follow up with a note or telephone call?"

He wrote a couple of times during the summer, but the correspondence seemed cold and formal, almost business-like. He closed one card with "Regards, Peter Marshall," hardly the complimentary close of someone interested in romance.

Once again, Catherine resolved during the summer to forget about Peter Marshall. It wasn't easy, because the memories of their times together stuck in her mind. "I must forget Peter Marshall," she determined and decided to reinforce it by not going to his church in the fall.

Her resolve lasted six weeks. On her first Sunday back at Westminster, he shook hands with her and remarked that it was the first time he had seen her that year. She was somewhat surprised that he had even noticed that she hadn't been attending. Then he said that he would get in touch with her. That night she wrote in her journal, "I shan't hold my breath until he does."

When they were together, he continued to express his enjoyment of her company, but he never pursued the relationship. Catherine couldn't figure him out.

Peter had reasons for not being too obvious about the relationship. As a thirty-three-year-old minister of a rapidly growing congregation, he didn't want to be aggressive in his display of affection for a college girl.

The turning point for Peter came near the end of Catherine's senior year. She had been asked to review a book on prayer at the church's fellowship hour preceding the evening service. As she spoke, she honestly confessed her own failings in prayer. She admitted her superficiality and expressed her hunger to know God better. It was a time of intense catharsis for Catherine, especially so since she knew that Peter was listening to every word.

The church's evening service followed. By the time Catherine entered, it was late and the only available seats were in the front of the church. As the church service progressed, Catherine started feeling ill. At first, she thought she could last through the service, but then she felt sicker and sicker. Finally Catherine had to walk out from her third row seat.

Something happened to Peter as he watched Catherine leave the church. From then on, she had his undivided attention. Catherine's journal took on a different mood; it recorded steady progress in the relationship:

"Terribly solicitous . . .

"I believe now he wants to be serious. . . .

"I think Peter is in love with me. . . .

"He kissed me. . . .

"We talked until three in the morning. . . .

"He proposed."

Yes, he proposed. She took a few days to pray about the proposal. It seemed strange to delay an answer, but she needed to be certain whether her dreams were just girlish fantasies or in keeping with God's will. As Catherine later wrote, "I saw how wrong it is to go after what we want and then—with considerable audacity—later ask God to bless it."

But by graduation day, the question was answered. She said yes.

That summer was far different from the previous two. Letters flew back and forth, combining passion, spirituality, and humor. "Darling, I am so happy! I love you so much," Peter now wrote.

Initially, they had planned to wait a year for marriage; Catherine would teach school. But Peter couldn't wait, and he talked Catherine into a fall wedding in her father's church in West Virginia.

When Peter came to visit Catherine at her home that summer, he earned his nickname, "The G.G.P." (The Great Game Player). Catherine enjoyed games too, but she admits, "I thought he was carrying it a bit too far when, thirty minutes before our wedding ceremony, he was so busy pushing his initial advantage in a game of Chinese checkers with my little sister that he still had not dressed."

The first night of their married life they honeymooned in Washington, D.C.—for a good reason.

Peter had agreed to meet with the pulpit committee of Washington's New York Avenue Presbyterian Church the following morning. He apologized to Catherine for having to leave her before breakfast. "Take your time dressing," he told her. "When the men want to see you, I'll telephone."

Only twenty-two, the bride was terrified to meet the auspicious committee of seven men and one woman. She prayed silently, "Please, Lord, don't let me embarrass Peter."

Apparently she didn't, because Peter received a call to the Washington church.

The question was: Should he accept the call? The answer didn't come easily. He told Catherine: "I do not sincerely feel that I am equipped for what they would need. I lack the poise, the balance, the preparation, the academic standing, the confidence, the discretion and the grace to be bridled in my pulpit utterances." In addition, the church in Atlanta had just added a balcony to accommodate the crowds that were coming to hear him preach. He couldn't leave Atlanta until the balcony was paid for.

So he turned down the call and the newlyweds set up housekeeping in Atlanta. But a year later, the New York Avenue Presbyterian Church of Washington renewed its call, and this time, after much prayer, Peter answered yes.

For the Scottish immigrant who had been working in a Glasgow factory only a decade earlier, it was frightening. "Catherine, I'm scared to death," he admitted. "Suppose I can't deliver the goods?" Catherine was scared too. Only eighteen months earlier she had been on a college campus wondering what life was all about. Now she was the wife of the minister of one of the most prestigious churches in the nation. The church was known as the church of presidents; eight presidents, including Lincoln, had worshiped there. She took a crash course in Washington protocol to help her through the maze of official niceties.

In Atlanta they had lived in a pleasant cottage. In Washington their manse was a ponderous red brick, three-storied house with ten rooms, including six bedrooms.

It didn't take long before the home reflected Peter's taste. As Catherine wrote, "To step into the living room of our home was like entering a marine museum. Seascapes were everywhere—Peter had seen to that." Catherine would have preferred a floral motif, but that wouldn't do, for Peter had a passion for the sea. Another passion was clocks; they had thirteen of them. He was also collector of stamps, pot lids, china, pressed glass, and, of course, games.

Fortunately, Catherine liked the color blue,

which was also Peter's favorite color. That solved many problems in decoration.

Neat and methodical, Peter trained Catherine in his ways.

When she left the top off the toothpaste or failed to close a dresser drawer, he let her know about it.

He was proud of how quickly his bride was becoming a good housewife. After Catherine had successfully cooked a Christmas turkey, he wrote his mother in Scotland: "Catherine is managing quite nicely. We are all proud of her. It amazes me the way she has taken hold and manages like a veteran. It was a proud moment for me to sit at that table, so tastefully laid out, and look at Catherine at the other end, and serve turkey, which I carved myself, believe it or not."

Peter had some definite ideas regarding the role of a wife, and in theory Catherine had no trouble in accepting them. He believed that a woman's place, no matter what education or talents she might have, is in the home. In one sermon he spoke of marriage as "a fusion of two hearts, the union of two lives, the coming together of two tributaries which after being joined in marriage, will flow in the same channel in the same direction . . . carrying the same burdens of responsibility and obligation."

Catherine had some reservations about his strong views; even before their marriage, she wanted to check on them. He assured her, "Darling, it is not that your life and love and gifts will be poured into my coffer . . . but that we both shall be poured into that new vehicle—and our joint lives—our blended hearts and fused souls—now one in the sight of God."

It sounded good to Catherine in theory. In practice, there were problems.

Ever since she began thinking of marriage to Peter, she had wondered how difficult it would be for him to adjust from his comfortable bachelor life to marriage. She thought that it might be better for him to remain a bachelor. "He seems to be altogether self-sufficient, independent, and perfectly happy that way."

Besides having an independent streak, Peter was a workaholic. He never took a day off. He worked long hours, usually attended committee meetings in the evening and for diversion accepted frequent out-of-town speaking engagements.

The out-of-town speaking engagements certainly bothered Catherine, but even more troublesome to her was Peter's inability to share his thoughts. Maybe it was his Scottish reticence; more likely it was that he had never had to do so before. When he talked about their lives being poured into a new vehicle, it sounded good, but Peter continued to operate his vehicle as he had always done before, with no help from Catherine.

Catherine was perfectly willing to subjugate all her desires to use her talents of writing and speaking and to throw herself into helping Peter as a minister. But she wanted Peter to share his ministry with her, and for the first few years of marriage he seemed incapable of doing it.

He had a divine call. His ministry came first. As she puts it, he was "at the beck and call of thousands of people," and all these thousands seemed to have priority over his wife.

That was a fact of her married life that she tried to accept. But resentment began to build. And at times she didn't know if she should be resentful against the church members, against Peter, or against God. The out-of-town speaking engagements were almost the last straw.

From his viewpoint, he was being charitable; after all, he received scores of invitations to speak and accepted only a relatively few of them. He thought she should appreciate the fact that he turned down many opportunities. She thought he still accepted far too many. He thought she was being self-centered and jealous of his ministry. She thought that he was being thoughtless and uncaring.

Despite the problems, the Marshalls had a good marriage. "We early discovered," Catherine writes, "that the important thing was not the differences between us, but the will, the determination to work them out. After all, every couple has difficulties. No two lives are fused into perfect oneness without a certain amount of painful adjustment."

Problems were dissolved sometimes by humor,

sometimes by the deep love and respect they had for each other, and sometimes, perhaps most importantly, by their custom of praying with each other every day.

Even though she was frequently frustrated with him, Catherine enjoyed Peter. She liked the way he laughed and the way he sang with such gusto. She even liked the way he dressed up in his kilt and entertained church socials with "Roamin' in the Gloamin'." He was fun to be with.

And of course, she also enjoyed his penchant for games, from Monopoly to baseball. "One might wonder how a busy minister could find so much time for game playing," Catherine writes. "The answer was that Peter stole the time from sleep."

Gradually, Peter made attempts to share. One way he did this was by reading his Sunday morning sermons to Catherine on Saturday night. For him it was a warm-up; for her it was an enjoyable preview. One Saturday night, as Peter reached the middle of his practice sermon, Catherine interrupted him. She hated to do it. But she had to tell him something important. She was having labor pains. And shortly before nine the next morning Peter John Marshall was born.

Peter was at the hospital for his son's birth; then he returned to church in time to teach the young people's Sunday school class at ten and preach his half-rehearsed sermon at eleven. To his congregation he never said a word about the excitement that had occurred in his household a few hours earlier. Some people mentioned to him that he seemed tired that morning, almost as if he had been up all night. He still admitted nothing. Then as he was shaking hands with his parishioners at the close of the service, one woman asked him about Catherine, who she had observed was absent that morning. Peter finally had to divulge the reason for Catherine's absence.

It had always been a policy for Peter not to mention his wife or his home life in his sermons. After Peter John was born, however, that policy was quickly forgotten. Peter John provided too many colorful sermon anecdotes to be neglected.

Peter enjoyed his son; there was no doubt about that. He felt guilty because his church responsibilities often kept them from spending more time together.

To work out a practical solution, the family purchased a summer home far away from the demands of a church and the endless stream of speaking engagements. Located on Cape Cod, it was close to the sea that Peter loved. Of course, Peter immediately had to paint the green shutters of the cottage his favorite Chatham blue. The cottage gave Peter a chance to spend more time with his son, to plant a garden of hybrid tea roses, to build some furniture, and to listen to the sound of the ocean. Catherine enjoyed antiquing on the Cape most of all. There was a lot of family togetherness. Peter and little Peter John would go blueberry picking together, and then Catherine would make deep-dish blueberry pies and blueberry muffins. At night Peter would read a book to his son and tuck him in bed.

Early in their married life, Catherine was a bit bothered because Peter was not more of a scholar. She thought that a minister should spend a part of his time studying the Greek and Hebrew root meanings of the biblical text. She tried without success to encourage her husband to be more studious.

She did succeed in making Peter feel guilty. So when they went to Cape Cod he brought books with him to study. But he seldom opened them; when he did, he usually fell asleep halfway through the first chapter.

Peter wasn't a scholar by nature. He was a poet, an artist with words. For instance, he likened doubt to cobwebs in the corners of our rooms. Our brooms of faith can't get into those corners. Only God's divine grace can.

"The use of the right word is the difference between a pencil with a sharp point and a thick crayon," he once said.

He told a group of seminarians, "If when you write your sermons, you can see the gleaming knuckles of a clenched fist, the lip that is bitten to keep back tears, the troubled heart that is suffering because it cannot forgive, the spirit that has no joy because it has no love, if you can see the big tears that run down a mother's face, preach for them—and get down deep."

Peter got his sermon ideas from anywhere and everywhere, and he took great care in selecting the titles. Since the church bulletin was prepared on Thursdays, he often discussed the subject of his sermon with Catherine at the Wednesday night dinner table. Sometimes, even though he had only a sketchy idea for a sermon, he would give a title to it with faith that sometime between Thursday and Sunday the sermon would become fully developed. Seldom could Peter develop sermon outlines more than a few days in advance.

Peter's responsibilities kept increasing. As the church grew, he began preaching identical sermons to two services on Sunday mornings. But still the crowds overflowed; people had to be turned away because the church could hold no more.

Catherine stayed behind the scenes, playing the role of a supportive wife. As she says in *A Man Called Peter*, she was expected to be "gracious, charming, poised, and equal to every occasion." And she fulfilled her role well.

Then when Peter John was three years old, Catherine was stricken by illness. At a church meeting she nearly fainted. Medical tests disclosed that she had contracted tuberculosis.

Because it was not infectious, she was allowed to remain home, but complete bed rest was required. She was not allowed to do work of any kind.

She lay in a large front bedroom. The room was pleasant enough with five windows letting in the sun's rays. She propped herself up in bed and started filling her notebooks with her thoughts. She scribbled that some day she wanted to "become a writer who will make a real contribution to my generation and to the world."

At first, it was thought that Catherine would be well within three or four months. And, she says, "the first three months were the worst. Every muscle in my body ached in protest." But when the time stretched month by month beyond that the x-rays showed the same spots, Catherine's discouragement verged on depression. Nor did she appreciate what she felt were trite words from her husband. "Catherine, you know perfectly well that all discouragement is of Satan." He also reminded her, "Some day you will look back with gratitude on these bleak days as some of the richest of your life."

Later she acknowledged that although she had resented his comments at the time, those "bleak days" had indeed proven to be some of the richest of her life. In them she found a relationship with Jesus Christ that she hadn't known before. For the first time in her life she developed an interest in the Holy Spirit. Understandably, she also became intrigued with the subject of healing. She struggled to understand what the Bible taught. Frequently her experiments with faith ended in dead ends, thus frustrating her further.

Catherine was struggling with other problems, too. She felt guilty that she could not spend more time with her son; and she was also concerned that she couldn't be the kind of wife that Peter needed. Instead of being a help, she was being a hindrance to him in the ministry.

Peter seemed sympathetic and caring; yet she was uneasy. She was concerned that he might lose interest in a wife who was an invalid. She dreaded that "someone else will usurp my place in Peter's heart." How could a virile man like Peter not become bored sooner or later with a "useless" wife? Especially when he traveled, she worried.

In late summer of 1944, after Catherine had been bedridden for seventeen months, the family situation was more desperate than ever. During her illness, the Marshalls had been served by fourteen different maids. It was the World War II era; and Washington, D.C., had plenty of high-paying jobs available; the Marshalls couldn't compete with the salaries the government offered. As a result, they couldn't keep a maid very long. Peter John was obviously feeling the effect of it; so were Peter and Catherine, not to mention their broken china and ruined linen.

The only alternative seemed to be to send Peter John to stay with Catherine's parents, for Catherine to go to a rest home, and for Peter to stay in a hotel until Catherine recovered—however long that might take.

Peter and Catherine prayed together fervently

for some resolution to the problem. "If You want us to stay together, Lord, then we will trust You to send someone to take care of the household." It was with considerable difficulty that they also prayed, "Thy will be done."

On the deadline day, a young woman from Kansas came to the manse, saying, "I don't really want the job, but here I am." She volunteered to help out for a few months, and they accepted her offer. She ended up by staying with them for four years.

In an article in *Presbyterian Life* Peter referred to this incident saying, "The greatest answers to prayer in our family have come at times when our faith was so small almost to expect the worst. Until we took hands off and really turned the problem over to God, He could not help us."

The final lesson that Catherine learned through her illness was obedience; as she committed herself to learning this lesson she began seeing some physical progress as well.

Her healing was not instantaneous, but she had no doubt that it was divine. It seemed to accompany a mystical experience in which she felt the presence of Christ as she never had before. "Why it should have happened to me, I had no idea. But I also knew that what I had experienced was real."

The years of Catherine's poor health taught both of them much. Peter worked to be more communicative, and she, no longer able to be involved in church activity, learned how to encourage him and to give him the understanding he needed.

They collaborated on writing projects, developing a Bible study on the Letter to the Ephesians and also preparing two issues of the devotional magazine *Today*. They discovered that they enjoyed writing together.

Peter involved her more with his sermons. Her convalescence gave her time for more reading; as she read she discovered fresh ideas to pass along to her husband. She often did research for him—"the spadework" she called it—and he did the final writing. Frequently, they talked through the sermon together before he gave it. Sometimes he would even phone her from the church office and ask for her help. "I'm stuck," he would admit, and he valued the creative suggestions that she offered.

He told friends, "My most effective sermons have been the ones Catherine and I have worked on together."

Her writing career and her natural desire to develop as a separate individual were set aside. As she put it in *To Live Again*, "All the ideas I possessed, all energy, all creativeness, were poured into the marriage partnership, and no effort was made to channel any part of it in other directions." She acknowledges that Peter's "strong views on the role of women in marriage" might have caused conflict if she had been unwilling to put aside any personal goals. She testifies that in thus losing her life in his, "I found it again in a fulfillment of every shred of femininity in me."

She also recognizes that her years of poor health "had given me a special kind of training in the quiet life."

Then one Sunday morning in the spring of 1946, halfway through his first Sunday morning sermon, Peter felt sharp pains in his chest. He clutched at his heart, stopped his sermon, and asked, "Is there a doctor in the house? If there is, I'd like to ask his help." He quickly pronounced the benediction and was helped off the rostrum.

At the age of forty-three, he was having a coronary attack. He was rushed to the hospital, where he was given a fifty-fifty chance to survive.

When Peter saw Catherine at his bedside, he took her hand in his and said, "You shouldn't have come, Catherine. You're not up to it." She was still recuperating from her illness, but this was a time that Peter needed her, and she had to come to his side.

She phoned a few choice friends who would spread the message that Peter needed prayer. Soon thousands across the country were praying for Peter. And in the following weeks, Peter gradually recovered. After ten weeks in the hospital, two weeks at home and then twelve at the cottage on Cape Cod, Peter was back in his pulpit again in September.

Catherine thought that he might slow his pace a bit, and for a couple of months he did seem to be more cautious. But soon he had resumed his usual hectic pace. "He had no desire to flirt with death," Catherine said. He really didn't know any other way to live. Along with a number of close friends, she tried reasoning with him. "But nothing really changed as a result of our talks. . . . It was like reasoning with a closed door," Catherine said. Peter didn't want a limited life.

More than anything else, Catherine wanted him to cut back on his out-of-town speaking engagements. The first year after his attack, he did; he took only ten of them. But the second year, he accepted twenty. "You should see the number I turn down," he told her. She had heard the same line before.

Then a few months later, much to his surprise as well as hers, he was elected chaplain of the United States Senate, a job he added to his regular church responsibilities.

In this capacity, he served as a personal chaplain to many of America's political leaders; his unique prayers become famous across the country.

Once he prayed, "Our Father in Heaven, help us to see that it is better to fail in a cause that will ultimately succeed than to succeed in a cause that will ultimately fail. . . . May Thy will be done here and may Thy program be carried out, above party and personality, beyond time and circumstance for the good of America and the peace of the world. Through Jesus Christ our Lord. Amen."

Peter's schedule was soon busier than ever. It

was true that his recovery from the attack seemed almost miraculous. He had no symptoms such as shortness of breath, dizziness, or swelling ankles. So he hadn't seen any reason to take it easy.

Besides that, he didn't know the meaning of the words, "Slow down." Catherine feared what was coming.

Early in 1949, in the middle of the night Peter called to Catherine, "I'm in great pain. Call a doctor." She wasted no time in calling for help. As the ambulance was ready to take him away, she whispered to him, "Darling, I'll see you in the morning."

By nine the next morning Peter had died. He was forty-six; he left his widow, thirty-four, and a nine-year-old son.

The church was packed for the funeral; people had to be turned away. *Time, Life,* and *Newsweek* all paid tribute.

The following Sunday, Catherine attended church as usual. On the surface she seemed strong. People remarked about how well she was taking it. Underneath, however, she was crumbling.

She should have taken better care of her husband, she told herself. After all, she had ample warning. He had had a heart attack three years earlier. Had she been a failure again?

After blaming herself, she heaped some of the blame on the church. After all, it was the congregation, no matter how loving the people seemed at times, that kept requiring more of him. "How selfish can human beings be?" she wondered.

Eventually, she got around to blaming God. "If God has the power to help us, why didn't he do something about Peter's heart?"

It was all part of the grieving process through which she had to work.

"I was a particularly ill-equipped widow," Catherine admits in *To Live Again*. She had never liked to face death. Peter had once said to her, "You act, Catherine, as if death can be avoided by willing it away."

But she was ill-equipped in other ways, too. Peter had handled not only the major decisions of their married life but the details as well. As a widow she was being called upon to make all sorts of decisions and she felt uncomfortable about it. "My ideal inner image of woman's role in the world—formed partly by the femininity with which I was born, partly by a Southern heritage and partly by the years of my marriage—was definitely not that of the career woman. . . . Yet now circumstances which I had not sought were thrusting this genuinely distasteful role upon me."

While Catherine was struggling to know how to pick up the pieces, three different book publishers wrote and asked her to compile and edit a book of Peter's sermons and prayers.

She couldn't say no. She had long dreamed of becoming a writer. Now, by putting her beloved husband's messages into print, she had the opportunity. That fall, *Mr. Jones, Meet the Master* was published. The first printing of ten thousand copies sold out on the first day; the book hit the best-seller list quickly and remained on it for a year. Less than two years later, the biography *A Man Called Peter* was published. It reached the best-seller list in ten days and stayed there for three years.

Overnight, it seemed, Catherine had become a nationally recognized writer. Twentieth Century-Fox released a film version of Peter's life in 1955. It too was successful.

During her long illness she had learned to write in bed, and despite the disadvantages of writing that way, she continued the habit. In *To Live Again*, she describes her unconventional style: "A woman propped up in bed writing, with scrapbooks and papers cluttering the bed and the floor; pencil smudges on her face and hands; on the floor beside her a cocker keeping sleepy sentinel. On one side of the bed was an olive-green filing cabinet; in a corner, a dictating machine. Sometimes the woman would jump up out of bed to get a cookie or an apple; at other times, to search the file for a missing paper."

But Catherine's life as a widow was not as idyllic as it might sound, especially after her son Peter John left her for a prep school and then Yale. Despite her best-sellers and her fame, Catherine was very lonely.

After Peter's death and during the time that she was writing his biography, she was convinced that she would never marry again. "This would violate something very precious," she said, "that my husband and I had had together."

She waged a "running battle with self-pity" for awhile, and talked herself into the idea that sooner or later she would get adjusted to this "doubtful state of single blessedness" and "inner peace will come."

Not too many months later, her journal indicates some wavering. "God has made me the way I am; he has made me for happiness and love. I do not believe that he means or wants me to stay by myself for the rest of my life."

There was no shortage of men. Several were interested in this attractive widow, now in her early forties. During one year she turned down three proposals of marriage. None of them measured up. "Somewhere there is a man whose life needs this lavish giving," she penned in her journal.

Loneliness increased. "I have felt defeated and frustrated," she wrote in her journal. "The zest has gone out of everyday life."

"It is especially lonely," she wrote in *To Live Again*, "when there is no one with whom to share what the world calls success."

Through her books she had become famous and had touched the lives of more people in less than a decade than Peter had done in two decades of pulpit ministry. Yet, she had to admit, "As a woman I was not impressed with any accomplishment of mine. . . . I felt drained, empty."

In 1957 she had to confess, "My personal answer to whether or not a woman can replace marriage with a career and find it satisfying was—no,
definitely not. The career left the woman still
wanting to be—only a woman."

Then one day in early 1959, *Guideposts* editor
Leonard LeSourd asked her if he could discuss an
article idea with her over lunch. To her it seemed
like only a business lunch.

But a few months later, in the summer of 1959,
Len asked her for a date. "I'll pick you up in the
morning in my car and we'll just take off to the
beach or to the mountains or whatever."

Catherine suggested the mountains, and off
they went. "We had an open, honest communication at a deep level," she reported.

This began a new relationship, a relationship
totally different from the one she had had with
Peter. When she was with Peter, he was the leader,
the decision-maker. He had all the spiritual answers too. With Len, it was different. "We were
both seekers," she says. And on their second date,
he proposed marriage.

It was a completely different kind of decision
than when Peter had proposed marriage more
than two decades before. She had been starry-
eyed in Peter's company; with Len she was more
analytical.

But as she analyzed him, she had to admit, "I
liked what I saw. He was a caring man, affectionate, comfortable to be with, mature. He ap-

proached problems calmly. He had a father's heart."

Yet on the other hand, marrying Len would mean moving to New York and raising his family of three young children—a daughter, ten, and two sons, six and three. Catherine's own son was now in college and she didn't know whether she wanted to take on the challenges of a young family again. What the decision boiled down to was this: She could stay in her sheltered, lonely existence and be comfortable, or she could make the difficult adjustment into Len's life and the tensions of involvement with a young and active family.

She chose involvement; she and Len were married in November.

Raising a family was indeed trying for Catherine. The children had been managed by six housekeepers in the previous two years. "How do you put families broken by death and divorce together again?" she asked herself. Fortunately, her new husband was extremely supportive.

One of the first things that Len did was to tell Catherine that he wanted her to keep on writing. "God gave you writing as your work in this world," he said. Catherine was even more impressed when he said that he thought she should keep on using Catherine Marshall as her writing name.

A methodical man, Len kept a notebook for prayer requests and answers. He listed the date of the request and the date of the answer alongside each request. One of Len's first entries in his little brown notebook was the prayer request "That household help be found so that Catherine can continue the writing of her novel 'Christy.' "

That prayer was answered when a housekeeper was found. Soon Catherine was back at work on her novel. But it still took a while for her to complete it. In 1967, *Christy*, her first novel, was finally published. The public thought it was worth waiting for; 250,000 hard-cover copies and 4,000,000 paperback copies were sold.

The following year she and Len founded the book publishing firm known as Chosen Books, which developed a reputation for producing carefully crafted Christian books.

By the time of her death in 1983 at the age of sixty-eight, Catherine had written or edited nearly twenty books; the sales of her books exceeded eighteen million copies. She endeared herself to her readers because she wrote from the heart and expressed herself honestly, clearly, and conversationally.

Her two marriages were poles apart in their dynamics; the two men she married were quite different. But both marriages were very successful.

Catherine, of course, was a different woman at the age of forty-five when she married Len LeSourd than she was when at twenty-three she married Peter Marshall. At twenty-three she was fresh from the campus, awed by the Peter Marshall mystique. At forty-five she was a best-selling author, known to Christians and non-Christians alike because of her books and the movie, *A Man Called Peter.*

Her first marriage lasted only eleven years before Peter Marshall was taken from her in death; her second marriage was more than twice as long before she was taken from Len in death.

Catherine Marshall was a strong woman. She used her strength in ways that reinforced the men in her life. And that made for two good marriages.

BIBLIOGRAPHY

THE BUNYANS

Bunyan, John. *Grace Abounding to the Chief of Sinners.* London: J.M. Dent and Sons, 1930.

Coats, R. H. *John Bunyan.* London: Student Christian Movement, 1927.

Day, Richard Ellsworth. *So Pilgrim Rang the Bells.* Grand Rapids: Zondervan, 1955.

Froude, James Anthony. *Bunyan.* New York: Harper and Brothers, 1880.

Furlong, Monica. *Puritan's Progress.* New York: Coward, McCann and Geoghegan, 1975.

Harrison, G. B. *John Bunyan.* New York: Doubleday, Foran and Company, 1928.

Loane, Marcus L. *Makers of Religious Freedom.* Grand Rapids: Eerdmans, 1961.

Winslow, Ola Elizabeth. *John Bunyan.* New York: Macmillan, 1961.

THE LIVINGSTONES

Blaikie, W. Garden. *The Personal Life of David Livingstone.* New York: Revell, 1890.

Campbell, R. J. *Livingstone.* New York: Dodd, Mead and Company, 1930.

Jeal, Tim. *Livingstone.* New York: Putnam's, 1973.

Northcott, Cecil. *Livingstone.* Philadelphia: Westminster Press, 1973.

Schapera, I., ed. *Livingstone's Missionary Correspondence, 1841-1856.* Berkeley: University of California Press, 1961.

Seaver, George. *David Livingstone: His Life and Letters.* New York: Harper and Row, 1957.

THE BRYANS

Bryan, Mary Baird. *The Memoirs of William Jennings Bryan.* Philadelphia: John C. Winston, 1925.

Koenig, Louis W. *Bryan: A Political Biography.* New York: Putnam's, 1971.

Macartney, Clarence Edward. *Six Kings of the American Pulpit.* Philadelphia: Westminster, 1943.

Russell, C. Allyn. *Voice of American Fundamentalism.* Philadelphia: Westminster Press, 1976.

THE SPURGEONS

Bacon, Ernest W. *Spurgeon: Heir of the Puritans.* Grand Rapids: Baker, 1967.

Conwell, Russell H. *Life of Charles H. Spurgeon.* New York: Edgewood, 1892.

Dallimore, Arnold. *Spurgeon.* Chicago: Moody, 1984.

Fullerton, W. Y. *Charles Haddon Spurgeon.* Chicago: Moody, 1966.

Ray, Charles. *Mrs. C. H. Spurgeon.* Pasadena, Tex.: Pilgrim Publications, 1979.

Spurgeon, Charles H. *Autobiography, Vol. 1: The Early Years, 1834-1860* and *Autobiography, Vol. 2: The Full Harvest, 1861-1892.* Carlisle, Pa.: The Banner of Truth Trust, 1975, 1976.

THE MARSHALLS

Marshall, Catherine. *Beyond Ourselves.* New York: McGraw-Hill, 1961.

———. *A Man Called Peter.* New York: McGraw-Hill, 1951.

———. *Meeting God at Every Turn.* Lincoln, Va.: Chosen Books, 1980.

———. *To Live Again.* New York: McGraw-Hill, 1957.

Marshall, Peter. *Mr. Jones, Meet the Master.* New York: Revell, 1949.

CHRISTIAN HERALD ASSOCIATION AND ITS MINISTRIES

CHRISTIAN HERALD ASSOCIATION, founded in 1878, publishes The Christian Herald Magazine, one of the leading interdenominational religious monthlies in America. Through its wide circulation, it brings inspiring articles and the latest news of religious developments to many families. From the magazine's pages came the initiative for CHRISTIAN HERALD CHILDREN and THE BOWERY MISSION, two individually supported not-for-profit corporations.

CHRISTIAN HERALD CHILDREN, established in 1894, is the name for a unique and dynamic ministry to disadvantaged children, offering hope and opportunities which would not otherwise be available for reasons of poverty and neglect. The goal is to develop each child's potential and to demonstrate Christian compassion and understanding to children in need.

Mont Lawn is a permanent camp located in Bushkill, Pennsylvania. It is the focal point of a ministry which provides a healthful "vacation with a purpose" to children who without it would be confined to the streets of the city. Up to 1000 children between the age of 7 and 11 come to Mont Lawn each year.

Christian Herald Children maintains year-round contact with children by means of a *City Youth Ministry.* Central to its philosophy is the belief that only through sustained relationships and demonstrated concern can individual lives be truly enriched. Special emphasis is on individual guidance, spiritual and family counseling and tutoring. This follow-up ministry to inner-city children culminates for many in financial assistance toward higher education and career counseling.

THE BOWERY MISSION, located at 227 Bowery, New York City, has since 1879 been reaching out to the lost men on the Bowery, offering them what could be their last chance to rebuild their lives. Every man is fed, clothed and ministered to. Countless numbers have entered the 90-day residential rehabilitation program at the Bowery Mission. A concentrated ministry of counseling, medical care, nutrition therapy, Bible study and Gospel services awakens a man to spiritual renewal within himself.

These ministries are supported solely by the voluntary contributions of individuals and by legacies and bequests. Contributions are tax deductible. Checks should be made out either to CHRISTIAN HERALD CHILDREN or to THE BOWERY MISSION.

Administrative Office: 40 Overlook Drive, Chappaqua, New York 10514
Telephone: (914) 769-9000